THE GAMES CHILDREN PLAY

will help you:

Understand the harmful patterns that sometimes arise in child-parent relationships

Develop more constructive communication with your children

Learn to cope with the disturbing implications of their "games"

Head off adolescent problems

Dr. A. H. Chapman is a graduate of Yale University, where he received his B.S. and M.D. degrees. Since 1951, he has been an active psychiatrist, and is currently in Brazil working in transcultural psychiatry. He is the author of many articles and a number of books, among them *Put-offs and Come-ons* and *Sexual Maneuvers and Stratagems (The Strategy of Sex)*.

ALSO BY A.H. CHAPMAN

THE STRATEGY OF SEX

PUT-OFFS AND COME-ONS

A.H. Chapman, M.D.

The Games Children Play

A BERKLEY MEDALLION BOOK
PUBLISHED BY
BERKLEY PUBLISHING CORPORATION

PREFACE

The material of this book is drawn from twenty-five years of psychiatric work with children, adolescents and parents. It deals with unhealthy child-parent relationships and the ways in which they warp children's personalities and destroy the comfort of families. At all times we stick closely to the day-to-day problems of children and parents and shun theory and speculation.

Child-parent problems fall into various patterns that are repeatedly encountered in psychiatric work, and these patterns are sometimes termed "games"; such games erode intimacy and tend to become ingrained in family life. In most instances neither the parent nor the child is aware of what is happening; he only knows that there is a nagging pain in his relationships with others in the home. He cannot define it, and his efforts to grapple with it often mire him more.

This book is written for parents in the hope that it will help them identify games and make such games articulate to both themselves and their children. Awareness helps. It offers the possibility that games can be stopped and that sounder parent-child relationships can be substituted. If this book helps some parents cope better with the opportunities and dilemmas of rearing children and of aiding adolescents to grow more comfortably into adults, it will justify the effort spent in writing it and the time required to read it.

A. H. C.

CONTENTS

1

HOW GAMES ARE LEARNED AND PLAYED

The emotional functioning and personality of a child are products of his interaction with the important persons in his life. His self-confidence or fearfulness, passivity or aggressiveness, and emotional comfort or discomfort are caused by what has gone on, and is going on, between him and his parents, siblings and other close persons. The harmony or chaos of a family is determined by the kinds of interpersonal relationships its members have with one another.

In addition, a child's past and present shape his future. The patterns of feeling, thinking and behavior that are ingrained in him during his formative years persist; they extend into adolescence and adulthood and affect success or failure in marriage, child rearing, making a living and other adjustments with people. Between infancy and middle adolescence a very skillful animal is molded into a person, and interpersonal relationships are the tools by which this task is accomplished.

Many children, adolescents and adults are unable to adjust in the environments they were reared to live in. They fail because of the warped patterns of dealing with people which they developed during their formative years. These inadequate patterns are sometimes called *games,* and games can be analyzed and healthier ways of adjustment can be substituted for them. To do so, four steps are necessary:

1. The unhealthy interpersonal pattern, or *game,* must be defined.
2. It must be made articulate (or aware, or conscious) to

one or more persons involved in it.

   3. It must be broken up.

   4. A healthy interpersonal pattern must be substituted for it.

Later in this chapter we shall more clearly define games, and in subsequent chapters we shall deal with many common games that occur during childhood and adolescence. However, we shall first discuss a few fundamental principles of emotional functioning and personality development.

In our discussions we shall use many of the principles developed by two psychiatric investigators. The first is Harry Stack Sullivan (1892-1949), probably the most influential and important of American psychiatrists. Starting with Freud's theories, Sullivan developed a broad *interpersonal* approach to psychiatry and human existence. Whereas Freud was interested in what went on *inside* people, Sullivan was interested in what went on *between* people. He is not well known to laymen, since he wrote only for the medical and social science professions. Although he published some of his points of view during his lifetime, a much larger amount of his material has been gathered from recorded lectures and seminars and has appeared in widely disseminated books since his death. To a large extent American psychiatry is gradually becoming a fusion of the points of view of Freud and Sullivan.

The second psychiatrist on whom we shall rely for some concepts is Eric Berne (1910-70), who studied various aspects of interpersonal relationships in a frame of reference he termed *transactional analysis*. Berne introduced the concept of *games* that, with some modifications, we shall employ in this book. In addition to writing for the medical and social science professions Berne wrote successfully for laymen. However, his influence on the general current of psychiatric development is small in comparison to Sullivan's. Since this book is a guide for parents, rather than a monograph for scholars, we shall not cite the places where we rely on these two psychiatric writers, but

12

the reader who is familiar with their works will note our dependence on them at many points.

Some Basic Concepts of Emotional Functioning

Personality consists of the relatively long-term ways in which a person engages in interpersonal relationships. The nature of a person's relationships with others characterizes him and enables us to discuss what kind of person he is. For example, we may conclude certain things about an adolescent who attempts to bully us. We may say that he is domineering and hostile and has a need to control people around him. If he becomes anxious and seems almost to beg for our compliance when we do not obey him, we may perceive that beneath his bluster he has insecurities that goad him into an urgent need to dominate people. If we spend a good deal of time with him, we may learn much more about him, and what we learn usually reveals that he has a mixture of aggressiveness, fear, and, at the same time, yearnings for closeness with people—little or none of which he may clearly perceive.

We learn these things about his personality only when he begins an *interpersonal relationship* with us. If he merely sits on the other side of a bus reading a newspaper and no interpersonal contact arises between him and us, we know nothing of him. *Personality can be studied, understood, and sometimes changed only in the context of interpersonal relationships.*

Whenever in this book we talk about the personality of a child, or an adolescent, or a parent, we are talking about what we can see in his relationships with others. By studying these relationships we may reach conclusions about what is going on *inside* him, but the avenue of our information is always observation of the interactions *between* him and others. Moreover, we may speculate about what has gone on in his life to make him the kind of person he is; our hostile, bullying adolescent was not born that way—relationships with people during childhood and early adolescence made him what he is. However, we never see those early relationships. What we conclude about him is based on what he *does* and *says* in the interpersonal relationship he has with us.

A person and his interpersonal environment are not two things—they are one process. Only death establishes a distinction; then interpersonal relationships cease and the *person* becomes a *thing* that we bury in the ground.

No interpersonal relationship, or set of interpersonal relationships, is ever static. It is a continual flow, sometimes turbulent, sometimes calm, but always moving and changing. This is particularly true of children and adolescents whose personalities are in the process of being formed. Although personality warps and defects may be improved throughout life, the best time is early; the helpful actions of parents have a much greater impact on a two-year-old than on a twenty-year-old.

The Principle of Communal Existence. A person cannot live healthily in isolation. Man requires a continuous interchange. And usually a live one, with people. Absence of interpersonal activity, or distortions of it, leads to personality sickness.

This can be seen in infants. An infant who receives little tender care often becomes apathetic and whining, and he may eat poorly and become emaciated. An infant who is cared for by an insecure, anxious mother or an angry, rejecting one screams, thrashes about, and sleeps poorly. For example, firstborn infants, whose mothers are tensely learning how to take care of children, have a much greater incidence of colic (howling spells of fretfulness with the legs doubled back on the abdomen) than second- or third-born children. Colic is less common after the first child because the mother is more relaxed and sure of herself, and she knows it—and more important, the child senses it.

Isolated children, shunned children, and rejected children are vulnerable to personality distortions because they are excluded from healthy interpersonal contacts, and, in addition, they often are subjected to damaging ones. Every person throughout his life, but especially during childhood and adolescence, needs a healthy, lively interpersonal environment.

14

Symbols and Abstract Ideas. An important part of human growth is the development of elaborate systems of symbols and abstract ideas related to interpersonal experience. This begins early and continues throughout life. Experience is too complex and varied to assimilate without condensing it into symbols and abstract ideas.

The first symbol in life probably is the nipple, and it seems to make little difference whether it is made of flesh, rubber, or soft plastic. What *is* important is the tenderness associated with it. An infant senses the gentleness or harshness that accompanies holding him and fussing over him when the nipple comes. A four-week-old infant has no concept of "mother," "world," or "interpersonal relationships." He feels only the comfortable sensation of the nipple between his lips, the cuddling that goes with it, and the end of a state of discomfort that years later he learns is called hunger. The nipple thus becomes the first symbol of "mother," "world," "interpersonal relationships" and many other things.

By the time he is five years old the child has acquired a large number of symbols, many of them tied to the development of speech. "Mother," "father," "toy" and "car" represent more than actual things in the child's life; they are symbols of untold thousands of separate experiences with these persons and things. Each time a child sees his father or thinks about him, he cannot say, "This is the person who did a thousand things with me, which I shall now remember." Instead, all these experiences are encapsulated in a word-symbol, "father," that designates this person, and that word-symbol embraces the love or rejection, security or desolateness, and reassurance or dread that the child has experienced with his father. Much of human life is dominated by the influence of such symbols.

In addition, the child forms abstract ideas. By the time he is five years old he has concepts, however vague and distorted they may be, of "good," "bad," "right," "wrong," "nice," "nasty" and countless other things. They grow more numerous and complex during childhood and adolescence and profoundly affect his thinking, feeling and personality structure.

Personality Development. The main qualities that characterize a person are gradually formed during his first ten to twenty years and depend to a large extent on his long period of reliance on others. A human being is biologically and socially tied to his parents and his home for the first 25 percent of his life, and this extraordinary reliance on them makes man the complicated social animal he is. His achievements or failures and his health or misery depend greatly on the kinds of relationships he had with people during his formative years.

The interpersonal patterns developed during childhood and early adolescence have a remarkable tendency to persist, even when circumstances change and they no longer work well, or not at all. They are mainly shaped by the intimate relationships of a child's life— those with his mother, father, siblings and other close persons. Broader social groups such as neighborhood and school groups also have impacts, but they are making their impressions on a slate already covered by designs sketched at home.

Awareness

The more a person's interpersonal processes are outside the range of his awareness, the more likely it is that unhealthy ones will arise. Moreover, unhealthy interpersonal patterns (which, if they become ingrained, may be called *games*) are particularly apt to occur during periods of stress either minor or major.

Consider the following exchange between a mother and a four-year-old boy:

MOTHER: Did you throw that fork into the baby's crib?

BOBBY: No.

MOTHER: Yes, you did. If you didn't, who did? Don't you know you could hurt her that way?

BOBBY: I didn't do it.

MOTHER: Then who did? You could kill her. How would you feel then?

BOBBY: Somebody else threw it in there.

MOTHER: Who? Just who? You're lying.

BOBBY: She didn't get hurt.

MOTHER: Then you admit you threw it in there.

BOBBY: I didn't do it.

MOTHER: Just wait until your father comes home and I tell him. Then you'll get it. I'll tell him you did it and lied afterward.

BOBBY: She hit me.

MOTHER: How could a baby hit you? You're lying again.

BOBBY: I'm not.

In this exchange neither Mother nor Bobby is *aware of the real issue.* Therefore, Mother deprecates Bobby and threatens him, and he lies and becomes frightened or sullen. *Nothing is solved,* and depending on Mother's alarm, she may continue to nag Bobby for minutes, or hours, or days, and Bobby's hostility toward his infant sister grows. If such dialogues between Mother and Bobby (also involving Sister, though she is as yet an inarticulate, unaware participant) are repeated often enough, they gradually form an entrenched, unhealthy pattern of interaction, or *game.* This pattern may continue throughout the childhood and adolescent years of Bobby and his sister, and it also may carry competition and hostility between them into adulthood.

Let us consider how this exchange might have occurred *if Mother had been aware of the real issue involved:*

MOTHER: Somebody threw a fork into the baby's crib. Since you and I are the only ones in the house and it wasn't there ten minutes ago, it must have been you.

BOBBY: She hit me.

MOTHER: That's a fib and we both know it, but we won't go into that now. The main point is that you're afraid Daddy and I won't love you as much since the baby came, and you're mad at her.

BOBBY: What do we need her for anyway?

17

MOTHER: To love. You are one of the bigger people in the family now. Just as Daddy and I love you (and we *do* love you as much as ever), we must all love the baby. Also, since you are one of the bigger people, you will have to help take care of her.

BOBBY: What can I do?

MOTHER: Get that giraffe doll Aunt Margie gave her and put it beside her. At her age she doesn't know what a giraffe is, but I think she likes the bright-yellow color.

BOBBY: I'll put it beside her.

MOTHER: Thank you.

In this exchange Mother *was aware* of what was troubling Bobby. She defined it to him and thus made him *aware* of it. Before she put his feelings into words, Bobby may not have been clearly aware of the insecurity and anger his newborn sister was arousing in him.

Then Mother reassured Bobby about his fears. She told him that the love of herself and his father for him were not diminished by the baby's arrival, and she gave him a non-competitive role with the baby—that of an auxiliary parent, one who loves the baby and helps take care of him. Thus, the baby ceased to be a threat to him, and his anger toward her subsided.

Last of all, Mother substituted a healthy activity with the baby in place of an unhealthy one. She asked Bobby to put a giraffe doll in the crib in place of the fork he had thrown in.

To recapitulate:

1. Mother defined an unhealthy interpersonal pattern that, repeated many times under different circumstances, might have become a *game*.

2. She made Bobby articulately aware (or conscious) of it, and in doing so she may have seen it a little more clearly herself.

3. She broke up the unhealthy interpersonal pattern by reassuring Bobby about the fears that were goading him.

4. She substituted a healthy interpersonal pattern by giving Bobby a reassuring, constructive role in relationship to the baby.

Much of this book is devoted to *increasing the awareness* of parents about a wide range of parent-child situations.

Self-Image Formation

Each person carries within himself a concept of what kind of person he feels he is. He may view himself as capable or incapable, worthwhile or worthless, lovable or unlovable, handsome or ugly, and strong or weak. This mental picture is termed his *self-image,* and it has a marked effect on his interpersonal life.

Although no one has an entirely accurate self-image, a person should have a reasonably valid concept of himself. An unsound self-image may lead to gross maladjustments. For example, the person who views himself as inadequate may not aspire to reasonable goals, and he may let others exploit him. A talented person may feel worthless; he feels that he succeeds only by extraordinary efforts and by hiding his defects, and he lives in constant dread of unmasking. A person with good capacities for giving and receiving affection may view himself as unlovable, and he may settle for a drab marriage, since he feels this is all he is capable of.

The most important factors in forming a self-image are the attitudes a person's parents and other close persons have toward him during his formative years. The child who is treated as a reasonably worthwhile person will tend to view himself as such, and the child who is browbeaten and constantly criticized will tend to view himself as unlovable and inferior. A child usually accepts as reality the things he continually feels and perceives, especially if no one expresses contrary opinions. Hence, a despised child tends to accept as reality that he is despicable, and a loved one that he is lovable.

Consider the following dialogue between a mother and a five-year-old girl:

MOTHER: Who spilled this detergent powder all over the kitchen floor?

19

DEBBIE: I don't know.

MOTHER: You did it. Look, you still have detergent powder stuck to your fingers.

DEBBIE: I guess I did.

MOTHER: I worked for a whole hour to clean this kitchen. Then you come in here, mess up everything, and all my work is lost.

DEBBIE: I'm sorry.

MOTHER: What good does that do? You're a nasty, sloppy girl. You don't care how much I work to keep this house in order. You don't care about anybody except yourself.

DEBBIE: I won't do it again.

MOTHER: You always say that. You don't mean it. You'll never be worth anything. You'll just go through life making a mess out of everything you touch.

DEBBIE: I'll really try not to do it again.

MOTHER: You're selfish and ungrateful. Your father and I work from sunup to sundown to make this home attractive, and you destroy everything.

In this dialogue the mother quickly forgets the issue, detergent powder on the kitchen floor, and goes into a harangue about the child's alleged personality defects. In her harangue the mother portrays the child as a destructive, self-centered, worthless person. The focus has shifted from detergent powder to the child's evolving self-image.

Of course, all mothers become angry and say unkind things once in a while. Occasional tirades do no harm if they occur against a general background of love and esteem for the child. It is daily hammering of this kind, especially if the father also does it or is a silent bystander, that gradually molds the child's self-image in unsound ways.

Let us now examine how this exchange might have occurred in a healthier manner:

MOTHER: Look at this detergent powder all over the kitchen floor. You spilled it there. You're not supposed to be playing with detergent powder, and you know it.

DEBBIE: I'm sorry.

MOTHER: I'm angry and I have a right to be. I spent a whole hour cleaning up this kitchen.

DEBBIE: I won't do it again.

MOTHER: You are a good girl, Debbie, but you did a wrong thing when you got into the detergent powder and messed up the floor.

DEBBIE: I'll clean it up.

MOTHER: Right! And do a good job. I'll be back in five minutes to see how it is going.

In this dialogue Mother sticks to the issue, the detergent powder on the floor. She points out Debbie's misbehavior, expresses her anger about it (which she is entitled to do), and sets Debbie to cleaning up the mess. However, in this exchange *she criticizes the act, not the child,* and *she deals with the problem without damaging Debbie's self-image.* The key to Mother's *healthy* approach to this situation lies in her words, "You are a good girl, but you did a wrong thing."

Expression of feelings

A child or adolescent should be able to give reasonable expression to his feelings in socially acceptable ways. He should be able to put into words, at least to some extent, his affectionate yearnings, anger, fear and other emotions. He should not be so uncomfortable with his feelings that he stifles them and crowds them out of his awareness, and he also should not be so driven by them that he acts them out in a self-defeating manner.

Children who are reared in loveless homes often are ill at ease with their affectionate feelings and unable to express them comfortably, and they tend to be awkward in close relationships during adolescence and adulthood. On the other hand, children who are reared in families in which there is an easy give-and-take of love tend to emerge from their formative years with good capacities for expressing it and receiving it from others.

Emotional health also requires that a person be able to express a certain amount of his aggressive feelings and that he not feel guilty and apprehensive when he does so. He should have the capacity to be comfortably angry when circumstances justify it; he should not be so ill at ease with his assertive feelings that he allows other people to dominate and exploit him. People who unduly bottle up their affectionate and aggressive feelings have a tendency to develop anxiety states, depressiveness, psychosomatic disturbances and other emotional problems in both childhood and adult life.

The inability to give adequate expression to feelings is usually produced by unhealthy parent-child relationships. Throughout his formative years the child is made to feel inadequate or guilty each time he puts his angry feelings into words, or he is told that he is "silly" and "mushy" each time he tries to express affection. These patterns may become so ingrained that as an adult the person is unaware that he represses his feelings. The passive person who can express no anger and hence lets everyone dominate him rationalizes by saying that he is "easygoing," "likes to get along with people," and "sees no point in arguing over things." The person who cannot express affection may rationalize that he "has self-control" and "doesn't get carried away by emotions." Much time in psychiatric treatment with both children and adults is devoted to helping them become aware of their feelings and comfortable in expressing them.

Let us consider the following exchange between a father and a five-year-old boy:

FATHER: What happened? Why are you crying?

BRUCE: Frank pushed me down and I hurt my leg. He's a dirty, stinking rat, and I hate him. I'm going to knock him down, and I hope he gets hurt.

FATHER: That's a terrible thing to say, especially about your brother. You should be ashamed of saying things like that. He probably didn't mean it.

BRUCE: Yes, he did.

FATHER: If you go around saying things like that, no one will like you. No one will want to have anything to do with you.

BRUCE: I don't care.

FATHER: Then you should care. Only good-for-nothing people say things like that. Decent people don't talk that way. Nobody loves a person who speaks like that.

BRUCE: I didn't do anything wrong.

FATHER: You did. You called Frank a lot of dirty, bad things, and then you said that you were going to knock him down and hoped he got hurt.

BRUCE: He hurt me.

FATHER: Don't let me ever hear you talk that way again. Get out. When you talk like that, I don't even want to have you around.

In this dialogue Father makes Bruce feel inadequate and guilty about his anger. He also threatens Bruce with loss of love and isolation if he continues to express such feelings. If Father and Mother persistently express such attitudes throughout Bruce's growing years, he will tend to be ill at ease with his assertive feelings and to suppress them. As an adult he may be a passive, exploited person, or he may be aggressive but wracked with guilt each time he asserts himself. In either case he is a possible candidate for a stomach ulcer, anxiety attacks, or occasional bouts of depressiveness.

Let us examine how Father might have handled this situation in a healthier way:

FATHER: What happened? Why are you crying?

BRUCE: Frank pushed me down and I hurt my leg. He's a dirty, stinking rat, and I hate him. I'm going to knock him down, and I hope he gets hurt.

FATHER: You're angry.

BRUCE: Wouldn't you be?

FATHER: Probably so.

BRUCE: He's a louse, a dirty louse. He's the worst kid I know. I hate him.

FATHER: Do you feel better now?

BRUCE: What?

FATHER: Do you feel better now since you blew off some steam about Frank?

BRUCE: No. My leg still hurts.

FATHER: You're not crying anymore.

BRUCE: It's because I'm so mad at him.

FATHER: You feel better since you got some of it off your chest. When you're mad it helps to blow off a little steam. However, I don't think you should knock him down. I'm the one who should punish him when he doesn't act right. Tell him to come here and we'll settle this.

In this exchange Father points out that Bruce's anger is understandable; he also indicates that expressing it is healthy and that talking it out opens the way to doing something about the cause of it. Father does not make Bruce feel guilty and inadequate about his anger, and he does not threaten him with loss of love or social isolation.

Identification

A child gradually assumes many characteristics and attitudes of his parents, and this process is termed *identification*. The child is not conscious that he is doing this; it is a slow, imperceptible process that goes on outside his range of awareness. The kinds of identifications a child makes constitute an important part of his personality development.

A child incorporates personality features from both his parents, but in healthy development he identifies to a larger extent with the parent of the same sex. Thus, a boy with a sound, warm relationship with his father takes on many of his father's qualities, and a girl assumes many of the attributes of her mother. To a lesser extent a child may identify with other significant persons in his environment, such as close relatives. Identification is a complex process that goes on throughout childhood and early adolescence.

Through identification a child usually assumes some of the moral standards and ideals of his parents. The child with a healthy relationship with his parents tends to take over their ethical standards, vocational aspirations and social viewpoints. However, the child with an unsound relationship with his parents may openly or deviously reject their way of life.

Moreover, he may incorporate the deceitfulness, callousness and brutality of maladjusted parents. The boy who identifies with a brutal father or the girl who identifies with a sexually promiscuous mother is said to have a corrupt identification.

Identification also plays an important part in determining a person's sexual orientation. The boy with a sound relationship with his father tends to take over his father's masculine qualities, and a girl with a healthy relationship with her mother assumes her mother's feminine orientation. However, when a boy is rejected by an indifferent father and hovered over by an engulfing mother, he may identify with his mother and incorporate many of her feminine qualities. If his identification with her is profound, he he may become homosexual. Similarly, a girl with a painful relationship with her mother may identify with her father and in adulthood follow a homosexual pattern. Unhealthy identifications may also contribute to other kinds of sexual problems.

In this light, let us consider the following exchange between a father and a nine-year-old boy:

MARK: Dad, the wheels on the cars of my electric racing-car set are getting stuck. They need oil, and I've read this page of the instruction book but I—

FATHER: Can't you see I'm busy working on these business reports?

MARK: It'll just take a minute to look at this drawing, and then I'll—

FATHER: This is the third time in the last hour you've come in here and bothered me. If it's not one thing it's another.

MARK: I'm sorry, but—

FATHER: How do you expect me to make the money to buy expensive toys like that if I never get a minute's peace around here to get some work done? I'm building up a business, and who's it for? It's for you and your brother to take over someday. But all you do is bother me when I'm trying to concentrate.

MARK: I'm sorry.

FATHER: All right, leave me alone. Ask your mother about it. Fran, see what this kid wants and do something about it. Keep him out of here.

When such father-son exchanges are characteristic of their relationship throughout the boy's childhood and early adolescence, his identification with his father often is defective. Many years later, when the father seeks out his son to interest him in the business, he may find in his place a bearded rebel or an effeminate stranger.

Let us consider a healthier way in which this interchange might have occurred:

MARK: Dad, the wheels on the cars of my electric racing-car set are getting stuck. They need oil, and I've read this page of the instruction book but I—

FATHER: I'm pretty busy.

MARK: This will only take a minute.

FATHER: All right. Let me see the car and the instruction booklet. Well, you get a toothpick or a straw from the broom, dip it in the oil, and put two drops, and only two, in each of these four axle holes. Get the oil and a toothpick and I'll show you how it's done.

In two or three minutes the job is finished.

MARK: Thanks, Dad. You're pretty smart.

FATHER: I'm glad you think so.

MARK: What's that you're doing?

FATHER: These are the plans for an office building they're going to put up in Westbrook, and I'm working out an estimate of how much the electrical installations will cost.

MARK: Why?

FATHER: Well, if I can give them a good price, maybe I'll get the job, and it will be a good thing for our business.

MARK: Do you think I could do that when I grow up?

FATHER: If you work hard and become an engineer,

you can. Now get along with you. I'm busy.

MARK: Thanks, Dad.

Anxiety and Security

Anxiety is a common feeling. It is the sensation a person would have if he were chained in the center of a busy intersection during rush-hour traffic. He would be flooded with painful apprehension and dread. The person with interpersonally caused anxiety feels similar, but as a rule he cannot identify the cause of his anxiousness. Anxiety may vary in degree from mild tension to disorganizing panic, and everyone has at least a touch of it now and then.

It may be caused by many things. Unsolved emotional problems from the past, unmet yearnings for affection, seething hostility that the person feels too guilty to express (or even to become aware of), sexual impulses which are crowded out of awareness because of shame and dread, and many other things may contribute to anxiety. *In each case anxiety is caused by past or present interpersonal stresses that usually are too painful for the person to deal with consciously.*

Anxiety is frequently encountered in children. It may be caused by the harshness of a rejecting parent, or the indifference of a loveless one, or the threats of a floundering one, or by countless other unhealthy parent-child relationships. Anxiety may be precipitated in an adolescent by his struggle to find acceptable expression for his sexual impulses, or by his tense search for prestige and love, or by his attempts to become gradually independent of his parents. In most cases unsolved problems from the past combine with current interpersonal difficulties to produce anxiousness.

To a greater or lesser extent, anxiety incapacitates a person for effective interpersonal action—it robs him of his comfort with people. He often cannot define its causes and cannot take appropriate steps to stop it. Severe anxiety also distorts a person's view of his past and interferes with judgment. Anxiety may occur in acute bouts that last a few minutes to several hours, or in a chronic form it may last for days, weeks or months. In many persons it becomes encapsulated in phobic fears, apprehensive obsessive thoughts, psychosomatic body disorders and other psychiatric problems.

Anxiety is so widespread that much of life is spent avoiding it, although few people are aware that they are doing so. For example, the child who is being reared in a loveless home may unconsciously attempt to quell his anxiousness by physical overactivity, aimless destructiveness, or severe nightmares. The child whose mother has tried to discipline him with daily threats of loss of her love may have phobic fears of the dark or of going to school. The anxious adolescent who is locked in a hopeless struggle with insensitive parents may seek release in drugs, or rebellion, or intestinal cramping.

Security is the opposite of anxiety; it consists of comfortable, tension-free interpersonal functioning. *Emotional security* is produced by the gentle cuddling a mother gives an infant, the companionship a father offers his son or daughter, and the judicious mixture of permissiveness and limitations a parent gives an adolescent. The secure person can talk out and solve most of his interpersonal problems, and he can form sound bonds with people. He has ways of dealing with the impulses and conflicts that arise within him; these methods are sometimes called his *security operations.* Much of this book is devoted to the many ways in which children, adolescents and parents seek emotional security.

Security and anxiety are inversely related. They are on opposite ends of a seesaw; when one is high, the other is low. However, no one is entirely secure emotionally, and at least some anxiety occurs at times in all people. The seesaw is rarely still—it is continually being tipped one way or the other by healthy and unhealthy interpersonal events. The ultimate goal of most interpersonal relationships is the control of anxiety and the preservation of emotional security.

In relationships between people anxiety and security can be produced without the use of words. For example, anxiety in a mother can induce anxiety in her infant through the inarticulate, unconscious process of communication we call *empathy*. The impatience or loathing a parent shows toward a child by the tightening of his lips or the narrowing of his eyes may often produce more anxiety than a torrent of words, and neither the parent nor the child may be aware of what is happening.

As we shall discuss later in this chapter and shall illustrate many times in this book, anxiety and security play important roles in molding the *games* that children, adolescents and parents play.

With these principles in mind let us consider the following conversation between a mother and her seven-year-old daughter:

MOTHER: Anne, go to bed. This is the fourth or fifth time I've told you.

ANNE: I'm going.

MOTHER: You're not. You're still playing.

ANNE: I'm putting my things away.

MOTHER: You're just stalling. I have to nag at you all day long to do this, to do that, to do anything. By the time the day is over I'm a nervous wreck because of you. Do you see these wrinkles and gray hairs? You're the one who's putting them there.

ANNE: I'm going.

MOTHER: What good does it do now? I've had to scream at you for half an hour and you've ruined my evening, and your father is annoyed with me and we'll probably fight over you. You're destroying my marriage, my health and my happiness. If I become sick and die, how will you feel?

ANNE: I'm sorry.

MOTHER: Sorry? That's all I ever get out of you. What good is "sorry"? You'll be the same tomorrow. If I have a nervous breakdown, I suppose you'll be sorry then.

ANNE: (beginning to cry): I'll be better.

MOTHER: Stop that crying. You don't mean it. If you really meant it, you'd be better. You're just crying so your father can hear you and fight with me about it. God punishes children like you.

ANNE: I'm afraid. It's dark in my room.

MOTHER: It's always something with you. Leave the light on, then.

In this dialogue Mother quickly leaves the problem at hand—getting Anne into bed—and accuses Anne of making her unhappy, old and physically sick. Mother also accuses Anne of destroying her marriage and pushing her toward emotional illness. In this harsh tug-of-war Mother lays the bases for much present and future anxiety in Anne.

Let us examine how this exchange might have occurred in a healthier way:

MOTHER: Anne, it's time to go to bed.

ANNE: I'm going.

MOTHER: This is the third time I've told you. Now march, young lady, or there's going to be a lot less television, or perhaps none at all, for you tomorrow night.

ANNE: I'm putting on my pajamas.

MOTHER: Here's a good-night kiss.

ANNE: What about television tomorrow night?

MOTHER: Up to now you still have it, but we get what we earn and tomorrow is a new day. Television is something you earn. It's not one of your constitutional rights.

ANNE: My what?

MOTHER: Never mind. Go to sleep.

In this dialogue Mother gets the job done by bargaining over television time. Threats of loss of television time do not precipitate anxiety, as all the threats in the first dialogue do.

Needs and Satisfactions

A great deal of human activity is directed toward the satisfaction of needs. Needs and their satisfactions play large roles in personality formation and constitute much of what is called experience. For example, one of the earliest needs of an infant is food. As the tension of hunger builds up, he becomes restless and cries, and this behavior evokes tender attention from his mother and satisfaction of his need. The infant's need for food is *both physical and interpersonal*. He needs more than calories and food values—he must have a tender, comfortable person to care for him. He requires more than an efficient incubator. The need for tenderness is the first and most basic interpersonal need. In the forms of affection, love, friendship and other kinds of interpersonal closeness, it continues to be a crucial need throughout life.

Similarly, all physical needs are closely connected with interpersonal ones, although from late childhood onward the relationship is more subtle. This union of physical and interpersonal needs leads to a special human characteristic, *foresight*. Each rising need stirs memories, conscious or unconscious, about how it was satisfied before in an interpersonal relationship, and the person makes plans to satisfy it again. Needs and satisfactions weave the past, present and future into a single process. Thus, a three-month-old infant with a tender mother cries lustily when he is hungry, and in a little while he is satisfied, but an infant with a cold, rejecting mother may whimper lowly and not be satisfied; in each case experience has already begun to mold personality structure and interpersonal functioning.

In our society the *interpersonal* needs of a child or adolescent go unmet more often than his *physical* ones; loneliness is more common than hunger. Interpersonal needs include love, esteem, prestige, reasonable limitations on undesirable behavior, and the freedom to grow comfortably through the successive stages of childhood and adolescence.

Reflection of Feeling Tones. A useful approach for parents in meeting the interpersonal needs of children and adolescents is the *reflection of feeling tones,* a technique first outlined in the writings of the American psychologist Carl R. Rogers. When a child has an interpersonal need, especially a painful one, the parents may approach it by putting into words what the child feels. For example, the parent may say, "You're angry," or "You're afraid and upset," or "You feel alone and left out."

Reflection of feeling tones accomplishes various things:

(1.) It lets the child know that the parent understands how he feels, and this creates an immediate bond. (2.) It often makes the child's feelings clearer to him. (3.) The parent frequently becomes more aware of what is going on in the child when he crystallizes it in spoken words. (4.) In many instances reflection of feeling tones opens the way to *satisfaction of the need connected with it.* The frightened child may be reassured, and the furious one given some outlet for his anger. (5.) Increasing the child's awareness of his feelings helps him understand himself and grow emotionally. (6.) The reflection of feeling tones at all times offers a parent a ready tool to use with an upset child. Often a parent does not know what to say to a crying child, a hostile one, or a terrified one. To say, "You're upset and sad," or "You're very angry," or "You're scared" opens the door to an effective and often healing parent-child exchange.

Let us examine how the reflection of feeling tones helps a parent approach an interpersonal need of a child.

In this first exchange the father does *not* reflect feeling tones, and he stumbles badly in handling a stressful situation with his son.

Father and four-year-old David are alone in the apartment. Father has just returned from taking Mother to the hospital for an emergency appendectomy. David is crying and Father is tense.

FATHER: What's the matter?
DAVID: Nothing.
FATHER: If nothing is the matter, stop crying. It doesn't help anything.
DAVID (still crying): I'm not crying.
FATHER: Stop that. You have to learn to face these things without bawling. It doesn't do any good, you just get more upset, and it bothers me.
DAVID: I'm sorry.
FATHER: Be a man, not a crybaby. Your mother will be back in a week or so, and tomorrow you'll go to stay with your Aunt Bella until she returns. It's time for bed.

This exchange creates no bond between Father and David, and it leaves David feeling inadequate, as well as desolate. *His needs are not met.* Also, Father becomes more upset as he hears David crying himself to sleep.

Let us consider how this interchange might have occurred if Father had met David's interpersonal needs by reflecting feeling tones. The reflections of feeling tones are in italics.

FATHER: *You feel lonely and sad because Mother went to the hospital.*

DAVID: I miss her.

FATHER: *Maybe you're also worried about what will happen to her there.*

DAVID: When will she come back?

FATHER: In a week or so. She's just going to have her appendix out; lots of people have that operation and there's almost no danger. *However, you're a little scared and worried.*

DAVID: I feel better now.

FATHER: *That means you don't feel so alone and afraid.*

DAVID: A week isn't so long.

FATHER: That's right. Besides that, you're going to your Aunt Bella's tomorrow morning, and you'll stay there until Mother comes home.

DAVID: I'll be all right.

FATHER: Of course you will. *You'll miss your mother and you'll feel a little worried at times,* but then you'll feel all right.

DAVID: I can take it.

FATHER: Sure you can. Maybe you should go to bed pretty soon. I have to get you up early tomorrow to take you to Aunt Bella's before I go to work.

In this dialogue Father meets David's interpersonal needs, and one of his main tools in doing so is the reflection of feeling tones.

Children and adolescents develop toward emotional health if obstacles are not placed in their way, and damaging interpersonal relationships are the main obstacle they may encounter. If they have secure love, reasonable limitations and the freedom to grow, children and adolescents have a basic tendency to develop into well-adjusted adults. Nature is on the parents' side.

This principle of *the tendency toward health* emphasizes that people do not have inborn inclinations to be hostile, destructive and callous in their interpersonal relationships. On the contrary, children have natural tendencies to respond to tenderness with love, to understanding with cooperation, and to reasonable limitations with compliance. The tendency toward health continues throughout childhood and adolescence. Early emotional damage, if it is not severe, can later be corrected by healthy relationships; in the same manner that personality can be distorted by harmful relationships, it can be mended by sound ones.

Individual incidents do not warp a child's personality. It is the daily hammering of long-term unhealthy relationships that damages a child. Screaming harangues once a month, or even once a week, by an exasperated mother do not harm a child if the mother-child relationship is sound most of the time. The indifference of a vocationally harassed father for a few weeks several times a year does not hurt a child if he gives the child love and companionship the rest of the time. The parent who says that his child was fine until some brief, upsetting event occurred and that since then the child has had behavior problems is merely seeking a scapegoat on which to blame personality difficulties caused by long-term defects in the child's relationships with his parents and other close persons. Children and adolescents are not fragile—they do not crumble when lightly tapped; they are sturdy and grow healthily if given reasonable chances.

The tendency toward health is an aspect of what Harry Stack Sullivan called the one-genus postulate: "that everyone is much more simply human than otherwise." By this Sullivan meant that the basic direction of human development is toward interpersonal health and that even very disturbed people have extensive resources that can be drawn upon to lead them back to sounder adjustments. Sullivan's one-genus postulate also implies that the lives of children and adults, even when they seem most pointless and self-defeating, make sense when viewed from the developmental point of view. The phobic fears of a child, or the self-defeating rebellion of an adolescent, or the repeated marital failures of an adult can be understood, and often helped, by comprehending and resolving the things that have distorted his emotional functioning.

The Backward Look. When an adult is dealing with an emotional problem of a child or an adolescent, he should take a *backward look* over previous events and relationships in the child's life to attempt to discern what has caused the difficulty. The backward look is systematically used by psychiatrists in working with disturbed children and adolescents, but it can also be employed by parents in dealing with minor upsets. When used by parents, the backward look covers relatively recent events—those of the preceding weeks or months; when employed by psychiatrists and clinical psychologists, it usually reaches back much farther.

Let us examine how the backward look may be used to clarify a problem that is more common than most parents realize. Mother is talking with four-year-old Susan. In the first dialogue the backward look is not used:

MOTHER: Go to the car, Susan. We're going to spend the afternoon at the Mortons'.

SUSAN: I don't want to go.

MOTHER: Why don't you want to go?

SUSAN: I don't know.

MOTHER: You're just being stubborn. We're all going, and you can't stay home alone.

SUSAN: I'm sick. I think I'm going to vomit.

MOTHER: You were perfectly all right a minute ago. You're just pretending to be sick because you don't want to go.

SUSAN: I'm really sick.

MOTHER: Let me feel your forehead. You have no fever. Go out and get in the car.

Susan begins to cry.

MOTHER: Stop that nonsense. You stop crying or I'll give you something to cry about.

Mother leads Susan, pale and sniffling, to the car.

Let us consider how this exchange might have occurred if Mother had used *the backward look:*

MOTHER: Go to the car, Susan. We're going to spend the afternoon at the Mortons'.

SUSAN: I don't want to go.

MOTHER: Why don't you want to go?

SUSAN: I don't know.

MOTHER: You usually like to go to the Mortons'.

SUSAN: I never want to go there again.

MOTHER: This is not like you, Susan. Whenever we go anywhere, you're usually the first one in the car.

SUSAN: I don't want to go to the Mortons'.

MOTHER: Is it just the Mortons' you don't want to go to?

SUSAN: Yes.

MOTHER (using *the backward look*): We went there three weeks ago. Did you like it then?

SUSAN: I don't want to go there.

MOTHER: Did anything happen there that bothered you?

SUSAN: No.

MOTHER: What did you do there three weeks ago? Martha was sick and you couldn't play with her. You stayed with us for a while. You went to George's room and listened to his stereo set with him. Then you came back and sat with us.

SUSAN: I don't like George [the Mortons' sixteen-year-old son].

MOTHER: Why?

SUSAN: I just don't like him.

MOTHER (exploring with *the backward look*): Susan,

did something happen between you and George?

SUSAN: No, nothing.

MOTHER: Susan, if you've changed so much about going to the Mortons', something must have happened. Did George do or say anything to upset you?

Silence.

MOTHER: What did George say to you?

SUSAN: He didn't *say* anything.

MOTHER: Did he *do* anything to you?

Silence.

MOTHER: Susan, honey, what did George do?

SUSAN: He felt me.

MOTHER: Where did he feel you?

SUSAN: Here. [She points to her genital area.]

MOTHER: Did he take your pants off?

SUSAN: He put his hand inside.

MOTHER: Did he do anything else?

SUSAN: He made me feel him.

MOTHER: Where did he make you feel him?

SUSAN: I can't say it. [She begins to cry.]

MOTHER: Did he take your hand and put it on his pants?

SUSAN: Inside his pants. He made my hand rub him there.

MOTHER: Did he do anything else?

SUSAN: He said that if I ever told you and Daddy, you'd hate me and send me away to live somewhere else.

MOTHER: Then what happened?

SUSAN: I got scared and came in and sat with you.

MOTHER: Susan, I'm glad this came out. You were right to tell me. You did nothing wrong, but George did, and we'll see that he never has a chance to upset you in this way again. Your Daddy and I love you, and we will never send you away to live anywhere else. I'll talk to your father about this right now. Your father will be glad you told us, and we'll never tell anyone else. I don't know what we'll do about our visit to the Mortons'. Maybe we'll make it a very short one, and you'll stay with us all the time we're there.

By using the *backward look* Mother discovered the problem behind Susan's upset and took steps to prevent it from being repeated.

Games

The word "game" has been used in psychiatry to designate commonly encountered patterns of interpersonal activity that have the following characteristics:

1. A game follows certain rules. In their interactions with one another the involved persons go through various steps, or "moves," in a more or less set sequence. Each action evokes a predictable response from one or more other persons, leading to a foreseeable result.

2. The person who plays a game frequently repeats it in his relationships with others, and it is characteristic of him. He may play it hourly, daily or weekly, depending on its nature.

3. A game, as defined in this book, is always unhealthy. It is a twisted substitute for comfortable interpersonal living.

4. The final result of a game is to block intimacy. By maintaining a rupture, or distortion, in an interpersonal relationship, it prevents people from being close. As such, it serves a sick need in one or more persons involved.

5. A game usually lies outside the conscious awareness of the person, or persons, involved. He does not realize that he engages in a repetitive, unhealthy interaction that destroys intimacy.

6. A person gets some type of unsound satisfaction from his game. For example, it may be a means of releasing hostility, or diminishing guilt, or fleeing a close relationship that frightens him. This is what Berne calls the "ulterior motive" or "payoff" of a game. A game is not "fun." Although a person "gets something" out of it, it gives him no persistent relief.

7. A game proceeds by various moves, or steps, which provoke each other in a regular sequence; these are what Berne calls "transactional stimuli" and "transactional responses." For example, player A makes a move, which

stimulates player B to respond with a particular countermove. A then makes another move, which causes B to react in a special way, and so the game proceeds.

8. Some games are expressions of the anxiety-security balance discussed earlier in this chapter. Such a game is fueled in the player by a basic anxiety, such as profound doubts about his adequacy or dread of hostile or sexual impulses. In such cases the game is a corrupt attempt to seek security (that is, emotional comfort), but it succeeds only briefly, or not at all.

9. Games are developed, or "learned," and incorporated into the person's patterns of emotional functioning during childhood and early adolescence. They begin mainly in the close relationship of life—those with parents, siblings and other important persons.

10. A game, once developed in childhood, tends to be carried into adult interpersonal relationships, whether it is relevant to them or not. For example, it tends to be carried into college associations, marriage, job situations and other interpersonal activities. Often the game dovetails with the games of other people. By trial and error the player goes from person to person until he finds one who will play his game with him, and this often determines whom he marries, for whom he works, and with whom he associates.

We shall illustrate the nature of games by describing a typical one.

A Game of Childhood: King on the Mountain

In this game a child and his parents go through a series of moves and countermoves, usually carried out one or more times each day, in which the child manipulates one parent to dominate the other. The child does not have a sound relationship with either parent; and if the game continues throughout his formative years, he develops an ingrained interpersonal pattern that may cause him much difficulty in adult life. King on the Mountain may be played by either a boy or a girl, but in the case we shall cite the player was a girl.

Nancy began her game between the ages of two and

three. Parents often underestimate the capacity of children to play games at early ages. The basic intelligence of a child is the same at three as at twenty; his information increases and his talents develop, but his intellectual potential, or IQ, remains the same. Also, many small children are very acute observers of the few close people in their lives. They cannot put their observations into words and cannot organize their thoughts into logical sequences, but their capacities to harness their observations into game playing are almost as great at three as at ten or twenty. In some ways children are more observant than adults; they see everything fresh and unclouded by the ideas and prejudices adults have developed.

Nancy's game of King on the Mountain was facilitated by her parents' personalities. Her mother was passive and felt guilty if she became angry, even when her anger was clearly justified; in addition, she felt anxious if other people became angry at her. Her domineering, guilt-slinging parents had made her so. Nevertheless, Mother at first could be firm with Nancy unless Father intervened. Father was an aggressive but affectionate man who had moved into the vacuum created by his wife's passivity. However, the marriage probably was reasonably happy for both of them until Nancy began her game.

Nancy learned early that Mother's firmness in restricting her could be wiped out by a sharp remark from Father, and she soon became skillful in mobilizing Father's irritability to dominate Mother. If Mother and Nancy were alone in the house and Mother disapprovingly tapped her hands when she began to open forbidden drawers and pull things out, Nancy pouted for a few minutes and then went back to her toys. However, if Father was home and this happened, Nancy ran screaming to him and clutched his legs or arms. Then the following exchange, or one of its many variations, took place:

FATHER (to Nancy): What's the matter, honey? (To Mother) Jane, what's happened to Nancy now?

MOTHER: She was getting into the cabinet where we

40

keep the good dishes and glasses; I told her not to and she began to cry.

Nancy shoves her hands toward Father's face and sobs loudly.

FATHER (becoming irritable as Nancy's sobbing begins to goad him): I suppose you slapped her hands again.

MOTHER: I tapped them lightly.

FATHER (annoyed and moving into the vacuum created by Mother's uneasiness with his irritability): Did a little tap produce all this sobbing? It seems to me, Jane, that there ought to be a more civilized way to tell a child to stay out of a drawer.

MOTHER: I'm sorry, but nothing else . . .

FATHER: This sort of thing happens frequently here. I don't want a daughter who is afraid of her parents and whose natural curiosity has been stifled by slapping her around because of perfectly normal, understandable childhood acts.

MOTHER: I'm sorry, Tom.

FATHER: Let Daddy see those hands. Now you go with Mother and she'll give you some pans and other things from the kitchen to play with.

Nancy screams louder and clutches Father tighter.

FATHER: Look how frightened the kid is. Jane, you have to stop hitting this child. [Father is now fairly upset.] I have enough trouble at the office all day long dealing with difficult people. When I come home and try to relax, these damn problems are thrown at me.

Nancy, seeing (inarticulately, or unconsciously, as it were) that Mother had been thoroughly cowed and that Father has done her work for her, and also sensing that Father has been pushed to the limit for the time being, knows that the game has been played out—successfully. Her sobbing stops, she allows Father to act as peacemaker by drying her tears, and she trots off to the kitchen sure that she can do whatever she wishes with Mother. She has paralyzed Mother and has dominated Father, although neither of them really understands what has happened. She is truly King on the Mountain.

As Nancy grew older, the issues and the techniques of the game changed somewhat, but the basic pattern remained the same. It was played daily or several times each week. By the time she was ten the pattern was ingrained. She used temper outbursts to tyrannize her mother and plaintive whimpering to manipulate her father. After the age of ten she needed the game only once a week or so to reinforce the well-established system. By the time she reached middle adolescence Nancy's ways of dealing with men and women were set, and she went on playing King on the Mountain, in one form or another, in various kinds of interpersonal situations. She was competitive with women and was disliked by them; she was charming with men and manipulated them to accomplish her ends.

However, she was close to no one. The game always interfered. It bred a cold, self-centered quality in her and corrupted her relationship with any man or woman with whom she had associated much. When the game did not work and many people would not play it with her, Nancy became frightened. She then played it even harder in her attempts to get rid of her anxiety and to obtain some degree of emotional security. The game was so deeply entrenched that she was unaware of it. Others occasionally discovered parts of it but could not piece together a complete picture. When she was twenty-eight, floundering in her second marriage and beginning to drink too much, she sought psychiatric help. It was time to stop the game.

We have described a game that proceeded unchecked throughout childhood and adolescence into adulthood to illustrate the origin, course and long-range results of games. In subsequent chapters we shall show how games can be stopped by the four basic processes outlined at the beginning of this chapter: (1.) The game must be identified. (2.) It must be interpreted. (3.) It must be broken up. (4.) A healthy interpersonal pattern must be substituted for it.

The Stages of Development in Childhood and Adolescence

We shall close this chapter by listing the stages of development in childhood and adolescence, and we shall indicate the chapters that cover the games relating to each period.

Infancy extends from birth to the appearance of articulate speech. Thus, it lasts until about the age of twenty-four months.

Childhood stretches from the appearance of articulate speech until the child has a strong need for companions of the same age group. Thus, it reaches from about twenty-four months to the age of five. The games of infancy and childhood are covered in Chapters 2 and 3 and in part of Chapter 4.

The juvenile period extends through most of the grade school years. It reaches from the age of about six through eleven. In the latter part of this period the person has a need for close comradeship with persons of equal status and usually of the same sex. The games children play in the juvenile period are discussed in Chapters 5 and 6 and to a lesser extent in Chapters 4 and 7.

Preadolescence, or *puberty,* extends from about twelve through thirteen. It is characterized by the emergence of genital sexual drives and the transfer of interest from persons of one's own sex to those of the other sex. Some of the games of preadolescence are outlined in Chapter 7.

Early adolescence reaches from the end of pre-adolescence until the person has established some pattern for the expression of his physical sexuality. The upper limits of this period are variable and are influenced by cultural and economic factors.

Late adolescence extends from the end of early adolescence until an individual's personality structure attains its more or less permanent adult form. The upper limits of this period vary from the late teens to the early, or even middle, twenties. Various games of early and late adolescence are described in Chapters 8, 9 and 10 and in part of Chapter 7.

Adulthood is characterized by the capacity to develop an interest in another person who is as important as oneself. The developing and broadening of such closeness, or intimacy, is a main feature of successful adulthood and the source of many of its satisfactions. The ways in which games may be carried from childhood and adolescence into adulthood, and thus impair it, are discussed in Chapter 10.

2

THE GAMES MY MOTHER TAUGHT ME

In the early weeks and months of life an infant has no concepts of "I," "other people" and "the world." He lives in an oceanic flood of sensations; he gradually forms a concept of himself as a person who is separate from his environment. The first figure who looms out of the mist is his mother or the person who takes her place. During this period his mother represents all interpersonal relationships to him, and his perception of her as a comforting or painful force affects to at least some extent his approach to all later persons in his life. His mother is the person who slowly draws him out of the *noninterpersonal* state in which he is born; his subsequent concepts of himself and other people depend much on how she cares for him as she feeds, bathes, cleans and cuddles him.

The mother is the first representative of what the child many years later will know as "reality," and she has a marked effect on whether he will find reality comfortable or frightening. The mother also is the main person who teaches the child many of the things he must master for social living. He must learn to communicate by gestures and speech, he must be toilet-trained, he must keep his clothes on, and he must not carelessly destroy the objects around him. In a period of a few years he must learn all that man in his social evolution required tens of thousands of years to master, and while teaching him all this, the mother must give him a reassuring view of the world and his place in it.

The physical equipment a child brings into the world, which is often labeled instinct and heredity, is so profoundly affected by his interpersonal life that it is difficult to know much about its influence on personality development. Human *instincts* are so quickly layered over by experience that we know little about them. We can talk about the instincts of young wolves to forage for food, but we cannot talk about the instincts of children to go to refrigerators for snacks; we can speak about kittens' instincts to pounce on mice, but we cannot speak of children's instincts to go to school so that many years later they can make money to spend on food.

The influence of *heredity* on a child's personality development is much less than the impact of how he is reared. The fearful child of a fearful mother got that way by being reared by her, not by being born of her. The assertive child of an outspoken mother developed this trait by associating with her after birth, not by genetic influences before birth. Human heredity is difficult to study because the life-span of the investigator is the same as that of his subjects; it is easier to study heredity in guinea pigs who have short life-spans and begin to reproduce at an early age. Rumors about the personalities of grandparents and great-grandparents who are said to have been alcoholics or judges do not constitute the stuff from which a science of human heredity can be built. At present most psychiatrists and social scientists feel human personality is determined mainly by interpersonal relationships and that the role of heredity is small.

We shall now discuss some games that children play in the first five or six years of life. However, the games that begin in the early years often continue during later childhood and adolescence. Brief games, which occur between all children and parents for a few hours or a few days, do no damage, although they may cause misery during that time. It is the long-term hard-fought games that warp a personality for life.

Early in life a child learns that he has a certain amoun of power. Even in infancy he senses that crying brings foo or cuddling and that thrashing and screaming mobilize hi mother to meet his needs. An equilibrium of power betwee mother and child slowly develops and persists throughou childhood and adolescence. The nature of this powe equilibrium has a marked effect on what kind of person th child becomes and how satisfying or miserable the mother child relationship is.

In this power equilibrium neither mother nor chil should be entirely dominant. A browbeating mother ofte rears a frightened or wildly rebellious child, and an undul passive mother may rear an unrestrained, temper tantrumish child who is ill fitted for the endless restriction that society puts on people.

Although perhaps uncomfortable to admit, a powe equilibrium is present to some extent in most human rela tionships. Thus, a mother has the power to satisfy or tor ment an infant by feeding him on time or not, and a fev years later the child has the power to respect or smash parent's furniture, although in most cases neither the paren nor the child has a clear awareness of the causes of his ac tions. Love and understanding in child rearing have bee rightly emphasized to parents in recent times, but a fran appraisal of the ways in which power is used and misuse by parents and children is also necessary.

A common disturbance of the power equilibrium be tween a mother and a child occurs in the childhood game o Ready or Not, Here I come.

Eric's game of Ready or Not, Here I Come began befor the age of three. He sensed early that fitful screaming trou bled and puzzled his mother. Although neither of them wa articulately aware of it, each of Eric's temper outburst caused his mother to feel, "What have I done wrong?" Th was not the right question. The right question would hav been: "What has gone wrong in our relationship?" The firs question directed attention only to Mother, but the answer did not lie entirely with her. The second question would have directed attention to the relationship *between* Mother and Eric, where the true trouble was.

Since Mother sought answers in the wrong places, she never found the right ones, and feeling that in someway she was at fault, she always gave in. By the time he was five Eric had acquired a good deal of power over her. His game consisted of two basic moves: (1.) aggressive behavior, both verbal and physical, when he wanted something and (2.) stopping this behavior when he achieved his object. Each new problem of childhood led Eric to play a round of Ready or Not, Here I Come, and Mother was never ready.

By the time he started school Eric's screaming and pounding on furniture had stopped, and his game had become entirely verbal. A typical round ran as follows:

MOTHER: Eric, come in and get ready for dinner.

ERIC: I'm playing.

MOTHER: Your father will be home soon. Please come in.

ERIC: I'm not ready to come in.

MOTHER: Please, Eric.

ERIC: Don't holler at me.

MOTHER: I'm not hollering, Eric. I'm just asking you to come in.

ERIC: You *are* hollering.

MOTHER: Eric, it's after five thirty.

ERIC: You butt into everything I do.

MOTHER (making a weak threat that both she and Eric know she will not carry out): Come in right now, or I'll come and get you.

ERIC (calling her bluff): I won't come in. It's too early. I'm going to play longer.

MOTHER: Please, Eric.

ERIC: In fifteen minutes I'll come in.

MOTHER: It will be dark then. [She goes into the house.]

Forty minutes later, when it is too dark to play longer, Eric goes in.

In Ready or Not, Here I Come the mother-child relationship is distorted, for in addition to love and understanding a mother should be able to give her child reasonable limitations and make them stick. The child who is reared without reasonable limitations on his behavior is unlikely to be able to adjust comfortably to the countless limitations society will later place on him. Society requires that a person stop for red lights, pay his taxes on due dates, get to work on time, deal tactfully with work superiors, and many other things; a person can meet these social requirements only if he develops the capacity to do so in the close interpersonal relationships of childhood and adolescence when his personality is being formed. Eric is not doing this.

Let us examine how this round of Ready or Not, Here I Come might have occurred if Eric's mother had handled it in a healthier way:

MOTHER: Eric, come in and get ready for dinner.

ERIC: I'm not ready to come in and don't holler at me.

At this point Mother asks herself the right question: "What is wrong with the relationship between Eric and me?" and she arrives at the correct answer: "He is bullying me and I'm being intimidated."

MOTHER: Eric, it's getting dark, it's nearly dinner time, and you must tidy up before your father comes home. Come in—right now.

ERIC: You butt into everything I do.

MOTHER (this time, no bluff): Come in right now or I'll bring you in.

ERIC (calling her bluff): I won't come. It's not time. I'm going to . . .

Mother pulls him in by the arm and wipes his face. Eric begins to howl.

MOTHER: Go to your room until that screaming is over, and close the door so you won't disturb everybody with the noise. We all love you, but we're doing you no favor by letting you grow up doing whatever you please and howling when you don't get your way.

ERIC: You wait until Daddy comes home.

MOTHER: I don't think that's going to change anything. Your father and I had a talk about you last night and neither one of us is going to be stampeded by your yelling and temper fits anymore.

ERIC: What?

MOTHER: You heard what I said.

ERIC: When did the new rules start around here?

MOTHER: Right now. Go in and watch television. I'll call you for dinner.

Throwing Mud Pies

Guilt is a particular kind of anxiety, a desolate sensation accompanied by feelings of unworthiness and failure. The painfulness of guilt molds many human actions.

A person may also use guilt as an instrument for controlling others. For example, a parent may use guilt to cow his child into submissiveness. A child may be reared in a hailstorm of "You are making me sick by all the bad things you do," "You are destroying our marriage by all the trouble you cause between your father and me," "You will cripple your sister for life if you go on hitting her like that," "You are bad and God will punish you for the way you're making us suffer," and many other guilt-laden accusations strung into painful harangues. Such guilt-throwing techniques often accomplish their objective: to whip the child into whatever pattern of behavior the parent wants. However, when such tactics are used hourly or daily in rearing a child, he often becomes anxious and guilt-ridden and is vulnerable to various kinds of emotional difficulties in both childhood and adulthood.

Guilt is an *interpersonal* phenomenon. An individual develops it because other persons produce it in him; it does not spontaneously occur within him. However, once guilt is produced in a person, it may become a persistent part of his personality. Thus, guilt which begins as an *interpersonal* process may become *internalized*, and the person carries his guilty preoccupations into each new relationship. The person into whom guilty feelings were drummed throughout his childhood years tends to feel guilty when problems arise in his marriage, his work situation, his friendships and other interpersonal contacts. Each time he asks, "What have I done wrong?" instead of "What has gone wrong in the relationship between him and me?" The first incorrect question frequently prevents people from solving the interpersonal problem, for the difficulty is often caused by *both* persons, or perhaps mainly by the other one.

Children may also use guilt as a tool to manipulate their parents. This is particularly apt to occur when parents are vulnerable to guilt throwing because of emotional damage sustained during their own childhoods. Moreover, modern parents, in contrast to parents of previous generations, are prone to feel guilty about their children. When anything goes wrong, from a temper tantrum of a two-year-old to the sexual promiscuity of a seventeen-year-old, a parent today usually asks himself, "What have I done wrong? How have I failed my child?" The parent of thirty or forty years ago usually asked himself, "What shall I do to get this child back on the right road? How shall I convince him that he is acting badly?" This shift in parental thinking has had a significant impact on the personality structures of children.

Regardless of whether or not it is theoretically correct, the readiness of modern parents to feel guilty about their children's problems has made the childhood game of Throwing Mud Pies common. Children quickly sense that they can manipulate their parents by blaming them for their own actions. They discover that the reasons "I did it because I was afraid of you" and "You made me do it" paralyze their parents. The parents' attention shifts abruptly from the child's undesirable actions to a guilt-ridden examination of what they themselves are doing, so the main issue of the child's actions is not dealt with. When this is an hourly or daily event in the child's upbringing, he may develop guilt manipulation as a fixed personality pattern in dealing with people. However, society will not usually play his game with him. Society is more likely to become angry and retaliatory than guilty and apologetic when he carries his game into his adolescent and adult years.

50

Four-year-old Vernon often played the game of Throwing Mud Pies:

VERNON (to his father): You're a liar.
MOTHER: Vernon, you shouldn't say such things to your father.
VERNON: That's the way you and he talk to each other.
MOTHER: We talk that way very little, but you do it all the time.
VERNON: If you can do it, why can't I?
FATHER (to Mother): Grace, we really should be more careful about what we say in front of the children.
MOTHER: I guess we should set a better example.

In this dialogue the central problem, that Vernon called his father a liar, is quickly forgotten as Vernon deftly mobilizes guilt in his parents and shifts their attention from his hourly misbehavior to their occasional spats. Vernon will probably call his mother and father many more ugly names in the future and will escape censure by the same game.

Vernon gives the vise another twist in the following exchange:

MOTHER: Vernon, eat your carrots and peas.
VERNON: They make my stomach hurt. Why do you force me to eat things that make my stomach hurt?
MOTHER: Carrots and peas ought not to make you sick.
VERNON: Then why do I have to go to the toilet so much when I eat them, or maybe even throw up?
FATHER: There are so many different kinds of food, Grace. Maybe the kid is allergic to carrots.
VERNON: Then why do you make me eat them?
MOTHER: Vernon, if I slice a tomato for you, will you eat it?
VERNON: I guess so.

The variations of Throwing Mud Pies are countless. Another goes as follows:

MOTHER: Vernon, you must stop breaking things. That ashtray is the third thing you've broken this week.

VERNON: I didn't mean to. I can't help it.

MOTHER: Well, you must learn. You can't go through life smashing things. There will be no television for you tonight.

VERNON: That's not fair. You're punishing me for things I can't help. Is it fair to punish me for things I can't help?

FATHER: Grace, he's only four. Four-year-olds break a few things.

VERNON: You both punish me all the time for things I can't help.

MOTHER: I guess we really shouldn't punish him for things that are normal at his age.

VERNON: It was an accident. Should I be punished for accidents? Is that right?

MOTHER: Well, maybe not.

FATHER: Vernon, you must be more careful.

VERNON: I'll try.

MOTHER: We'll not punish you this time, but if you break one more thing, there will be no television for two days.

Vernon knows this is an empty threat. He has been playing Throwing Mud Pies with his parents for two years.

Let us examine how Vernon's parents might have handled this last exchange if they had understood his game. The dialogue begins as above:

VERNON: That's not fair. You're punishing me for things I can't help. Is it fair to punish me for things I can't help?

MOTHER: Vernon, this business of blaming your father and me for everything you do wrong is going to stop.

VERNON: Huh?

MOTHER: I said that you have developed the habit of

blaming your father and me for everything you do wrong. That's out from here on.

VERNON: You both punish me all the time for things I can't help.

MOTHER: That's not going to work anymore. You're not going to throw mud at us every time you do something wrong, or if you do, it won't stick.

VERNON: You're unfair. You're cruel. You're . . .

MOTHER: And you're throwing mud at me again. I'm not perfect—nobody is—and maybe I'm wrong sometimes. But blaming everything on us is not going to work anymore. It's no good for you and it's no good for us.

VERNON (beginning to sniffle loudly): Dad . . .

MOTHER: And it's no use turning to him. We've talked it over and we agree. No more blame-slinging at us.

FATHER: Go to your room for half an hour, Vernon, and think it over.

VERNON: You're ganging up on me.

MOTHER: To help you—yes.

Vernon's mud-throwing days are numbered, to the benefit of his personality structure and the harmony of his home.

One Potato, Two Potatoes

A child's refusal to eat often upsets his parents and may lead to the common game of One Potato, Two Potatoes. In some families the dinner hour degenerates into a session of pleading, threatening and bribing as an anxious mother and father beg a foot-dragging child to eat. The child auctions off each plate of food for privileges and presents, and in time this pattern usually spreads from the dinner table to other activities such as going to bed and taking a bath.

Sandra, age four, was an expert at One Potato, Two Potatoes. Let us examine a typical round of her game:

MOTHER (whose face reveals her fear of what is going to happen, and so she is beaten before she begins): We have a delicious dinner tonight, Sandra.

SANDRA: I'm not hungry.

MOTHER: Let me give you some potatoes and chicken.

SANDRA: I don't like potatoes and chicken.

FATHER: (who has had a bad day at the office and will do anything to avoid an unpleasant scene): All children like potatoes and chicken.

SANDRA: Says who?

FATHER: Well . . . uh . . . everybody says so.

SANDRA: Harold Michelson doesn't eat them. [A skillful stab, since Sandra's parents scarcely know Harold Michelson who lives six doors up the street, and hence they cannot refute this statement.]

MOTHER: Come on, Sandra, I'm going to put some potatoes and chicken on your plate.

SANDRA: That's too much.

FATHER: Please try them, dear. Make a start.

MOTHER: I'm eating mine. Oh, they're so good!

SANDRA: Eat mine then. [Sandra now has the situation completely under control. The dinner table conversation will be entirely devoted to her eating. The time during which Mother and Father should be talking about things that interest them will be occupied by Sandra's game of One Potato, Two Potatoes. This goes on every night, and soon Mother and Father will be numbing themselves each evening with a couple of pre-dinner martinis to endure the ordeal. The game goes on.]

MOTHER: Eat some of your asparagus, Sandra.

SANDRA: They make my stomach ache.

MOTHER: That's nonsense.

SANDRA: How do you know how my stomach feels? [Mother is checkmated. Now the game moves into its final phase. The parents begin to bribe Sandra to eat.]

MOTHER: Just eat a little of everything, Sandra, and we'll let you watch television half an hour later tonight.

FATHER: Yes. *The Marty Montague Show* is on tonight.

SANDRA: Who likes him? [Mother and Father do, but they're about to be maneuvered into watching a program they detest.]

MOTHER: All right, eat your dinner and we'll let you

watch the program you want.

SANDRA: I like *The Vampire Hour*.

MOTHER: All right. We'll watch *The Vampire Hour*. Now please eat some of your dinner.

Sandra begrudgingly eats a dozen or two mouthfuls. She then dallies, and the whole sequence begins again and continues until a new bribe is offered—and sullenly accepted.

Six months later, when Mother takes Sandra to see Dr. Shapiro for her booster shots (which, incidentally, Sandra has agreed to take in exchange for a new doll, since she is now playing One Potato, Two Potatoes in many other situations), Mother brings up the eating problem. Sandra is sent to the waiting room, and the doctor spends ten minutes talking with Mother. Mother later discusses with Father what Dr. Shapiro said.

The dinner table scene that evening proceeds as follows:

MOTHER (calmly puts a reasonable portion of each food on Sandra's plate, smiles, says nothing to her, and turns to Father): Walt, how did things go at the office today? What are the prospects for getting the Thompson-McDonald contract?

FATHER: We've practically got it all sewed up. Old Montgomery is so pleased that he called me in today and said that—

SANDRA (she's not going to let them get away with this): I don't like any of this stuff.

MOTHER: Eat what you want, dear. You were saying, Walt, that Mr. Montgomery called you in.

FATHER: Yes. He said to me, "Walter, this contract is going to mean a great deal to—"

SANDRA: I can't eat a thing.

MOTHER: You mustn't interrupt when your father is talking, Sandra.

SANDRA: This food makes me sick.

MOTHER: I doubt that. However, eat what you want and when you're through, excuse yourself and go play. But if you can't eat your dinner, you of course can't have dessert and there will be no snacks between meals. As you were saying, Walt, Mr. Montgomery was pleased with this deal and he—

SANDRA: I'm sick.

MOTHER: You were well enough a minute ago. However, if you are sick, go to your room and lie down for a while, but no toys and no radio. Yes, Walt, go on.

SANDRA: I'm going to vomit.

MOTHER: Do that in the toilet.

FATHER: The company's volume this year will reach a total of—

SANDRA: I'm going to my room.

MOTHER: Excuse yourself, Sandra.

Sandra is so dumbfounded that she actually says "Excuse me" and wanders off.

If her parents can persist in this manner for five days, Sandra's animal hunger will take over and she will begin to eat. Several days of not eating do not harm a child. The main problem is the parents' anxiety, and Mother had to make two telephone calls to Dr. Shapiro, who reassured her that she was doing the right thing. Thus, Sandra's game of One Potato, Two Potatoes was broken up, appreciably benefiting her developing personality structure and also making the dinner hour a pleasant occasion for her parents.

Carrousel, or the Merry-Go-Round

Some games are more complex than these so far discussed. For example, in the game of Carrousel, or the Merry-Go-Round, a vicious circle occurs in which the unhealthy attitudes of the parents toward the child produce in the child emotional disturbances, which in turn increase the parents' irritability and revulsion. For example, a rejecting parent who chronically accuses his child of misconduct and malice may in time produce in the child the things he accuses him of. The child's misbehavior in turn increases the parent's rejection of him, and the game goes on in an endless circle. Let us examine a typical example of this game.

Larry was unexpected and unwanted. His brother and sister were nine and fourteen years older than him, and several years before his birth his mother had gone back to work selling cosmetics, a job she had held before she married. She did well in sales work and liked it, and the money she made paid for vacation trips, new carpeting, a second car and other things her husband's salary could not cover. She was depressed and angry for a few weeks when she discovered she was pregnant, and her husband accused her of negligence with her contraceptives. After Larry's conception their marriage was never quite as harmonious as it had been before. In addition, Larry's older brother and sister shared, though to a lesser extent, their parents' irritability toward him; he was an expensive inconvenience and a burden.

Mother's rejection of Larry was expressed in her impatience in feeding, bathing and caring for him during his early months, and he became a whining, restless baby. He ate poorly, he awoke screaming two or three times each night, and he was unaffectionate when handled, and the irritability of his parents toward him sharpened. Even in the first year of his life their attitudes were beginning to make him what they accused him of being: "A difficult child—stubborn, irritable, unaffectionate and not like the other two." Toilet training was an angry struggle, and Larry broke his toys, tore his clothing, ate capriciously, and spilled food. He wet the bed until he was six, and each morning began with Mother scolding him for wet sheets and blankets and Larry staring sullenly back at her. He screamed in supermarkets if Mother did not buy something he wanted, and he sulked when relatives and company came to the house. He was unloved and he became unlovable.

When Larry was four, his mother put him in a nursery school and returned to work, but after a few weeks his persistent aggressiveness toward other children forced the nursery school to request his removal. The same thing occurred in three other schools. Larry's behavior seemed to justify the attitude of his family toward him, and they felt no guilt about their revulsion and irritability. In addition, throughout his growing years Larry's inner fury was made greater by observing the affection with which his older brother and sister were treated and by the fact that they were frequently held up to him—at home, at school and in the neighborhood—as models he should follow.

A typical episode of Merry-Go-Round would go as follows:

MOTHER: Larry, your shirt is torn. Why do you always tear your clothing? [An unanswerable question. Neither Larry nor his parents understand why he tears his clothing, or any other aspect of Merry-Go-Round.]

LARRY: I didn't tear it. It was torn when I put it on. You never fix my clothing.

MOTHER: Why do you lie all the time? That shirt didn't have a hole in it when I put it in the drawer two days ago.

LARRY: It did have a hole. I saw it.

MOTHER: Lies, lies, lies! Your brother and sister don't lie. Why can't you be like them?

LARRY: They're no angels. I saw Betty with her boyfriend last Saturday, and he had his hands all over her.

MOTHER: You have a filthy mind. You exaggerate and you don't respect anybody.

LARRY: Ask her. She'll just lie about it.

MOTHER: You spoil everything here. Nobody can stand you.

LARRY: I'm not the only one who yells around here.

FATHER (hearing the noise and coming in from the next room): What has he done now?

MOTHER: He's lying as usual and causing trouble for all of us.

FATHER: Where did you get that pen in your shirt pocket?

LARRY: I found it.

FATHER: Where?

LARRY: I don't remember.

MOTHER: Have you stolen something more at the drugstore?

LARRY: I didn't swipe it. A kid gave it to me.

FATHER: You're lying. You just said you found it. Now you say a kid gave it to you.

This exchange continues for twenty minutes more, as Larry and his parents release some of their hostility toward each other. As the Merry-Go-Round spins endlessly on, it becomes probable that Larry will carry this game, or variations of it, into most of his adolescent and adult relationships.

Larry will be seven in two months, and the years in which the Merry-Go-Round can be stopped are quickly passing. To end it—and it is actually a family game rather than a child's game—the parents must be helped in dealing with their unhealthy feelings toward Larry, and Larry must resolve some of his fury. Advice rarely accomplishes this; the parents and the child have been playing a hard game for seven years. Without the kind of professional assistance outlined in Chapter 11, Larry's later childhood will probably be crisis-strewn and his adolescence chaotic.

The Checkerboard

When Cathy was five years old, her mother enrolled her in the kindergarten of the public school in their suburban neighborhood; but when the first day of her attendance arrived, Cathy sobbed and said she didn't want to go. Her mother scolded her for such timidity and took her to the school, which was three blocks away. At midday Cathy's ten-year-old brother, who attended the same school, brought her home.

However, Cathy's fear of attending school continued. At school she huddled in a corner of the room, stared around in a scared way, and cried occasionally. The teacher tried to interest her in various activities, but Cathy only sobbed and said she wanted to go home. Each morning, when the time came for her brother to take her to school, Cathy became panicky, cried, and complained of an upset stomach or a sore throat. Most days her mother or her brother took her to school anyway, but she remained frightened and inactive. Sometimes, however, her mother let her stay home, and, once relieved of the prospect of attending school, she relaxed and played quietly.

After two months Mother took Cathy to their pediatrician about this problem. He found nothing physically wrong with her. He said she probably had a "school phobia," and he explained that it was fairly common in children. He urged Mother to keep Cathy in school, since in many cases school phobias are mild and clear up spontaneously in time. The doctor also recommended that if Cathy's school phobia didn't clear up in a month or two, Mother ought to take her to a child guidance clinic to find out what was causing it. He explained that the true problem in a school phobia is the terror of leaving home for a period of several hours. The child, consciously or unconsciously, fears that some disaster such as the death of a parent or the destruction of his home by fire will occur while he is away, and he feels comfortable only at home, since he thereby is continually reassured that everything is all right. Reassurances to the child help mild school phobias, but in severe ones they are of no avail.

Mother struggled with Cathy for another month. Finally, the teacher and the principal had a conference with Mother and urged strongly that she seek help for Cathy at a child guidance clinic, since the problem was not diminishing and Cathy's sobbing in class was interfering with activities.

Mother took Cathy to a child guidance clinic, which was affiliated with the school system in their district. Cathy was interviewed in two play-therapy sessions and was tested by a clinical psychologist; during the same hours that Cathy was being seen, Mother was interviewed by a psychiatrist. Cathy's father was also interviewed in one session. The evaluation of an emotional problem in a child requires assessment of the family environment in which the child is being reared and out of which the child's difficulties arise in most cases.

A case conference concerning Cathy was held by the psychiatrist, the clinical psychologist and the psychiatric social worker who had interviewed the various family members. They felt that Cathy was a frightened, emotionally insecure child and that she had a great deal of unconscious hatred, which seemed particularly directed toward her mother. On the surface Cathy clung desperately to her mother, seeking the love and security she never truly felt from her. From Cathy's confused hostility and guilt came a fear that her mother would abandon her or die—events which Cathy unconsciously both wished for and dreaded. She had to stay home to be constantly reassured that her fears and guilt-laden wishes were not coming true.

Cathy's father did not seem significantly involved in her emotional turmoil; he was affectionate toward her and concerned about her. However, he pointed out that there was something strange in the relationship between Cathy and her mother and that it had been present all of Cathy's life. His wife had always been irritable with Cathy, but in addition she seemed afraid of the child. Sometimes he caught her staring at Cathy with what seemed terror in her eyes. He had tried to talk to his wife about this a few times, but she became so upset that he stopped. He found all this especially peculiar since Mother was affectionate with their other two children, a girl of eight and a boy of ten, and she got along well in the marriage and other relationships. Although Father was a reasonably observant man, he could find no explanation for the unusual relationship between his wife and their youngest child.

Treatment was set up in the child guidance clinic for Cathy and her mother. Cathy was seen once a week in play-therapy sessions using a dollhouse and a doll family consisting of a mother, a father and three children, which matched her own family. In her doll play Cathy acted out family situations while a clinical psychologist sat with her and made occasional comments about the conflicts she portrayed.

While Cathy was with the psychologist, a psychiatrist spent an equal period of time with Mother trying to explore the roots of her unhealthy attitudes toward Cathy. In time Mother could talk about her feelings of hostility and rejection toward Cathy and her guilt about them, but her behavior with Cathy remained the same. As time went on, the psychiatrist perceived that Mother also dreaded Cathy and that hidden within Mother were guilt-ridden wishes that Cathy had not been born or that she had died in infancy. However, despite months of patient exploration, the causes of Mother's dread of Cathy became no clearer.

Cathy's sessions at the clinic were at four o'clock, and one overcast winter afternoon, as the psychiatrist watched Cathy and her mother part in the waiting room, the shadows for a moment played on Cathy's face in an unusual manner, and the psychiatrist saw her profile in a way he had not noticed before. There was a flaring of the nostrils; it was very slight, but it was there. The lips thickened a little in the midline, the chin receded somewhat, and the forehead slanted slightly backward and did not have the bulbous contour of most small girls. The psychiatrist watched her as she turned and disappeared down the clinic corridor hand in hand with the psychologist, who was chatting with her, while Mother was picking up Cathy's coat and overshoes and preparing to enter the psychiatrist's office. The psychiatrist was not sure, but he thought he now knew the cause of Mother's terror of Cathy and the origin of the diseased mother-child relationship that had produced Cathy's school phobia. Cathy and her mother—indeed the whole family—were caught on a checkerboard.

If the psychiatrist had abruptly led the course of their interviews to the Checkerboard, Mother would only have fled treatment. He waited, and in time the game was revealed.

Mother was born in Chicago. Her mother and father separated during her infancy, and she never knew her father. When Mother was four, her mother was struck by an automobile and died, and after that Mother was reared by a cousin. Mother completed high school, got a job as a clerk in a store in her neighborhood, and at night attended business school for two years. When she was twenty-one, she went to a distant city, where she got a job as a secretary in a large corporation. She was bright and able, and in two years she became secretary to one of the sales managers. She lost contact with her cousin in Chicago and had no other close relatives. In time she began to date her boss, and after a year's courtship they were married. She was pretty, she loved him, and with the marriage came a life she had only dreamed of and had felt was impossible for her—a suburban house with two cars in the garage, country club parties, and red-faced children with freckles who play with the kids next door.

Mother did not have the courage to tell her future husband a central fact about herself. She feared, and probably correctly, that if she told him, he would not marry her, even though he loved her. Like tens of thousands of other Americans each year, she was able, with her very light skin and straight hair, to cross the color line; when she left Chicago, she passed from a black community into a white one.

Her first two children were red-faced and had light-brown hair, gray eyes, thin lips and thin nostrils. But in the first few months of Cathy's life Mother saw other features—features that only the informed eye can see. When Cathy was sleeping and the light caught her face at an oblique angle, Mother could see that the lips widened a little in the midline and the nostrils spread slightly. The eyes were brown and the emerging hair was black. For months Mother watched the hair in secret dread to see if it would grow straight. It did. Cathy's skin was light, but Mother knew that all human pigment—eyes, hair and skin—tends to grow continually darker to a certain extent during the first fifteen years of life and that a child who passes for white at two may not be able to do so at fifteen. After Cathy's birth Mother insisted that they have no more children, and Father, well satisfied with three, agreed.

For five years Mother watched her child grow older, and out of her horror, hatred and guilt came Cathy's school phobia.

Beyond the family lies society, and society often determines the games families play.

3

THE GAMES MY FATHER TAUGHT ME

During the first two years of life a child's period of necessary physical dependence on his mother ends, and the father becomes increasingly important. By the time a child reaches the age of three or four the father should occupy a role equal to the mother's in his emotional growth.

In the first year or two, the father exerts a large part of his influence on the child indirectly through the mother. For example, the father who gives his wife a secure, affectionate marriage contributes to the comfortable tenderness she in turn can give to the child, but the father who causes his wife continual turmoil may rob her of the ability to give gentle mothering. After the first two years the father's direct relationship with the child becomes a decisive factor in forming his ingrained interpersonal patterns, or *games*.

Reverie and Distortion. Anyone who carefully observes a small child soon notes that an appreciable part of his life is spent in reveries. The term "reverie" is used here to mean the same thing that many psychiatrists and social scientists mean by the word "fantasy"; a "conscious reverie" is synonymous with the lay term "daydream."

The play of a small child, especially when he is alone, consists of a rich world of make-believe in which reality is carelessly pushed aside as he becomes a spaceman, a sheriff, a television star or some other person. He weaves complicated plots and acts them out. Several children playing together quickly assume roles and in their *joint reveries* act out extravagant wishes and fancies. This capacity for *flight into reverie* continues throughout life, but by middle adolescence it no longer is jointly acted out with others. It has become hidden and private, and often it is largely unconscious. Intellectual creativity depends heavily on a person's capacity to harness this *flight into reverie* and to direct it toward purposeful goals. It is the source of imagination, a crucial ingredient in most successful ventures in science, art, professional work, business and many other areas of living.

Comfortable reveries usually remain conscious, but fearful or guilty ones tend to become unconscious. Painful reveries that have been pushed out of awareness back into unconsciousness nevertheless often disturb a person's emotional functioning. For example, a child locked in a hostile relationship with loveless, rejecting parents may for fleeting moments have conscious reveries of cruelly revenging himself on them or even of killing them. However, the anxiety and guilt that flood the child during the moments he is aware of such reveries usually cause them to be repressed quickly out of his awareness. They persist nevertheless, and even though the child cannot consciously come to grips with them, they may contribute to emotional problems in both childhood and adulthood.

Reveries sometimes distort a child's views of the close people in his life and of the world around him. A child with sound interpersonal relationships tends to see people and things more or less as they are, but an emotionally damaged child may flee into distorted views. For example, a child with a cold, rejecting father may be unable to face this painful reality, and he may escape into the false but comforting reverie that his father is a strong, good person who loves him but has little time to spend with him. A child with a hostile, deprecating mother may flee into the distortion that she is a loving mother whose stern attitudes are justified by his own shortcomings and her earnestness to correct them. Such a distortion temporarily solves the child's immediate problem; he escapes dealing with harsh realities and the anger, anxiety and guilt that confrontation with reality might precipitate in him. However, although a distorted view may for a while alleviate the child's dilemma, it does not solve it; the facts of his day-to-day living and his distorted views of them breed continual conflicts in

him. Such conflicts contribute to some of the games w
shall discuss in this chapter and in later ones.

We shall now consider five games that occur betwee
fathers and children.

The Shell Game

Elaine's father had an urgent need to feel that his chi
dren loved him. If they did not continually reassure him c
their love by both words and actions, he felt that he wa
failing them and was damaging their personalities. He ha
been reared in a home where duty was better understoo
than love, and he had emerged from *his* formative year
with an aching need to love and be loved.

Although love *is* a basic requirement in rearing a healtb
child, the parent's need for it should not be so urgent that
makes him vulnerable to a Shell Game. The parents shoul
be able to tolerate confortably the brief quarrels an
misunderstandings that are inevitable in the day-to-da
problems that all parents encounter with their children.

By the time she was three Elaine sensed her father
inability to tolerate coldness, even briefly, in their relatio
ship. Although she could not have put it into words, sh
had grasped that pouting and a sullen withdrawal pushe
him into compliance with her wishes. By the time she wa
four she had learned some of the verbal maneuvers tha
made her Shell Game even more effective. By trial and e
ror she had found that "You don't love me," "I hate you,
and "If you loved me, you would do that" coerced him int
giving in to her demands. He was rewarded with a smile an
occasionally with a kiss if he pleaded a little.

A typical exchange between Elaine and her father ran a
follows:

ELAINE: (pointing to a large doll in the drugstore):
want that doll.

FATHER: It costs twelve dollars, honey. That's to
much. You have lots of dolls.

ELAINE: Wilma Sutton has one like that. I want on
too.

FATHER: But, darling, you have so many dolls and there's a limit to how much we should spend on them.

ELAINE: (the Shell Game begins): Wilma Sutton's daddy gets her things she wants. He loves her.

FATHER: Oh, Elaine, don't talk like that and don't look so sad. You shouldn't be so unhappy over such a little thing.

ELAINE: It's not a little thing.

FATHER: Darling, I don't like to see you like that. Please. I'll get you something else.

ELAINE: You don't love me.

FATHER: Elaine, I do. It's just that this doll is very expensive and—

ELAINE: You don't care whether I'm happy or not. You don't care at all.

FATHER: All right, honey, I'll get it. Now brighten up and don't look so hurt and sulky. Daddy loves you. He loves you very much.

ELAINE: I want it now.

FATHER: The salesgirl is wrapping it up. Now give Daddy a big smile and a kiss.

ELAINE: All right.

When a Shell Game is a frequently used technique by which a child manipulates a parent, it in time destroys the love a parent is seeking. The game is often played several times a day on both minor and major issues, and love becomes something that is bought and sold—a commodity, not an emotional bond.

A Shell Game corrupts both the child and the parent. The child does not develop the capacity to give and receive love; he learns only to bargain with it, and he does not grasp that love is an end in itself. The irony of a Shell Game is that the parent's desperation to secure love from his child produces an inability to love. In addition, the unloved parent in many cases eventually develops feelings of despair and hostility (about which he feels guilty) toward the child. By middle adolescence the parent-child relationship is bankrupt.

Let us examine how Elaine will probably play her Shell Game when she is fifteen:

FATHER: Elaine, honey, you took the car out again last night. You don't have a driver's license and you're going to get into trouble.

ELAINE: All you do is criticize me. Don't you ever have anything good to say to me?

FATHER: Darling, don't talk that way. I only want what's best for you. You didn't come in until four in the morning, and your mother and I feel you're going with the wrong kind of boys.

ELAINE: You don't trust me. You don't like me. You don't like anything I do.

FATHER: Oh, Elaine, don't say that. We've always done everything we could to make you happy.

ELAINE: You hate me. Both of you do.

FATHER: I'm sorry I said anything that sounded cruel. I just want what's good for you.

ELAINE: I can take care of myself. I'm almost old enough to drive, and I haven't been caught yet.

FATHER: Well, darling, just be careful, and stay away from those boys who have dropped out of school.

ELAINE: OK, but don't nag me about it.

FATHER: Now brighten up, honey. Let's see a smile. That's my girl.

Webster's Dictionary defines a Shell Game as a type of fraud in which a small pellet or pea is hidden under one of three halved walnut shells or other kind of small inverted cup. The operator of the game quickly shifts and reshifts the positions of the shells, and the duped person tries to guess which shell covers the pea; he rarely succeeds. The operator of a Shell Game has only contempt for the person whom he tricks and exploits for money; he is interested only in what he can get out of him and has no interest in him as a person. A child who plays a Shell Game with his parents feels similar, though he is usually not clearly aware of it. Moreover, the child who is reared to play a Shell Game as a rule carries it into later relationships with overs, marital partners, work associates and many other persons, and they often refuse to play.

Let us examine how Elaine's father might have ended her Shell Game if he had better understood his own needs and hers:

ELAINE: I want that doll. Buy it for me.

FATHER: It's a fine doll, but you have eight of them already. Besides, it costs twelve dollars and that's a lot of money.

ELAINE: Wilma Sutton has one. Her daddy loves her.

FATHER: I'm glad to hear that. I also love *you* very much.

ELAINE: If you really loved me, you'd buy me the doll.

FATHER: I really love you, but it doesn't work that way. A daddy who really loves his daughter doesn't need to show it by buying her everything she wants.

ELAINE: You don't care whether I'm happy or not.

FATHER: Yes, I do care, but I'm not helping you by giving in every time you pout and sulk.

ELAINE: You hate me. You don't love me.

FATHER: Honey, that's not going to work anymore.

ELAINE: What?

FATHER: I said that this business of telling me "You don't love me" is no longer going to get you everything you want. I love you, and you must learn to love me without bargaining about it.

ELAINE: You're an awful father. I hate you.

FATHER: You're very angry because you didn't get the doll.

ELAINE: Please get it for me.

FATHER: Don't pout. It doesn't work any longer. It's no good for you and it's no good for me.

Elaine is four. By the time she is five the Shell Game will be over.

Ugly Duckling

About 10 percent of children have physical disorders,

and in some cases these disorders may cause unsound rela tionships between them and their parents. For example, parent may have feelings of hostility and revulsion toward child with cerebral palsy, and these feelings may poison th parent-child relationship. In other cases a parent may b overly indulgent toward the child and allow him to contro the family. Oversolicitousness may be caused by parenta guilt about the child's defect. For example, a mother ma anxiously ask herself, "If I had been more careful durin pregnancy, maybe Barbara would have been born normal. Another parent may feel bitterness—"Why did this have t happen to me?"—and such bitterness may be open or hid den behind overprotectiveness. These parental reaction frequently cause unhealthy personality development in th child; the child with a physical disorder should be reared i the same way that other children are reared.

In some instances a child with a physical difficulty per ceives at an early age that his defect causes his parents t treat him in special ways, and this may lead to the game o Ugly Duckling. Kenneth was such a child.

When Kennth was three, his left foot and leg were i jured in an accident while riding in a car that his father wa driving. Kenneth's foot and leg were in a cast for fou months, and afterward he had physiotherapy and wore brace for six months. By the time he was four he coul walk well and had no serious residuals from the acciden However, he had a slight limp and some awkwardness wit his leg that prevented him from successfully participatin in athletics.

Kenneth's father felt guilty about his son's defect; h thought that if he had been more careful while driving, th accident would not have occurred. In time Kenneth sense that his father was ill at ease when this subject rose an that if he referred to his difficulty, his father became tro bled and did whatever he wanted him to do. Thus, th game of Ugly Duckling began. A characteristic episod went as follows:

FATHER: Kenneth, put on another shirt and wash uj We're going over to your Uncle Fred's.

KENNETH: I never have any fun there.

FATHER: Nonsense. You always have a good time with Mike and Charles.

KENNETH: No, I don't. I can't play the games they play.

FATHER: Son, you can play *almost* everything they do. [He is visibly troubled.]

KENNETH: I can't run as fast as they do. When we play games I always lose. [Not strictly true, but this is the move that routs Father.]

FATHER: But you can play ping-pong, badminton and tetherball as well as they can, and they like those games.

KENNETH: Maybe they won't want to play them.

FATHER: I'm sure they will.

KENNETH: I like ping-pong best.

FATHER: I'll speak to your Uncle Fred, and he'll see that Mike and Charles play that with you. Is it all right now?

KENNETH: I guess so.

FATHER: Then run along and get ready to go.

Father spoke to Uncle Fred, who spoke to his sons, mentioning "Kenneth's problem," and so they played what Kenneth wanted. Kenneth thus used his defect to manipulate his father, his uncle, and his two cousins. The issue was a small one, but it followed a pattern that was to become ingrained in Kenneth's relationship with his father.

As Kenneth grew older, the stakes became larger, and he developed into a peevish tyrant who dominated his parents (he also played Ugly Duckling with his mother) by his limp. His parents got him special exemptions at school, extra favors in the neighborhood and other privileges. "Kenneth's problem" was always their excuse for intervening and arranging what he wanted. Sometimes relatives pointed out to Kenneth's parents that perhaps they were making too much of his limp, but Father's guilt feelings about the injury and Kenneth's skill at Ugly Duckling always carried the day. By the time he was ten he was self-centered, becoming sullen and demanding when his wishes were not met and self-pitying when circumstances prevented him from fulfilling them. During his adolescence his parents were continually less able to arrange things for him. The community usually refuses to play Ugly Duckling.

Ugly Duckling, or varieties of it, is fairly common between parents and children with convulsive seizures, mild or moderate degrees of mental retardation, orthopedic defects, facial birthmarks, cleft palate and many other minor and major physical difficulties. Medical care in many cases corrects the physical problem or reduces it to minor dimensions, but the personality damage from an entrenched game of Ugly Duckling goes on.

Let us examine how Kenneth's father might have broken up this game. The dialogue begins as previously:

KENNETH: I never have any fun at Uncle Fred's. I can't play the games Mike and Charles play.

FATHER: Son, it's time for you and me to have a little talk. Every time something comes up that you don't like, you try to make me feel sorry for you because of your limp. You use it to get me to do what you want or to get other people to do what you want.

KENNETH: But I can't run as fast as they do. When we play games . . .

FATHER: That isn't going to work anymore.

KENNETH: Huh?

FATHER: I said that using your limp to push me around isn't going to work anymore. It only makes you feel sorry for yourself and makes me your puppet, not your father.

KENNETH: My what?

FATHER: Never mind. Your limp is not a big problem. You can do almost everything any other kid can. I love you, but I'm doing you no favor letting things go on this way. Now go get ready to go to your Uncle Fred's.

KENNETH (beginning to sniffle loudly—he hasn't given up yet): But when I get there, Mike and Charles won't want to play with me because of . . .

FATHER: That's not so. You're no ugly duckling and you might as well know it right now. You can do about as much as any other boy. A kid who can't play center field

72

can still be a great catcher on anybody's ball team. [Father's affectionate but firm tone of voice is as important as his words.]

KENNETH: You mean that a kid with a limp could be a great catcher?

FATHER: He could if he worked at it. Now go get ready to go to your uncle Fred's.

Kenneth's game is over. Father won't play anymore.

Bang, Bang, You Shot Me Down

Many parents are aware that emotional problems in children arise to a large extent from interpersonal stresses in families, and such parents often feel much guilt if their children develop even minor emotional difficulties. The parents' reaction to small problems such as mild phobias or transitory nightmares is "My Lord, what have we done to damage our child?" The child may sense that his symptoms disturb his parents, and this sometimes precipitates a game of Bang, Bang, You Shot Me Down.

In considering this game it is necessary to examine briefly the meaning of the words "symptoms" and "normality." All human beings have at least minor emotional problems, and most people occasionally have tension symptoms. Many medical studies have shown that between 30 and 50 percent of all the symptoms for which people consult physicians are largely or entirely caused by emotional factors, and at least 25 percent of the symptoms for which parents take children to pediatricians are similarly produced. These symptoms include emotionally caused gastrointestinal disturbances, headaches, fatigue, pain in various regions of the body, and many other physical complaints. They also include minor psychiatric difficulties such as mild anxiety states, insomnia, small phobias, mild depressiveness, occasional nightmares, and many others. In addition, pediatricians are often consulted about behavior disturbances such as overactivity, aggressiveness, school difficulties, and eating disorders.

Since most adults and children have occasional mild

symptoms that are caused by day-to-day stresses, our concept of "normality" must be fluid. Many psychiatrists hesitate to use this word; they prefer to say that a person is "within normal limits" because this phrase allows for a wide range of minor emotionally caused symptoms.

Many parents do not realize this; they begin painful self-questioning if their children develop even minor emotional symptoms; and their guilt feelings often block them from solving the causative interpersonal stresses in their children's lives. In some cases the children in time sense that they can use their symptoms to manipulate their parents. When this occurs, the original symptoms (such as mild phobias and psychosomatic stomach upsets) are much more difficult to remove because they have become important elements in the interpersonal dealings between the child and his parents.

Let us examine a typical game of Bang, Bang, You Shot Me Down.

When Sharon was three, she developed a mild fear of the dark. Such minor phobias are so common in childhood that if they last for only a few weeks or months, they usually do not indicate significant emotional problems; they are brief reactions to small interpersonal stresses. However, Sharon's father was troubled by her fear of the dark. He knew enough about child psychology to be alarmed but not enough to see the problem in its proper perspective. He felt that he and his wife were failing as parents and that grim psychiatric problems lay ahead for Sharon. Sharon saw their alarm, and in time she found that she could use her phobia to control them; Bang, Bang, You Shot Me Down began.

By the time Sharon was four the game was a firm part of their family life. A sample conversation went as follows:

FATHER: Sharon, it's past your bedtime. When you're in bed, call me and I'll give you a good-night kiss.
SHARON: I'm afraid. It's dark in there.
FATHER: There's nothing to be afraid of. Please go to bed.

SHARON: I'm afraid. Come in with me.

FATHER: Sharon, I'm watching TV. Honey, please go to bed. Leave the light on in your room. Nothing bad will happen.

SHARON: I won't go. I'm afraid. [She now makes the crucial move of Bang, Bang, You Shot Me Down.] *It's not my fault I'm afraid of the dark*.

FATHER (very uncomfortable and troubled): No, I guess it's not. [The game is over. Sharon will watch television until eleven o'clock, when she falls asleep on the couch, and her father will then carry her in to bed.]

In time Sharon found more symptoms to use in Bang, Bang. Vomiting, complaints of stomach aches, headaches and fears of various things were added to the game, and by the time she was five a significant percentage of her interactions with her parents centered on her symptoms. Repeated checkups by pediatricians and four hospital workups revealed "nothing wrong." Such reports increased the parents' feelings of inadequacy and guilt, and the game became more entrenched.

In time Bang, Bang may become a standard part of the interpersonal equipment a child uses, and he often carries it from childhood into adolescence and adulthood. However, most people refuse to play. Nevertheless, the player sometimes finds a marital partner who will continue the game, and then it goes on for life.

Let us examine how Sharon's father might have handled her game if he had had a broader perspective on it. The interchange begins as the previous one:

FATHER: Sharon, honey, it's time you and I had a little talk about this fear of going to bed in the dark.

SHARON: I won't go. I'm afraid.

FATHER: Now listen to me, darling. Lots of kids have a fear of the dark for a while. Your brother Ronald had it when he was your age, and it went away after a couple of months. Your cousin Valeria had it for a while, and it went away. If we make a big thing out of this, it will only get

75

worse. We're not going to do this.

SHARON (making her major move): *It's not my fault I'm afraid of the dark.*

FATHER (refusing to be stampeded by her move): No, and it's not my fault either. There are lots of little stresses and strains in life, and we all have a few fears and tensions now and then.

SHARON (trying again): But it's not *my fault* I'm afraid. [Begins to sniffle.]

FATHER: No, and it's not my fault either. Perfection is for the next world, not this one.

SHARON: I don't get it. [Only partially true. Although she does not get Father's philosophical allusions, she grasps the absence of alarm and guilt in his tone of voice, which carries much more meaning than his words.]

FATHER: No, I suppose you don't. But what you *are* going to get is into bed. You can leave the light on, and I'll turn it off after you drop off to sleep. When you're in bed, call me and I'll give you a good-night kiss. I love you, but I'm not helping you by letting you make a big deal out of this fear of the dark.

The game is over, or will be in a few months.

Hidden Faces

Between 15 and 20 percent of children reared in America today have little contact with their fathers. About 30 percent of marriages end in divorce, and in most cases the children remain with the mother. Although many fathers maintain close relationships with their children after divorce, others have little interest in them, or move to distant cities and see them infrequently, or become absorbed in the children of subsequent marriages. In addition, a few children are abandoned by both parents and live with grandparents or others, or are taken from negligent parents by courts and are placed in foster homes. Also, here are the special problems of slum children who are reared by unmarried mothers receiving Aid to Families with Dependent Children and whose fathers are shadowy figures appearing only occasionally in the home.

However, the absent father may still play a significant role in the child's emotional life. In the child's reveries, or daydreams, he may assume whatever form the child needs. He may be envisioned as an affectionate person who will one day rescue the child from a loveless home, or he may be viewed as a wealthy person who in time will take the child from a squalid one, or he may be seen as a menacing person whom the child fears. In other cases the father remains a cloudy figure, neither affectionate nor threatening, but only a source of doubt and curiosity. The absence of fathers allows children to play various games that may be grouped under the name of Hidden Faces.

A common form of Hidden Faces is the game If My Daddy Were Only Here. Let us examine a typical case.

Randy's mother and father had been divorced when he was two. His father drank, spent little time with his wife, and when she was pregnant with Randy, he began to have affairs with other women. He had little interest in Randy and after dissolution of the marriage saw the boy only once or twice a year. By the time Randy was five his mother had remarried and his father was living in a nearby city.

Randy's stepfather was good to him, but this did not prevent Randy from playing If My Daddy Were Only Here in his relationship with his mother. His mother had a deep-seated fear that Randy would be attracted to his likable but irresponsible father during later childhood and adolescence and would leave her in preference for him. She knew that Randy's father, by carelessness and lack of interest, would let Randy do whatever he wanted, and this might appear attractive to Randy in adolescence. Out of his mother's fear grew Randy's game of If My Daddy Were Only Here, and by it he overcame her opposition to whatever he wanted.

A typical exchange of If My Daddy Were Only Here went as follows:

MOTHER: Randy, you can't play outside today. It' cool and wet, and you still have a bad cold.

RANDY: The other kids are out playing.

MOTHER: But they don't have bad colds. Your throa is sore and you're still coughing a lot.

RANDY: You never let me have any fun. You spoi everything I want to do.

MOTHER: Randy, we try to let you do everthing that' reasonable.

RANDY: If My Daddy Were Only Here, he'd let me d the things the other kids do. I'm going to run away and g live with my real daddy. He loves me.

MOTHER: You're much better taken care of here, Ran dy.

RANDY: Says who? When I'm older, I can live where want* and I'll go live with my real daddy. [This is the blov that annihilates Mother.] He knows what kids need an wouldn't tell me all the time, "You can't do this" and "Yo can't do that."

MOTHER: Oh, Randy, we love you. It's just that you'v been sick and it's too early to go out and play in the . . .

RANDY: I'm all right and I want to go out.

MOTHER: Well, please put on your overshoes, you heavy jacket and your leather cap with the earflaps.

RANDY: OK. [He puts on none of these things and rur out to play.]

Randy's stepfather in time understood Randy's game which occurred one to several times each day, and he sav that it was eroding Randy's relationship with both hi mother and himself. By use of his game Randy wa dominating his mother and chronically irritating his step father. Moreover, the stepfather foresaw that the gam would become much worse during late childhood an

---

* There is a factual basis for Randy's threat, since man state laws allow the child after the age of fourteen to decid with which parent he wishes to live.

adolescence. Finally, after he watched Randy and his mother go through a particularly hard-fought round of If My Daddy Were Only Here, he intervened:

STEPFATHER: Dorothy, I've had enough of this. Pack a bag for the kid, and I'll drive him over to spend a week with his father.

MOTHER: What's that?

RANDY: Huh?

STEPFATHER: I said, pack a bag for the kid. I'm taking him over to spend a week with his father.

MOTHER: Yes, Randy, if you don't straighten up, we'll send you to live with your father. You'll find out what really goes on there. So, if you don't . . .

STEPFATHER: No, Dorothy, I'm not threatening. I'm doing it. Go pack a bag for him.

RANDY: I can go next week.

STEPFATHER: You're going today. It's only an hour's drive to where your father lives. In one week I'll pick you up. We love you, Randy, but it's time you found out a few of the facts of life.

MOTHER: But, Carl, you know what goes on there, especially with that woman he's living with now.

STEPFATHER: Exactly. But maybe it would do Randy some good to get a glimpse of it, too. As I said, Randy, we love you, but you boss your mother and cause a lot of turmoil by continually threatening to go live with your first father. That has to stop. It's no good for anybody, including you. Dorothy, go pack a bag or I'll pack it myself.

Randy spent a bad week with his first father and his current wife. They were frankly dismayed when Randy arrived, and during the week they quarreled endlessly with each other and with him. Much of the time he was left alone in their apartment while they went to work during the day and went to bowling alleys and bars at night. Twice during the week both of them were drunk. At the end of the week Randy clutched his stepfather and gratefully returned home. His game of If My Daddy Were Only Here was over.

Mother and Stepfather could have now turned the tables on him and played If You Don't Behave, We'll Send You to Live with Your First Father, but they were healthy enough not to do that.

There are many variations of the game of Hidden Faces, and some of them may be played even when the father is living in the home. He may be so caught up in an endless round of work, business conferences, entertainment of customers, civic activities and social life that he has little contact with his children. In such cases a child may attribute to his father ideal qualities that he does not have or he may resent him as a malicious or menacing person who does not meet his emotional needs. In other instances the absent father remains a blank—an unknown person, a Hidden Face.

During his child's adolescence a parent needs a sound relationship with him as the basis for moderating the normal turmoil of the period. When there is no relationship, or when it is defective, adolescence often becomes a troubled experience for both the parents and the child.

An Old-Fashioned Game

Matthew was born fourteen years after his sister at a time when his parents, then in their middle forties, were not expecting more children. His parents had so long accustomed themselves to the idea that they would have no more children that they didn't know how to adjust to him, and they reared him in an odd, mechanical way. They lived in a large house on half an acre of land in an old suburb, and Matthew saw little of other children during the first few years.

Matthew was reared with careful attention but little cuddling. He was fed, bathed, dressed, toilet trained, and taught to talk by his mother and the middle-aged housekeeper, but they treated him more like a miniature adult than a child. There was neither tenderness nor harshness in Matthew's upbringing. It was as if someone from another country had entered the house and had to be instructed patiently in the ways things went on there. He was always called Matthew, never Matt.

He grew into a well-behaved boy. When he was four, he ate properly at the table, said "please" and "thank you" at appropriate times, and played quietly by himself. He talked with good diction and used no slang. His parents and their middle-aged friends found him an excellent child and a pleasure to be with, but his sister and her friends, who had little to do with him because of the age gap, referred to him as "the judge."

Matthew sat with his parents and their friends after dinner and listened to talk about business, vacation experiences, golf games, politics and household decoration. He was bright, and sometimes his parents showed him off by asking him what he thought about a topic, and he parroted back some of the things he had heard. He went promptly to bed when told, but sometimes he lay awake for a long time.

He was always neatly dressed, and he kept his toys in tidy order on the shelves of a large bookcase in his room. He did not like disorder, dirt, dust or mud. He could not sleep if his room was untidy; he got up, put things in order, and then went back to bed. Matthew rarely got angry, but when he did, it was as often at things as at people. He might stare at a toy if it didn't work and tell it it was "bad," or he might frown at the housekeeper or the yardman if they did something he didn't like. He seldom laughed or got excited. His father commented that he "took his pleasures soberly," but his sister's boyfriend said, "The kid isn't a kid."

Occasionally Matthew showed some resistance to the way he was being reared. Once while his mother was straightening his clothing and prompting him on how to behave on a visit to some friend's house, he asked why. When his mother replied that these were the rules people followed when they visited others, he asked, "Who made the rules?" He usually sat silently in the barber chair, but when the barber asked him how he liked his haircut, he sometimes said, "It's too short. Other children have longer hair." His comments occasionally puzzled his parents, but more often they quoted them to friends as examples of "hi inquiring mind" and "his powers of observation."

When Matthew was five, a crisis occurred. He entere kindergarten at a private boys' school, and he didn't kno what to do with the other boys. When he tried to play wit them, he didn't fit and they excluded him, and in time the made fun of him. The teacher repeatedly tried to get hi involved in activities with other children, but it neve worked. Finally, she gave up and gave him projects wit modeling clay and crayons and paper. In school he was isolated as he had been at home.

When Matthew's sixth birthday came, his parents tol him he could invite all his friends to a party. He thought fc a moment and said, "I don't think I have any."

"Nonsense," his mother replied, "there are all the boy in your class at school." Mother called the school and g the names and telephone numbers of the boys in his clas they were invited, and the day came.

It was a disaster. It occurred on a Saturday and bot Mother and Father were there to supervise the party. Ma thew welcomed each child at the door, opened his present and placed them on a table in the family room. From the on, Matthew was uninvolved. He watched the other boys play. When his father went to him and said, "Matthev why aren't you playing with the other boys?" he said notl ing. His face was as restrained as ever, but he brushed o one or two tears that started to run down his face. He ble out the candles on his cake and cut it, but he left half of h piece on his plate. When the party was over, he stood at th door and thanked each child for coming. Then he went t his room, put his new toys away, and sat down on the flo to play silently with one of them. His father came to th door and looked at him for a while. Matthew looked u and said, "I'm playing."

The birthday party troubled Matthew's father. He spo of it to his wife, but she brushed his comments aside, sa ing that the other boys were rowdy and were not the litt gentlemen that Matthew was. Father closely watched Ma thew for a few weeks and one day announced to Mothe that he was going to take him to a child guidance clinic fc evaluation. "Whatever for?" Mother inquired.

"To calm me down, if nothing else," Father answered.

Matthew was seen at the clinic, and his parents were interviewed separately and together. When the evaluation was over, Matthew's parents had a conference with the psychiatrist. He explained what the clinic staff thought about Matthew and outlined a plan of counseling for the parents and group-play therapy for Matthew. "You've reared him to be a very well-behaved person," he said. "Now you must try to make a child of him."

Matthew's game is sometimes labeled *pseudomaturity*. The pseudomature child retreats from the pain and emptiness of his interpersonal environment into a caricature of adulthood. He seeks the affection of adults by mimicking them, and he may be partially successful. He may acquire patronizing attention that passes for love and a kind of comradeship that seems to be acceptance. However, in doing so he becomes incapacitated for comfortable living with other children, and he is vulnerable to later interpersonal problems.

The title for this game, An Old-Fashioned Game, is derived from the description of the four-year-old Paul Dombey in Charles Dickens' novel *Dombey and Son*. Dickens frequently used the term "old-fashioned" in speaking of Paul (one chapter is titled "Paul Grows More and More Old-Fashioned"). Dickens presented an astute study of a pseudomature child and the interpersonal forces that made him so. In describing the relationship between Paul Dombey and his father Dickens wrote:

Paul had a strange, old-fashioned, thoughtful way. . . .
He would frequently be struck with this precocious mood and lapse into it, but at no time did he fall into it so surely as when, his little chair being carried down into his father's room, he sat there with him after dinner, by the fire. Mr. Dombey so erect and solemn, gazing at the blaze; his little image with an old, old face peering into the red perspective with the fixed and rapt attention of a sage. . . . Mr. Dombey stiff with starch, the little image in unconscious imitation. The two so very much alike,

and yet so monstrously contrasted.

On one of these occasions, when they had both been perfectly quiet for a long time, little Paul broke silence thus: "Papa, what's money?" . . . How old his face was as he turned it up toward his father's.

A large part of *Dombey and Son* deals with the perils of An Old-Fashioned Game.

4

THE GAMES WE PLAYED AT HOME

In this chapter we shall deal with the relationships a child has with his brothers and sisters and the impact these relationships have on his developing personality and the games he plays. However, relationships with siblings cannot be separated from relationships with parents; they all are knit into a single fabric.

In the past some psychiatrists and social scientists felt that a child was prone to have special types of emotional problems because of his position in the sequence of siblings. For example, particular kinds of problems were felt to be more common in the firstborn child, the middle child, the only child, the youngest child, and so on. However, today most students of child psychology believe that such concepts are not valid. The attitudes of various parents differ too much to allow descriptions of standard problems a child will face because of his age position with respect to his siblings.

For example, a firstborn child may be planned and eagerly awaited, or he may be an unwanted economic burden to a working mother whose husband is attending college. Similarly, a last-born child may be desired and loved or unwanted and rejected. Such variations in parental attitudes may also apply to middle children. A child's sex, moreover, sometimes affects parental attitudes. For example, when the third child is a girl with two older brothers, she may be eagerly received by parents who wanted a girl; on the other hand, she may be treated with hostility by a mother who, because of personality problems of her own, does not feel comfortable rearing a girl.

A family has some similarities to the general structure of society. Parents occupy positions of guidance and *authority* during a child's formative years, and his siblings are his *peers*, or equals. As the child passes through adolescence and into adulthood, society gradually takes over the authority his parents had. Society exercises its authority through governmental, vocational, educational and other organizations. The individual must adjust to a wide range of authoritative social organizations; these include the business firm for which he works, the labor union to which he belongs, the government whose laws he must respect, the social club whose rules he must obey, and the neighborhood group whose codes he must observe.

A person does not escape the authority of social organizations by rejecting the usual patterns of life; slum gangs and hippies have strong unwritten codes, and they often reject members who violate them. A slum gang member who refuses to take part in a gang raid may be brutally beaten by his comrades, and a hippie in a white shirt and a necktie would probably be shunned by his associates. In many cases the authoritativeness of these socially deviant groups is much harsher than that of conventional society, a fact conveniently overlooked by their members who proclaim their freedom from the establishment.

A person's attitude toward social authority is affected a great deal by the kind of relationship he had with his parents and siblings. A child reared by affectionate parents who nevertheless can place reasonable limits on his behavior is more likely to adjust to social authority than a child who is reared in chronic conflict with hostile or negligent parents. The child who chronically played his parents and siblings off against each other to get what he

wanted is likely to carry this pattern into his adult relation
ships with work superiors and peers in his job. In general
the games we learn at home are the ones we play in life.

Baa, Baa, Black Sheep

In most families there is a certain amount of com
petitiveness, or *sibling rivalry*, among brothers and sisters
When parents treat their children with equal love an
privileges, this rivalry remains minor; but when parent
favor one child, sibling rivalry may become intense. Th
favored child is quick to exploit his advantage and to us
his parents as tools against the less-favored children. /
vicious circle is set up in which the favored child become
steadily more esteemed and the unfavored child mor
deprecated. The preferred child becomes the "good" child
and the unfavored one is pushed deeper into the role of th
"bad" or "difficult" child. Let us examine a typical gam
of Baa, Baa, Black Sheep.

Pamela was a wanted baby and was affectionatel
reared. Her parents planned to wait several years befor
having a second child and were dismayed when Pamela'
mother became pregnant again five months later. The sec
ond child forced them to move from a small apartment t
a suburban home before they had enough money to bu
and furnish the type of home they wanted. The pregnanc
also put a strain on the parents' marriage, and the
bickered throughout it. They offered themselves the con
solation that the new baby might be a boy and that h
would thus round out the family. However, the baby wa
a girl. No name was given to her until the day Mother lef
the hospital. The nurse said they needed one to fill out th
birth certificate, and Mother told her to put down "Ruth.'
Mother's impatience in feeding, bathing and handlin
Ruth produced problems that increased the parents' ir
ritability toward her. She cried a great deal, awoke scream
ing several times each night, ate poorly, and was restless
The parents labeled her "a difficult baby" and often com
pared her with Pamela who "had been a good baby." Toile

training was a battle between an exasperated mother and a resistant child, and Ruth broke more toys and other things than Pamela had broken at the same age. By the time Pamela and Ruth were four and three a game of Baa, Baa, Black Sheep was ready to start in earnest.

Pamela sensed early her favored position and Ruth's vulnerability, and she learned that she could manipulate her parents' prejudices to her own advantage. In doing so she also increased her parents' irritability toward Ruth and her own esteem in their eyes. By the time Pamela and Ruth were seven and six this vicious circle was entrenched, and it invaded every aspect of the relationships between Pamela and Ruth and their parents. A typical dialogue was as follows:

MOTHER: This room is a mess. You girls clean it and get ready for dinner.

PAMELA: I told Ruth not to spread toys all over the floor and not to leave scraps of paper there, but she wouldn't listen.

RUTH: You did as much as I did.

PAMELA: I did not.

MOTHER: Ruth, stop blaming everything on your sister. She's always been neat, and you've always been the messy one. Clean up this mess right now.

RUTH: Pamela took out those—

MOTHER: You're lying and you know you are. On top of everything else you lie, lie, lie.

RUTH: I don't lie.

MOTHER: Why can't you be like your sister? How can two sisters be so different? And don't make those ugly faces at me, young lady.

RUTH: I wasn't making a face.

MOTHER: You were. You're lying again.

PAMELA: Ruth, you shouldn't upset Mother so much.

RUTH: I didn't do anything.

MOTHER: Clean up this room right now.

PAMELA: I've always done my share. [She has put away two or three things.]

RUTH: All you did was to put away—

MOTHER: That's enough. Pamela always does her part without being told, but it's a struggle to get you to do the least thing.

PAMELA: I'm going to get ready for dinner.

MOTHER (leaving the room): Ruth, I'm coming back in five minutes and I want everything in order.

The parents' attitudes and the skill with which Pamela played her game affected the other people's opinions of the girls. The grandparents and other relatives accepted Pamela as a pleasant child and Ruth as a sullen one, since they frequently heard this from the parents and observed the cheerfulness of Pamela and the sullenness of Ruth. These roles were also carried to some extent into school, where Pamela was the teacher's helper and Ruth was an unresponsive pupil. Schoolteachers who had Pamela one year and Ruth the next sometimes asked Ruth, "Why can't you be cheerful and helpful like your older sister?"

By the time they reached early adolescence Pamela was a smug, self-centered girl who had a large repertory of techniques for manipulating people, whereas Ruth was a resentful rebel with underlying feelings of inadequacy, and she was estranged from her family and their way of life. During middle and late adolescence Ruth settled her scores with a delinquent rebellion, and for years she was her parents' agony and her sister's embarrassment.

Let us consider how Pamela and Ruth's mother might have handled the scene above if she had had more insight into her own feelings and Pamela's game:

MOTHER: This room is a mess. You girls clean it up and get ready for dinner.

PAMELA: I told Ruth not to spread these toys all over the floor and—

MOTHER: Pamela, I think some things are going on in this family that are bad for you, for Ruth and for your father and me. One of them is that you are not the one to tell Ruth what to do, I am.

PAMELA: Yes, Mother, but she's the one who spread the scraps of paper all over the—

RUTH: I did not.

MOTHER: Well, both of you can clean them up.

PAMELA: But Ruth is the messy one.

MOTHER: Maybe she's that way because we tell her that all the time.

RUTH: Yeah, and Pamela's not the angel everybody thinks she is.

PAMELA: There she goes again, blaming everything on me.

MOTHER: That's enough. Your father and I have had a few talks about you girls, and from now on we're going to see that both of you get the same deal here.

PAMELA: I don't get it.

RUTH: What?

MOTHER: I said that we've been too quick to assume that Pamela's the good one and Ruth's the bad one whenever there's trouble here. Neither one of you is an angel and neither one is a black sheep. Both of you clean the room, and neither one is to leave until it's tidy.

PAMELA: But Ruth is always the one who—

MOTHER: I'll be back in five minutes, and if this room is not clean, neither one of you will see any television tonight, and Dick Barbizon is the guest singer on the *Don Walker Show* tonight.

PAMELA: Let's get this room cleaned up.

RUTH: OK.

My Team Against Your Team

Unsolved emotional problems from childhood may be reawakened in a parent as he watches his own children grow up. For example, a woman may become anxious as she sees in her relationship with her five-year-old daughter certain problems that are reminiscent of difficulties she had with her own mother. In most cases this is an unconscious process; the parent cannot connect his child's present with his own past. However, in other instances the parent is aware of the connection and can say, "I'm not going to let what happened between my parents and me occur between me and my child."

89

In some instances a parent unconsciously sees in his children a reenactment of aspects of his own childhood, as if he were watching a play portraying his early years. For example, a father who fought chronically with his mother throughout his childhood may see in each spat between his wife and his four-year-old son a repetition of what went on between his mother and himself. Watching such events may stir much unresolved turmoil in the father, and he may find himself entering into these quarrels as the protector of his son and the antagonist of his wife. The anger he releases toward his wife arises mainly from unresolved hostility toward his own mother. Usually he is unaware of this connection, but in some cases he can see it, though distortedly, and say, "I don't want my wife to do to my boy what my mother did to me."

In such cases the parent *identifies* with his child and through him may relive much unresolved fear and hatred. A parent most often identifies with a child of the same sex, but identification with a child of the opposite sex can occur. When a parent's unresolved childhood conflicts are severe, he may push his children and his marital partner into a reenactment of his childhood traumas, almost as if he had a compulsive need to relive them. For example, a woman who was brutally dominated by a harsh father may unconsciously incite her husband and daughter into chronic conflicts, re-creating between them the relationship she had with her father. Psychiatric theory holds that in doing so this woman is trying to solve, or at least to exorcise, the unresolved turmoil within herself. She rarely accomplishes this, however, since she is groping in the dark.

Various other factors such as his physical appearance and his position in the family structure may influence parental identification with a child. For example, a woman who was a bullied, despised youngest child in a family of four children may feel special sympathy and overprotectiveness toward her youngest daughter.

Children quickly note such differences in parental attitudes. For example, the overprotected child by the age of three, and often before, perceives that his mother or father is particularly solicitous toward him and intervenes on his side when he has conflicts with his brothers and sisters. The child may exploit his parent's attitudes, and often he unconsciously takes cues from the parent and acts out the role he casts him in. These unhealthy situations are common sources of games.

In some cases unhealthy parental identifications divide a family into two hostile camps in a game of My Team Against Your Team.

Let us consider a family caught in this situation.

Mother was the youngest of two children; she had a brother six years older. The brother had been eagerly wanted, but Mother had arrived at a time when her parents were having severe marital problems and were considering divorce. Her birth tipped the balance in favor of continuing a marriage that neither parent wanted but to which they felt chained by the children. Her parents were divorced when she was sixteen, but by then their rejection and hostility toward her had scarred her. To her parents she was only an annoying accident that had bound them for sixteen years to a marriage each detested. She sensed from an early age that her parents disliked her, and her bitterness was increased by seeing the affection they gave her older brother. Two years after her parents' divorce she went away to college in a distant city and after that saw little of her parents and her brother.

At twenty-three she married, and her marriage was happy during its early years. Her first child was a boy, Ralph, and her second child born three years later was a girl, Louise. Although she made no conscious connection, her home now had a cast of people similar to that of her childhood home—Mother, Father, older boy and younger girl. The family relationships were good until Louise was three and Ralph was six. At about this time Mother began to be very upset by the common childhood quarrels that arose between Louise and Ralph, and she invariably took Louise's side. In time Louise started to pit her mother against Ralph, exploiting them both, and Ralph became sullen and resistant. Father, in turn, tried to defend his son against his wife's irritability and protested that Mother's overprotectiveness of Louise was making her a demanding, shrewish child. The bickering between Mother and Father over the children became chronic. Thus, Mother, by identifying herself with Louise, was casting old, pent-up hostility toward her brother and her parents onto her son and husband.

Father fell into the role his wife had cast for him, and he became his son's defender and her antagonist. The situation grew steadily worse over a two-year period until they were divided into two hostile camps. A representative exchange in their game of My Team Against Your Team went as follows:

MOTHER: Ralph, are you picking on Louise again?

RALPH: She took my truck from me and I took it back.

LOUISE: I had it first.

MOTHER: What else did you do? Look at how upset she is.

LOUISE: He hit me, too.

RALPH: Liar!

MOTHER: How dare you call your sister a liar. You're the constant troublemaker here. I have to come in here ten times a day to stop you from bothering her.

RALPH: She always starts it.

LOUISE: No, I don't.

FATHER (entering): What the hell is going on here now? Can't you ever leave this boy alone?

MOTHER: Stay out of this. You don't know anything about it.

RALPH: Louise started a fight, and Mother's taking it out on me.

FATHER: I'm not going to stand by and watch you push this boy around while that precious little brat of yours gets away with anything she pleases.

MOTHER: And I'm not going to let you and that bully blame everything on Louise. You're always. . . .

Such interchanges, sometimes stretching out into long quarrels, occurred once to several times a day, and the marriage, as well as the parents' relationships with their children, deteriorated. "Why don't you get a divorce if I'm so awful?" Mother sometimes yelled at Father, and Father shouted back. "And leave this boy in the hands of you two castrating females?" In time each child became an expert in pitting his respective parent against the other.

When Ralph was eight and Louise was five, their parents sought marriage counseling, and in time the marriage counselor referred them to a child guidance clinic, for their marital problems could not be solved until their family game of My Team Against Your Team was ended. However, mild games of My Team Against Your Team can sometimes be stopped without professional help if the parents realize what they are doing.

Let us consider how early insight into the nature of their game might have changed the family dialogue given above:

MOTHER: Ralph and Louise, what's all this racket about?

RALPH: She took my truck.

LOUISE: I had it first.

FATHER (entering): What's going on here?

RALPH: They're picking on me again.

LOUISE: He started it.

MOTHER: I think we won't interfere this time.

RALPH: Won't do what?

LOUISE: You mean you're going to let him . . .

FATHER: Your mother means we're not going to take sides anymore. Your mother is not going to take Louise's side and I'm not going to take Ralph's side.

LOUISE: He hit me.

RALPH: She bit me.

MOTHER: Show us the marks.

LOUISE: There weren't any.

RALPH: She bit through my shirt.

FATHER: Then I don't think either one was very bad.

MOTHER: Give me the truck. [Hands it to Father.] Jim, put this away for three days. Then we'll see if they can play with it without fighting.

FATHER: That's a good idea.

LOUISE: You're ganging up on us.

93

MOTHER: No. For the first time we're both doing the same thing to the two of you.

FATHER: And that's the way it's going to be from now on. It's six o'clock, Helen. Let's have a cocktail before dinner.

MOTHER: I'll make a couple of martinis.

Make-Believe

In every game but one described in this book we deal with a child's interaction with an actual person. In one game, Make-Believe, the child has a relationship with a nonexistent person. This person is an imaginary companion, in some instances an imaginary brother or sister. The child talks with him, plays with him, eats with him, and shares most of his activities with him. He may for a while be the most important person in the child's life.

Various psychiatric studies have shown that about 15 percent of children have imaginary companions for a few weeks to a year or two at some time during childhood. The most common age period is between three and six, but they may occur until ten. An imaginary companion usually has a definite name, and the child may talk openly to him in front of his parents. As a rule the imaginary companion is of the same sex as the child and has the same interests. Their relationship is harmonious in all respects; they rarely quarrel. If the imaginary companion is a sibling, he usually is slightly older than the child.

If parents or other adults press the child, he usually admits that the imaginary companion is "not real," but he prefers not to make such an admission. Follow-ups in late adolescence and early adulthood indicate that children who have imaginary companions have no higher incidence of psychiatric problems in later life than the general population. Some investigators believe they tend to have above-average intelligence and in adulthood preserve a superior level of creative imagination. Make-Believe is a harmless game.

Imaginary companions usually occur in children who lack close associations with other children. They are more common in firstborn children and children separated by several years or more from their next-older siblings. Lacking relationships with other children, the child fills the gap by inventing a companion and clings to him until he no longer needs him.

Gregory, an only child, was typical of children who play Make-Believe. His parents were fond of him and had reasonable ideas about how to rear children, but they simply had no time for him. His father was a busy orthopedic surgeon, who was active on committees at the hospitals he attended and played golf on weekends. He was pleasant with Gregory but saw little of him. Gregory's mother had been a nurse, and she fitted well into her husband's life. She was the perennial vice-president or secretary of the women's auxiliaries of two hospitals. Gregory's parents dined out and entertained at home frequently and were dependable fixtures at the cocktail parties in the medical circles of their city. Their vacations usually combined the sands of Miami or Honolulu with medical conventions in those cities. They were constructive members of society and generous with their time—to everybody except Gregory. He was cared for by a middle-aged housekeeper and a twenty-year-old sister of Mother's who lived with them while attending college.

When Gregory was four, he stunned his parents by the appearance of Todd. One night, when the entire family gathered for dinner (which happened about twice a week), Mother noted that an extra place had been set at the table. "Who's that for?" she asked.

Gregory looked up and said in a matter-of-fact way, "Todd."

"Who's Todd?" Father inquired.

"My brother," Gregory replied.

Mother's sister stammered out that this was a "thing" Gregory had developed during the past month. This night he had insisted that a place be set for Todd at the table, and the housekeeper, after a long argument, had complied.

From then on Todd was a member of the family. If Mother told Gregory to eat his salad, Gregory would turn to Todd and ask what he thought. After a moment's silence Gregory would indicate that Todd approved and then he would eat his salad. Gregory consulted Todd on what clothes to wear, what games to play, and what television programs to watch. He chatted amiably with him while he played in his room and put an extra pillow for him beside his own at bedtime. He once asked the housekeeper to put another blanket on the bed because Todd had complained that he was cold the night before.

At first Mother and Father were somewhat amused, but when several months went by and Todd was still with them, they became uneasy. Mother scolded Gregory a little, and Father told him it was time to "get over this." Gregory accordingly did not speak of Todd for a week or so, but when the housekeeper asked if he was gone for good, Gregory replied that he was at scout camp and would return on Saturday. He did. Thereafter, Mother's pleadings and Father's annoyance did not budge Todd. In fact, Gregory one day told them that Todd was getting tired of their attitude and that if "they don't get off his back," he was going to run away and take Gregory with him. This nonplussed the parents.

Mother and Father held earnest conversations on what to do about Todd. Mother suggested that maybe they should talk to a child psychiatrist, but Father was hesitant to lay his family problems before a colleague. So they did nothing. The shoemaker's child is often the last to be shod.

Finally, after a particularly bad breakfast in which Mother had to talk to Todd directly to get him to tell Gregory to eat his cereal, Father spoke to a child psychiatrist. He accidentally met the psychiatrist in the coffee shop of a hospital, got him into a corner, and had what is known in medical circles as a curbstone consultation. The psychiatrist reassured Father, explained that Gregory needed a lot of vibrant activity with other children, and suggested two or three good preschools with well-organized programs. The psychiatrist also suggests that maybe the parents should spend more time with Gregory.

Mother and Father did what the psychiatrist recommended, and four months later Father noted hopefully that

place was set for Todd at the table. Two weeks after
that Mother took courage and inquired if Todd had gone
way. "He's staying with Aunt Margaret. She has no kids
home since all of her's are at college," Gregory
answered.

"Is he going to stay there permanently?" Mother asked.

Gregory said he wasn't sure; he said that when Todd left
he told Gregory that any time he needed him Gregory
would telephone him and he would come right back.
Mother and Father made sure that that need did not arise.

One Little, Two Little, Three Little Indians

A parent sometimes enters a room and finds two or
more of his children quarreling loudly. Each child blames
the other for the disturbance, and usually it is impossible to
determine who started the trouble and where justice lies. In
some instances this frequent situation leads to the game of
One Little, Two Little, Three Little Indians in which the
children use this kind of turmoil to manipulate their
parents and dominate the household.

Mrs. Adams was a conscientious mother. She was a
tense person with a few minor phobias, and she was determined that her children should not be emotionally
damaged, as she had been. She had half a bookshelf of
laymen's guides on how to rear children, she consulted
them often, and she had mastered them well. She knew that
There is no such thing as a bad child. only a misunder-
stood or unloved one." She also knew that words like "bad"
and "good," as applied to children, are "value judgments,"
and she did not use them. Instead of "bad" she used the
phrase "has problems," and instead of "good" she used the
term "well-adjusted." She knew that when children quarreled, or were rebellious, or were frightened, they needed
emotional security," but frequently she was not sure how
to convert this term into concrete acts with her children.
When her child screamed in a supermarket because she
wouldn't buy him Candy Crackles, she struggled to give
him "emotional security." She explained, pleaded, coaxed,
and usually ended up buying Candy Crackles. When one of

her children refused to go to bed, or pounded on his brother, or hammered on the new glass-topped coffee table she rarely knew what to do. Although the books were not too clear about how to deliver "emotional security" at such times, they emphasized that failure to do so led to painful personality problems.

Although all the statements in the books were more or less valid, they had an unfortunate effect: They incapacitated Mrs. Adams each time she faced a crisis with her children. She was so anxious not to damage them that she usually did nothing at all. She knew that she should not nag them, should not spank them, should not make them feel guilty, should not mobilize anxiety in them, should not threaten them, and should not make vague references to what her husband would do to them when he came home. However, she had only the foggiest ideas about what she *should* do. She knew that she should "respect the child's individuality," that she should "give the children equal love," and that she should "understand the child's needs." However, she floundered badly when the hour of decision was upon her and her seven-year-old daughter Elizabeth had just hit her five-year-old son Norman and he, with the aid of his twin brother Russell, was attempting to pull Elizabeth's hair and rip her dress.

In time Elizabeth, Norman and Russell learned that they could rule the household by well-timed turmoil, and the game of One Little, Two Little, Three Little Indians became a standard fixture. Although they had no articulate awareness of what they were doing, they had grasped that a violent quarrel among them brought a flood of concessions from their parents (Mr. Adams' reactions were the same as his wife's). Whenever the parents demurred about taking the children to the swimming pool or the movies or failed to oblige them in any other way, they retired to the family room or one of their bedrooms, and within five to ten minutes the uproar began.

A typical scene went as follows:

MOTHER: Elizabeth! Norman! Russell! What on earth is going on in here?

98

ELIZABETH: They started it. They hit me.

NORMAN: She called me a name.

RUSSELL: She pushed me.

MOTHER: Children, please. Norman, take your hands off Elizabeth. Now, what . . .

ELIZABETH: They were taking my dolls off the shelf.

NORMAN: She pushed me down.

ELIZABETH: You tore the doll's dress.

RUSSELL: You always push us around.

FATHER (entering): Oh, Lord, are you kids fighting again?

ELIZABETH: Give me my doll. Look, you tore her dress.

NORMAN: It was already torn.

FATHER: Think of all the children who have less than you do. Besides that, you're making nervous wrecks out of your mother and me, and furthermore . . .

MOTHER: Oh, Ed, don't make them feel guilty. Let's show them how to live together without . . .

RUSSELL: She pinched me.

ELIZABETH: I did not.

NORMAN: I saw you. You did.

ELIZABETH: Liar!

FATHER: Children, stop that.

MOTHER: Please!

NORMAN: You're the liar around here.

ELIZABETH: Shut up, you dirty little rat!

FATHER: Oh, Elizabeth, you never hear your mother and me talk that way.

NORMAN (to Elizabeth): Just because you're older than we are you think that . . .

MOTHER: Children, I tell you what we'll do. Let's all get our swimming suits and go to the pool at the club, like you suggested earlier this afternoon.

FATHER: But, Marie, I have these reports to get out.

MOTHER: I'll help you with the typing tonight. Besides, what's more important . . .

ELIZABETH: We're ready to go.

NORMAN: Get the floater.

RUSSELL: I'll get the water ball.

When a game of One Little, Two Little, Three Little Indians becomes fixed in family life, it has deleterious effects on both the children and the parents. The children adopt turmoil as their means of getting what they want, and chronic dissension is poor preparation for future social living. The parents become irritable and exhausted, and, in addition, they feel guilty and inadequate about their inability to handle their children. Moreover, they lose their ability to distinguish minor problems from major ones, and when important decisions must be made, their judgment is askew.

The game of One Little, Two Little, Three Little Indians is best handled by the approach outlined below. It is simple and does not make children (or parents) feel guilty or anxious. In the vast majority of cases, when applied consistently over a period of several weeks to several months, it works. The scene begins in the same way. Mother and Father enter:

MOTHER: Children, from now on we're going to handle these problems in a new way, and it's starting right now. Elizabeth, you stay here in this room. Russell, you go to your bedroom. Norman, you go the living room. Each of you is to remain in his place for two hours. At the end of that time—which I will announce, not you—you can play together again.

ELIZABETH: That's not fair. It was Norman who started it.

NORMAN: I did not . . .

RUSSELL: Norman and I didn't do anything. How do you know how it started?

FATHER: We don't, and it would be impossible to find out. Therefore, we shall separate the three of you. If you can't play peacefully together, you can play apart.

MOTHER: And after you're together again, if you start quarreling once more, you'll be sent off to separate rooms for another two hours.

FATHER: And furthermore, every time one of you calls to ask if the two hours are over, we'll add five minutes to

he time he stays in his room. Now each of you go off to his
:parate room.

ELIZABETH: But they were the ones who . . .
NORMAN: She was the one who . . .
RUSSELL: This isn't fair . . .
MOTHER: The sooner you're in your places the sooner
we'll start counting the two hours.

When handled in this way, the game of One Little, Two
Little, Three Little Indians is soon over. The children will
refer to play peacefully together, or at least to keep the
noise down to a dull roar, than to sit separately.

The Four-Legged Sibling.

There are 60,000,000 dogs in American homes, and
many of them have roles, though admittedly peripheral
ones, in the emotional lives and games of families. Sig-
mund Freud was so fond of his Chow Chow dogs that for
decades he customarily had one at his feet while treating
patients, and his principal biographer, Ernest Jones,
describes as "heart-rending" Freud's reaction in the last
month of his life when his favorite Chow Chow shrank
from him because of the offensive odor of the cancer of
the jaw from which he was dying. Harry Stack Sullivan often had a dog at his side during many of the tape-recorded
seminars and lectures that form the basis of the greater part
of his published works.

Probably the most thorough psychiatric article dealing
with the roles of dogs in the emotional life (and games) of
families is "The Mental Hygiene of Owning a Dog" by J.
H. Bossard; it is published in Volume XXVIII of the
Journal Mental Hygiene. Bossard discusses eight main
ways in which dogs contribute to the mental health (and
thus decrease the incidence of games) of families.

1. Bossard states that a dog is an outlet for affection
and often helps tide a child over during a period of irritable
rejection by his parents.

CAROLYN: Look, Mother! Look Dad! I just ma this . . .

FATHER: Damn it, Carolyn, can't you see I'm bu going over these end-of-the-month bills?

MOTHER: Carolyn, why must you interrupt us wh we're busy?

CAROLYN: (turning to her dog): Come on, Fritz. I show *you* what I did. *You* love me. [She leaves.]

FATHER: Now about this fifty-four-dollar bill from t Bon Ton Beauty Shop. . . .

2. Bossard points out that a dog serves each person a cording to his individual emotional needs and that there c ten is a significant emotional relationship between a chi and his dog.

FATHER (to Mother): Hurry up, Thelma. We're : hour late already, and some important customers are goir to be at this party.

MOTHER: You don't want me to wear the same dre twice with the same crowd. This is the third company par we've gone to this week.

FATHER: I'll get the car out.

MOTHER (to ten-year-old Gary): Your dinner is on t table in the kitchen.

GARY: I'm all alone.

MOTHER: Nonsense. You have Fritz. Take the po table TV to your room and curl up in bed with hii [Leaves.]

GARY: Come on, pal. We'll eat and then watch T There's a Tarzan movie on tonight.

3. In the article Bossard notes that a dog can be used help develop habits of responsiblity in a child.

MOTHER: Arnold, I have to tell you the same thing dozen times every day. Can't you ever remember to do tl things you're supposed to do?

ARNOLD: Whenever I do them, you bawl me out b

cause they're not done right.

FATHER: The only thing you remember to do around here is to take care of that damn dog.

ARNOLD: He's a good dog.

MOTHER: Well, I must admit you take care of him. However, right now he smells.

ARNOLD: OK. Come on, Fritz, I'll give you a bath.

4. The dog is a useful agent in teaching children about sex. Even in our sophisticated, frank society many parents stumble when they come to the point where they explain "how the little seed gets from the daddy into the mother."

JUDY: How does the seed get from the daddy into the mother?

MOTHER: Well . . . er . . . uh . . . you see . . .

FATHER: Well, you remember how Fritz mounted on top of Flossie and you asked what they were doing and we said they were making baby dogs?

JUDY: Yeah.

FATHER: Well, that's how.

JUDY: People do it just like that?

MOTHER: People face each other when they do it.

JUDY Why?

MOTHER: Because they like to look at each other and sometimes kiss each other while they're doing it.

JUDY: Oh.

5. In the article Bossard emphasized that dogs help many children feel worthwhile and important.

FATHER: Why can't you ever do anything right? There's not a single thing you do around here that helps keep this house going.

DOUGLAS: I feed Fritz. I wash him. I trained him not to dig in the flower garden and I housebroke him. Besides that, I taught him . . .

FATHER: All right, all right. I admit you do accomplish a few things around here.

DOUGLAS: You wanted to sell him if he didn't stop barking at people on the sidewalk and I was the one who taught him not to . . .

FATHER: OK. Drop the subject.

6. Bossard notes that a dog helps accustom children to the normality of defecation and urination.

MOTHER: Anita, I called you four times. Where were you?

ANITA: I was on the toilet moving my bowels.

MOTHER: Don't say that. It's ugly and horrid. Just say you were busy in the bathroom.

ANITA: If it's so ugly and horrid, why does Fritz do it all the time?

FATHER: I think the kid's right, Norma. It's not ugly and horrid. You got that from your mother and father, who in my opinion have kooky ideas about some things.

MOTHER: Well, maybe so. All right, Anita, I take it back.

7. A dog sometimes serves useful interpersonal purposes in the neighborhood.

FATHER: We've lived in this neighborhood for four months, and we don't know anybody yet.

MOTHER: This is the coldest town we've lived in. I wish your company didn't transfer you every few years.

STEPHEN: I know the Johnsons, and the Kings, and the Goldmans, and the Clauses, and the Spinellis, and the Freemans, and the . . .

FATHER: How the hell did *you* get to know so many people?

STEPHEN: I don't know. Well, when I take Fritz for a walk, Mr. Goldman always comes out and brings his dog so they can get to know each other, he says. And Mrs. King invites us in and sometimes I have cookies and . . .

MOTHER: You're not supposed to eat between meals.

STEPHEN: And the Claus kids and I play with Fritz, and there was the time Fritz got into the Johnsons' garage and I went in and the Johnson kids said . . .

FATHER (to Mother): Maybe you and I should take Fritz for a walk once in a while.

8. A dog is always a conversation opener between parents and children.

MOTHER: You never spend any time with Linda, and you never talk with her.

FATHER (whose mind is full of debentures, golf handicaps, the problems in the Pittsburgh branch office and related topics): Well, to tell the truth. I don't know what to say to the kid.

LINDA (enters with Fritz): Fritz has a sore paw.

MOTHER (to Father): Here's your opening.

FATHER: Let me see that paw.

LINDA: Come on, Fritz. Get up on Daddy's lap. It's this one. See?

FATHER: It's badly swollen and there's pus coming out. He ought to see the vet.

MOTHER: There's no time like the present.

FATHER: I don't know where the vet's office is.

LINDA: I do.

FATHER: Well, let's go.

LINDA: Gee, Dad, you're great.

FATHER: When I was a boy, I had a dog named. . . .
[They leave.]

5

SCHOOL GAMES

In the first four chapters we have considered the child's relationships with his parents and siblings and the ways in which these relationships mold his personality and games he plays. In the current chapter and in succeeding ones, though we shall continue to discuss family influences, we shall examine the impact of school relationships, neighborhood associations, and other social forces on personality development. In the present chapter we shall deal with school experiences from the ages of five through eleven, and all the children discussed have average or better intelligence.

The Interpersonal Features of the School Experience

School is the first prolonged interpersonal venture of a child outside his home, and he carries into the school situation the personality structure and interpersonal patterns he has so far developed.

School is to some extent an interpersonal replica of the home situation. Teachers and principals take the place of parents, and schoolmates take the place of siblings. In addition to testing the soundness of the child's personality development until this time, school also offers the child new relationships that can help or harm him. In general, school is more often a helpful than a harmful influence, for the child has many opportunities to compare what went on at home with what goes on among people generally and to correct any emotional warps he has formed.

At about the time he begins school, the child has an increased need for relationships with persons of his own age—that is, his peers—and school offers an important opportunity for satisfaction of that need. It is his first major move into the community, and over the next ten to fifteen years the importance of family relationships gradually decreases and nonfamily interpersonal relationships take their place. The child thus begins a slow odyssey that, extending onward into adolescence and young adulthood, ends in the establishment of another home in which he in turn becomes a parent.

Constructive Interpersonal Aspects of the School Experience

In his preschool interpersonal life, both at home and in the neighborhood, the child was always more or less under parental supervision. However, when ne enters the classroom and the school playground, his parents surrender much of their capacity to supervise him and to intervene directly in his relationships; they surrender this capacity to a social institution that after a year or two occupies the major part of the child's daylight hours. The ability of interpersonal relationships at school to correct homebred games and personality problems depends on how severe these difficulties are. If they are mild, the school situation may have a beneficial effect, but if they are severe, school relationships are less likely to improve them.

The possible benefits of the school experience (and other broader social experiences) arise from the fact that *the people at school usually refuse to play the game the child learned at home,* and a child whose game is not too deeply entrenched tends to modify or abandon it to achieve interpersonal satisfactions in this new environment. For example, a child who has been playing a Shell Game or Bang, Bang, You Shot Me Down soon finds that his game does not work with teachers and principals, and if his game is not severe, he tends to develop healthier ways of relating to adults. Similarly, a child who has been manipulating his siblings and parents with a game of My Team Against Your Team finds himself shunned by his schoolmates and ignored by his teachers, and he tends to seek sounder patterns for interacting with them.

In addition, in school a child has opportunities to see and experience the ways in which many other children get along with each other and with adults. For example, the child who has been constantly bullied by his siblings at home finds that this does not occur among most children, and the child who has been chronically assailed with parental criticism finds that teachers do not repeat this unhealthy pattern.

This is one aspect of what Harry Stack Sullivan called *consensual validation.* By the multiple senses of seeing, hearing and feeling—in brief, experiencing—many interpersonal relationships in various social situations, the person begins to correct his personality warps. This is mainly an *unconscious* process and it proceeds slowly.

However, occasionally it becomes conscious, and the person can put it into words: "The people in the world are not as they were at home, and I perhaps am different than I was considered there." The child, of course, puts it more simply: "Things are better at school, and I'm not as bad as I thought I was."

Interpersonal Problems That May Occur in the School Experience

Although a child who plays mild or moderate games may be able to modify or abandon them in the school experience, the child with ingrained games cannot. He comes into abrupt conflict with teachers and schoolmates who do not deal with him as his parents and siblings did. This social conflict often is the first of a long series of maladjustments he will have in many situations in childhood, adolescence and adult life.

A child with a deeply engraved game may come in conflict with teachers and schoolmates in various ways. For example, the child who plays a hard game of Merry-Go-Round may provoke continual hostility in his teachers and classmates, and this pushes him into further rebellion. His increased rebellion isolates him even more from those at school until he and his teachers and classmates have mutual contempt for one another. This vicious circle often extends into adolescence and adulthood, and if he finds other persons who are playing the same game, they may become allies (though never friends, since they are incapable of true interpersonal intimacy) in their antagonism toward all social institutions.

In other instances children with deeply ingrained games withdraw socially because they are ill-equipped to deal with people. They become silent and isolated, and though they attend school, they do not truly participate in its interpersonal life. For example, a child who plays an Old-Fashioned Game often is considered odd ("a kooky kid") by other children, and their attitudes make his game even more entrenched and block the relationships that might help im. Also, teachers may find him unreachable and hence may not establish helpful contacts with him.

In some cases children with severe games deteriorate when they encounter the school situation; they find that people there will not play their games, and, knowing no other ways to establish interpersonal bonds, they cling more tightly to their home situations. For example, the child who has controlled his parents with a hard game of Bang, Bang, You Shot Me Down soon discovers that his flurries of symptomatology arouse neither the compassion nor the compliance of the people at school, and he may retire into an even more dependent attachment to his home. He misses much school because of his symptoms, clings to his parents, and shuns the school situation; he becomes a semi-invalid with hovering parents intervening frequently on his behalf to get concessions from the teachers and principals. He becomes steadily more dependent on his parents at a time when he should be moving toward independence and self-reliance.

By trial and error a child with a severe game sometimes finds people who will play his game with him, and he thus establishes a workable but sick way of dealing with the school situation. Such a child may also go on to find similar sick relationships in neighborhood groups, adolescent contacts, marriage and vocation. However, each new situation requires finding someone who, because of his personality problems, will play the game, and this is a risky search. The player is only dimly aware, or not aware at all, of the game he is playing, and when he makes a mistake in his choice of a partner—the situation often deteriorates into misery, and sometimes the result is disastrous.

Possible Harsh Effects of the School Experience. Although unpleasant experiences with some of his teachers and fellow students may make a child miserable, they rarely cause games; the variety of interpersonal experience at school is too wide. For example, if the child has difficulties with one or two teachers, he usually has better relationships with others, and if he cannot get along with some schoolmates, he finds others with whom he is congenial.

Home experiences have a much greater capacity to produce games because *the child has no choice of associations at home*.

However, there is one aspect of the school experience that may have damaging effects on some children and may lead to game formation. The child who comes from an outgroup—that is, a nonpreferred social group that is considered different and inferior—may for the first time encounter ostracism and contempt from the in-group, the more numerous group that considers itself desirable and superior. This confrontation may be brutal or subtle. The differences involved may be racial, or religious, or economic, and they may lead to various kinds of unhealthy interpersonal patterns. Extensive consideration of this subject is beyond the scope of this book, but we should note it as we discuss possible effects of school experiences.

The Problem of Authority and the Theory of Psychic Determinism

In dealing with teachers, principals and school regulations the child has his first encounter with the wide range of *non-parental* authoritative forces he will face for the rest of his life. In later years he will have to observe traffic regulations, pay taxes on due dates, obey Army sergeants, follow union and work regulations, get to work on time, and respect his neighbors' property and privacy, or he will suffer reprisals from many kinds of authority. The justice and logic of social authority may be debated, but the person who defies it often has much trouble.

The authority that the child encounters in grade school, which includes the unwritten but powerful codes of his playmates, is gentle and flexible in comparison with the authoritative forces he will face from middle adolescence onward. In grade school he is still considered to be in the period of personality formation; whereas from middle adolescence onward, society assumes that he is more or less responsible for his actions. Grade school, at least in theory, is adapted to meet *his needs,* but from middle adolescence onward, he is expected to conform to *society's*

110

needs. The punishments that society imposes on the non-conforming grade school child are minor in comparison with its reprisals against the rebellious adolescent or adult. Hence, the games which bring a grade school child into conflict with authority have far milder consequences than the same games carried into adolescence and adulthood.

In the last thirty years, and especially in the last decade, the problem of the relationship of social authority to the individual has been greatly complicated by what in psychiatry is called *the theory of psychic determinism.* Simply stated, this theory postulates that an individual's personality and actions are produced by a parental home situation he did not choose and a childhood social environment that he could neither control nor modify. Hence, any social troubles the individual has during childhood, adolescence or adulthood are the fault of his home situation and social environment. If he cannot adjust to grade school, or if he drops out of high school and becomes delinquent, or if he rebels against society in young adulthood, the theory of psychic determinism states that it is society that has failed him, not he who has failed society.

Although the theory of psychic determinism is rarely defined this clearly, even by those who accept it, it has a marked effect on attitudes toward children, adolescents and young adults. Moreover, the degree of acceptance of this theory is closely related to differences of social class. It is held mainly to the well-educated, the well-read and the well-to-do. It is not accepted, by and large, by the working classes and the educationally unsophisticated. A university professor is more likely to accept it than a sheet-metal worker.

The consequences of these facts are far-reaching, and, among other things, they contribute to the understanding of conflicts between upper-middle-class college students and working-class people such as construction workers and policemen. The college students question society's authority, while the construction workers tend to accept it. The students have been reared according to the precepts of psychic determinism (though rarely stated as such), and the construction workers have not. Thus, university students

111

tend to feel that society is to blame when trouble arises between the individual and society and that society should be changed, whereas construction workers and policemen tend to feel that the individual is to blame and should modify his behavior.

The problem is serious because almost all forms of existing social and legal authority do not accept the theory of psychic determinism. The law courts, the police, most religious bodies, business organizations, labor unions, social clubs and all the other groups that constitute what is carelessly called the establishment assume that a person has *freedom of choice* to conform or not to conform and that if he freely chooses to flout authority, he must be punished. Society also assumes that it is *morally obligated* to punish him in order to prevent the community from disintegrating into licentiousness, disorder and chaos.

This subject is complex and urgent, but extensive coverage of it is outside the focus of this book. However, it should be noted at this point because those games that bring the person into conflict with authority may begin to produce problems during the grade school years.

The Educational Aspects of the School Experience

The interpersonal and *educational* aspects of school are tightly interwoven, since unhealthy emotional patterns may distort or block the child's capacity to learn. For example, a child who pits his parents against his teachers in a hard game of King on the Mountain often learns poorly; his game disrupts the educational process. On the other hand, the child who can identify with the teacher and accept the teacher's goals, and who can form sound bonds with his classmates, learns better than the child who cannot do these things because of games. Thus, the child who carries the stringent sibling rivalry of Baa, Baa, Black Sheep into his relationships with schoolmates often performs below his intellectual capacities.

The Goals and Techniques of Education

We shall briefly inventory some of the things a child should learn in school, keeping always in mind our main focus on the child's interpersonal life and games.

The acquisition of information and basic scholastic techniques is a primary goal in grade school. However, in his studies the child must learn to distinguish what is important from what is unimportant. In reading a story, in doing a thought problem in arithmetic, and in getting some concepts about what caused the American Revolution, he should be able to concentrate on the central facts. Games can interfere with this. For example, the child caught in an Old-Fashioned Game may have much difficulty distinguishing important points from unimportant ones; all facts merge into one dull, gray blur to him, and though he may know a lot, he often cannot use it well. He may do well enough with *noninterpersonal* things like addition and long division, but anything that involves human relationships and emotions is difficult for him. His concepts of children's stories, history, art and music have a mechanical, feelingless quality.

Developing *the ability to analyze problems* is a basic task in school. The analysis of even the simple problems dealt with in grade school involves three main steps: (1.) Asking the right questions, (2.) outlining simple steps to find the answers, and (3.) creative imagination, a complex process in which both personality and intelligence play roles. Games can interfere with all three steps. The frightened child cannot decide what question to ask, or he is indecisive and afraid to deal with it once he has formulated it. The distractible child is unable to devise steps to answer questions, and the emotionally disturbed child's creative imagination is either stifled or wildly rampant. Moreover, when children are organized into small teams to solve problems, their capacity to work comfortably with others greatly affects their ability to participate in such projects.

Developing *the capacity to see the relatedness of things* is crucial in education, and games can impair it. For example, a child reared in a harsh game of Merry-Go-Round often is in such confused rebellion against his parents and society that he cannot organize material and see the logical

113

connections of things. He cannot join pieces into wholes. He seizes a fragment, often one that serves his hostile needs, and only that has meaning for him. For example, the political and economic causes of the American Revolution make no impression on him, but the bloody fighting at Trenton and Saratoga fascinates him.

A reasonable capacity to endure tedium is necessary in education. Education should be made as interesting and stimulating as possible, but some drudgery is inevitable. All education, like all life, is not "fun." A person should be able to go through the boring but necessary tasks of education while keeping in view the eventual satisfactions. Various kinds of games impair children's capacities to do this.

Cooperation rather than competition should be stressed in education. Of course, some competition is inevitable, but the emphasis should be on learning rather than on beating one's companions. Education is a journey in which one should observe all one can, not a horse race to see who can get there first.

Learning by trial and error is an important concept. The child should grasp that he often can learn as much from his errors as from his successes, that it is as important to know what will not work as what will, and that error is not necessarily defeat nor success victory. This is a basic aspect of the "laboratory method" of education, and it can begin in the first grade. For example, children can plant beans in jars and keep some under paper hoods and others in the sunlight and thus by trial and error learn that sunlight does something that makes beans grow. However, games can make learning by trial and error difficult. A child with profound feelings of inadequacy and a desperate need to succeed does not learn well by trial and error; his emotional problems do not allow him to tolerate mistakes comfortably, and fear of failure casts him into anxious indecision.

Multiple sensory educational techniques are best. The child who sees, hears, feels, smells and tastes in his educational experiences learns more than the child who merely repeats what he is told. For example, the child who feels the texture of a flower, smells it, and tastes the fruit of its plant understands more, and remembers it longer, than the child who only sees a picture of the plant and hears his teacher tell him its name. Moreover, the same subject should be repeatedly approached from different aspects. For example, if the child over periods of months and years returns from time to time to the subject of the flower—studying its pollination by bees, the uses of the fruit of the plant, the place of the plant in the ecology of the field it grows in, the problems caused by insecticides, which kill not only the insects that harm the plant but also the bees that pollinate it, and many other related subjects—he gradually develops a much broader concept of what this plant and its flower are. Many games interfere with such understanding because they constrict the child's vision and limit his flexibility in perceiving and experiencing. Games can put blinders on children.

Intelligence and Judgment

Intelligence. Although there is no entirely satisfactory definition of intelligence, the one I prefer is that it is *the ability to see the relatedness of things and to express such relatedness in interpersonally workable symbols and ideas.*

We shall illustrate the terms used in this definition by some examples. An example of *seeing the relatedness of things* is the capacity of an eighteen-month-old child to see that his mother's relationship to his father is different from her relationship to his grandfather or the boy who cuts the grass. A *symbol* is a convenient sign for something else. For example, the word "Lily" may represent a two-year-old child's older sister; the word "Lily" is *not* his sister, it is a symbol for his sister. In later years the child also learns that this word is the symbol for a white flower he sees in church at Easter, and still later he may grasp that the lily is a symbol of the renewed life of a resurrected divine person.

By *idea* is meant such things as justice, love and divine Providence; an idea is purely a mental thing composed of many words and symbols woven together. However, effective intelligence requires that the child have *interper-*

sonally workable symbols and ideas that help him get along with people. A schizophrenic has many symbols and ideas, but they are not interpersonally workable, and hence his total adjustment is grossly impaired.

These criteria define intelligence, but they do not really tell us very much about it. Most psychiatrists and clinical psychologists feel that the concept of intelligence is an elusive one; although we use the term freely, it is hard to nail down exactly what we are talking about. However, most authorities agree that it is closely interwoven with personality structure; unhealthy interpersonal patterns—that is, games—therefore can severely impair intellectual functioning, as we shall see in some of the games discussed later in this chapter.

The various intelligence tests merely compare children with other children in the performance of standard sets of verbal and manual tasks. Their value in informing us about a child's ability to see the relatedness of things and to express that relatedness in interpersonally workable symbols and ideas is quite limited. Hence, the results of intelligence tests can be very misleading if taken too seriously. Highly effective people often have mediocre scores on intelligence tests, and people with high scores may be crippled by games. To cite two extreme examples, a person with an IQ so low that diagnosticians call him mentally retarded may get along well with his family and be comfortable in a job he does well, whereas a brilliant corporation lawyer may be enmeshed in the misery of his third marriage and chew pills all day long to decrease the distress of his stomach ulcer.

Judgment. Although less often discussed than intelligence, judgment is equally important. It also is hard to define, but it may be described as the *ability to consider a wide variety of factors and possibilities and to choose the most workable course of action.*

Personality stability often is more important than intelligence in determining a person's judgment. For example, a person with an IQ of 70, which technically places him in the range of mental retardation, may obey traffic regulations and be a good driver, whereas a person with an IQ of 160, who would be considered a genius, may race along trafficways at 100 mile an hour, maim pedestrians, and cripple himself for life. The first person had good judgment and the second did not. Probably the most important single thing (and there are many) that establishes good judgment is *the absence, or at least the mildness, of the unhealthy interpersonal patterns we call games.*

School Games

The remainder of this chapter will be devoted to presenting five games that demonstrate the ways in which unhealthy interpersonal patterns may cause disturbances in both the scholastic achievements and social adjustments of children during the grade school years.

Twenty Questions

The game of Twenty Questions is fairly common in professional- and business-class families who put a high value on education. In it the child unconsciously uses school failure as a means of expressing hostility toward parents who have not met his emotional needs, and the game sometimes has marked effects on the lives of both the child and his parents. The following game was particularly hard fought.

In almost all ways Warren's parents found him a satisfactory child. He was well mannered, obedient and quiet; he was not a "roughneck" or a "spoiled brat" like the sons of many of their friends. He got along well with adults, played well with other children, and did not tear his clothes. He kept his room neat, ate well, was healthy, and went to bed when sent. He gave his parents no trouble—except in school.

He did badly in the first grade, but after a few visits by Mother to the school he was passed on to the second grade, although the principal said that he "wasn't quite ready for it." In the second grade he floundered. He couldn't read, or spell, or do arithmetic. He was tested by the school psychologist, who reported "normal intelligence, but with

117

some emotional blocking." Warren's parents were unable to get an exact IQ number from the school; they were told that it was against school policy to release IQ figures, since they were useful only to cast children into broad groups such as "normal," "very superior" and "slow."

Warren's parents then took him to another psychologist who spent two sessions with him, did many tests, and came up with an IQ of 121. This, the psychologist assured them, was good intelligence and would carry him not only through the second grade but also through college. However, the psychologist said that the other tests he gave Warren showed that he had a "learning block," and he started to talk about "emotional factors that interfere with the educational process." The psychologist invited them back for a second session to explore this further, but they did not return.

Warren failed the second grade, and this put his parents over a barrel. Mother and Father were on the rise; Father had worked his way through college and had used his engineering education to become a fast-climbing executive in a large manufacturing concern, and Mother, who had been reared on the shabby fringe of the fashionable well-to-do, had finally made the Junior League and her name appeared with increasing frequency on committees that devoted themselves to tea and genteel charity. Warren's school problems put them on the rack.

After a certain amount of negotiation and telephone calls by two of Father's friends to the headmaster, Warren was admitted as a day student to an exclusive private school dedicated to getting students into the "right universities." However, despite special tutoring and all the ingenuity of the school staff, Warren still read, spelled and added so poorly that he failed the second grade again.

Father decided to take the situation in hand, and nightly sessions were held that went about as follows:

FATHER: Now, Warren, we're going to sit down and go over this material. We know you can do it, so let's get on
WARREN: Yes, sir.
with it.

FATHER: I go to the store. I buy four eggs at five cents each. How much did I spend?

WARREN: Huh?

FATHER: Warren, pay attention. How much are four eggs at five cents each?

WARREN: Uh . . . er . . . ummm . . . four eggs . . . five cents . . .

FATHER: Don't count on your fingers, Warren. Do it on the paper.

WARREN: Yes, sir.

FATHER: Well, do it.

There is a long pause during which Father gets increasingly upset.

FATHER: Well, why aren't you doing it?

WARREN: I'm thinking.

FATHER: Damn it, there's nothing to think about. Just do it.

WARREN: Fifteen.

FATHER: No, no, no. Twenty. Put down twenty. Four fives are twenty.

WARREN: Twenty.

FATHER: Twenty what?

WARREN: What?

FATHER: Oh, hell. I said, twenty what? Twenty eggs, twenty cents, twenty football fields—twenty what?

WARREN: Twenty eggs.

FATHER: No, Warren, no! Twenty cents. Oh, Lord, Angela, see what you can do with this kid.

This interchange was then repeated between Mother and Warren on the subject of six bananas at four cents each, with similar results, while Father paced the living-room floor. Warren was compliant, earnest and unperturbed. Father slept poorly that night and Mother had a headache. In one version or another this nightly torture became part of their family life.

In brief, Warren was playing a good game of Twenty Questions. Reared by ambitious, socially rising parents who viewed him not as a child but as part of the paraphernalia that went along with their increasing status, they had little affection and time for him. He in turn unconsciously had found their weakest point and the most painful way of getting revenge for having been robbed of his childhood. While other fathers boasted of their sons' prowess on the school athletic field, Father had to remain glumly silent, for Warren spent his athletic time inside the school receiving special tutoring. Mother and Father had to sit through the thrice-yearly school programs for parents and watch their son, three inches taller and two years older than his classmates, stumble through his few lines. What galled them most, however, was Warren's serenity; he failed continually, but he never seemed defeated. Mother and Father had one other child, a four-year-old girl who had temper tantrums at the poolside and feared the dark and dogs.

Finally, Warren's parents returned to the psychologist who tested him again and came up with the same results. This time they returned for a second visit, and the psychologist explained as gently as possible what Warren's game of Twenty Questions was all about; he recommended treatment at a child guidance clinic that, he explained, would consist to a large extent of counseling them. Six months later they did as he recommended, and in time Warren's game of Twenty Questions ended. In the process, however, Mother and Father had to learn how to become parents to their children instead of co-conspirators in an assault on the bastions of social and economic prestige.

Mirror, Mirror, on the Wall

Every game requires intact brain tissue, especially the thin outer layer of the brain called the cortex. When we talk about parent-child relationships, affection, hostility and fear, we are talking mainly about things that go on in the brains of one or more persons. All ideas and most feelings depend, in the final analysis, on complex chemical events in brain cells and nerve fibers. If something goes wrong in these chemical processes, a disturbance in interpersonal relationships occurs, and in some cases a game is produced.

The human brain has an unusual capacity: It can affect

120

the chemistry of the brains of other people. For example, as you read this book your brain is acting differently than it would if you were watching television or driving your car. The chemical things going on in your brain as you read this page are being affected by the chemical things that went on in my brain when I wrote it. When you tell your child that he is "good," or "did a bad thing," or should go to bed, your brain chemistry is causing immediate changes in his brain chemistry, regardless of whether or not he agrees with you and whether or not he goes to bed. Your brain is the only part of your body that has such effects. Your liver, spleen, colon and other organs cannot change the chemical functioning of other people's bodies.

If an anatomist cuts a human brain down the middle, he sees with the naked eye and with a microscope that in every respect except one the right and left halves of the brain are exactly alike. The one difference is that the right half is what the left half would look like if you held it up to a mirror; in other words, the right and left halves of the brain are in every detail *mirror images* of each other. The brain is the only organ of the body with this quality. Your liver, heart, lungs and other organs have small or large differences between their halves.

If the anatomist then gives the halves of the brain to teams of biochemists and physiologists, they can find no differences between the two sides. However, neurologists and psychiatrists know from experience with patients that there is one important difference between the two sides of the brain. The person's special abilities for talking, reading, writing, doing arithmetic, and all the other things that go into education are contained *in only one side of the brain.* This side is opposite to the side of the dominant handedness of a person. Thus, the abilities to read, write, and so forth of a right-handed person are in the left side of his brain, and in a left-handed person they are lodged in the right side of his brain. Experts disagree on exactly where these abilities are in that particular half of the brain, but all authorities agree that they are only on one side.

The side of the brain in which these special abilities are lodged is called *the dominant side*. Thus, in a right-handed person the left side of the brain is dominant, and in a left-handed person the right side is dominant. As noted above, no ones knows *why* one side of the brain is dominant over the other, but a great deal of neurological and psychiatric evidence demonstrates that this is so.

Like everything else in humans, something occasionally goes wrong in this process, and neither side becomes clearly dominant over the other. They exist in uneasy competition with each other. This may cause many problems in the person's efforts to read, write, spell, and master other educational skills. This lack of dominance of one side of the brain over the other is called *mixed cerebral dominance* or, more simply, *mixed brain dominance*. It also is called *strephosymbolia,* from the Greek words meaning "the twisting of symbols," since, as we shall see, children with this condition tend to have trouble with the symbols used in reading and writing.

Although it is not clear what causes mixed brain dominance in most children who have it, in some cases it is produced by a specific kind of interpersonal act or series of interpersonal acts between a mother and her child. Less commonly, it is caused by similar interpersonal acts between a teacher and a child. When this happens, a game of Mirror, Mirror, on the Wall occurs. Let us examine Mirror, Mirror, on the Wall between Paula and her mother.

Paula's mother was a very neat, orderly woman. She could not stand unemptied ashtrays, disarranged shelves, or dust. She could not sleep if there were dirty dishes in the sink; she had to get up, wash them, and put them away before she could relax. She always arrived for appointments on time and was impatient if others were late. She said she liked everything to "run on schedule" and considered "order, system and method" to be cardinal virtues. She had two spotless children, a well-regulated husband and an immaculate house.

Her older child was a boy who survived all this compulsive devotion to order and cleanliness in reasonably good shape, largely due to much comradeship with his father. From the time the boy was four years old, they escaped Mother's war against germs and disarray by weekend fishing trips, camping forays, hunting, and frequent attendance at baseball games and other sports events. They were "pals," and Mother found that appropriate. Father confided to his son that Mother was a little nutty about the way she kept house but that she was a good woman and it was all right.

When Paula was born four years after her brother, she was staked out as Mother's child and in time she was compressed into the same mold. Paula was born left-handed. Mother dutifully read books on how to rear children and knew that you shouldn't force a left-handed child to be right-handed. If you did so, the books said, the child had a greater than average probability of stuttering and having reading problems. However, Mother simply couldn't stand Paula being left-handed. It was disorderly, it wasn't as it should be, and it annoyed her so much that when Paula was twenty-four months old, Mother began to shift her to right-handedness. By the time Paula was four she was completely shifted over to right-handedness, and she did not stutter or have the physical awkwardness the child-rearing books warned about. Mother and Paula were good friends and did many things together, but they always had to do them Mother's way.

Paula got along well in kindergarten, and her teacher praised her for her neatness and industriousness. However, in the first and second grades many problems began to crop up. Paula could not tell the difference between a *b* and a *d*, and she could not distinguish between "was" and "saw" and between "no" and "on." Her writing was an illegible scrawl, and she had a tendency to write everything backward and from right to left. In time her second-grade teacher observed that if left to herself, Paula could write backward very well. If she wrote a sentence such as "I see a cat and a dog," she wrote it from right to left and reversed all letters and word sequences in a mirror-image fashion. Thus, if you held her writing up to a mirror, the image reflected was clear and well written, but seen without such a device, it was incomprehensible. No matter how hard Paula tried, she could not write legibly in the ordinary way, but her mirror-image writing was always correct and well executed.

The teacher kept Paula after school for several days and examined her problem more. Paula was a very poor reader, but if the teacher held the page of a book up to a mirror and let Paula see the reflected image, she read well. The teacher also studied Paula's drawings. If Paula was shown a picture of a bird and was told to draw it, she drew it correctly but as if it were reflected in a mirror. If the bird the teacher showed her was pointing its beak to the left, Paula drew its beak pointing to the right, and all other details were similarly reversed. If Paula tried to draw the bird exactly as it was in the teacher's picture, it didn't look like a bird at all. The teacher recognized Paula's trouble and sent her to the school psychologist, who confirmed the teacher's opinion.

Most children with this condition today are correctly diagnosed within the first two or three grades. However, when the problem of *mixed cerebral dominance* is not recognized, the child may be considered mentally retarded or educationally blocked by personality problems. He may end up in special classes for the mentally retarded, or he and his parents may be counseled for emotional problems unrelated to his learning difficulty, or he may struggle through regular classes year after year, always at the bottom of his class and sometimes repeating grades.

In this condition the child sees everything as if it were a *mirror image* of itself. Neurologists, psychiatrists and educators do not understand just how this happens, but some of them speculate that it is related in some way to the fact that anatomically one side of the brain is the mirror image of the other. This condition is statistically more common in children who have been forcibly shifted from left-handedness to right-handedness, but (as is more frequent today, since parents and teachers have been educated on this subject) this difficulty also occurs in children, who, to the best of everyone's knowledge, were never shifted in handedness. Of course, brief confusions of *b* and *d* and "was" and "saw" are common in children in the first and second grades, but they soon get over them. *Mixed brain dominance,* or *strephosymbolia,* is a different matter.

Mixed cerebral dominance is perhaps fairly common in mild and moderate degrees. Children with moderate degrees of it progress through school, but they perform below their intellectual potentials. One of the original pioneers in studying this subject cited the case of a medical student who wrote so illegibly that he had trouble passing examinations. Upon discovering that he was a strephosymbolic, the investigator suggested that the student write his examinations with a sheet of carbon paper face up underneath the examination paper and that he write from right to left in his comfortable strephosymbolic manner. The carbon paper impressions on the underside of the written sheets were quite legible, and the medical student eventually became a physician.

These problems are sufficiently common to justify special classes in all large school districts for the children who have them. In such classes special techniques are employed, and many of these children completely get over the difficulty. Others improve but remain awkward writers and somewhat slow readers for the rest of their lives.

The alertness of Paula's teacher led to conferences with Mother, special education for Paula, and clearing of her problem over a three-year period. In this case Mirror, Mirror on the Wall was a game, since it arose out of unhealthy aspects of Mother's relationship with Paula. Mother's compulsive need for uniformity and order caused her to shift Paula from left-handedness to right-handedness, and this did something to Paula's brain and produced a disturbance in her educational process.

Tug-of-War

The school experience does not remain confined to the classroom; it invades the home in the form of homework. This often begins in earnest in the fourth or fifth grade and sometimes before that. The homework burden of grade school children has greatly increased in recent years. The effects of tightening competition to get into the better colleges, the greater emphasis on technology in our economic system, and many other things have filtered down to even the grade school level, and in many communities grade school education has acquired an intensity it did not have thirty years ago. The number of hours the grade school child spends in class each day have not increased, but his amount of homework has.

This change involves many parents directly in their children's grade school studies. Children ask them how to do "modern math" problems, how to organize short essays, where to find pictures for scrapbooks, and many other things. In my opinion, parents can play useful roles in orienting their children and helping them over rough spots, and they can be even more active in homework when the child has missed school due to illness or when he is beginning a new type of schoolwork. *However, the parent should be an occasional helper and not a constant supervisor of homework.*

In many homes the parent's role in homework deteriorates into that of a nightly tutor of his child. Each night the child, or children, and the parent, or parents, settle down for an hour or two to do *their* homework at the dining-room table. The architecture of suburban homes tends to involve everyone in this process. The dining area, the family room and the kitchen space are often divided only by waist-high partitions or wide passages. Hence, what goes on at the dining-room table is fully audible and visible to everyone else.

In my opinion *the roles of parent and nightly tutor are incompatible.* The parent deteriorates into an irritable nagger and the child into a sullen foot-dragger, and the total parent-child relationship degenerates.

Let us examine a home in which a game of Tug-of-War has been going on for six bitter months.

Scene: Father is seated at the dining-room table with neat piles of fifth-grade books, paper and pencils before him. It is 7 P.M. Mother and six-year-old Marilyn are in full view in the adjacent family room.

FATHER: Keith! Keith! Where is that boy?

KEITH (distant voice): I'm in the bathroom.

FATHER: Well, hurry up. It's time to do your homework.

KEITH: OK.

Father fidgets for three minutes.

FATHER: All right, you've been in there long enough. Come on, stop stalling.

KEITH: I'm coming.

The sound of distant flushing of the toilet momentarily encourages Father, but he gets visibly upset as two more minutes go by.

FATHER: Keith, damn it, you come here right now or I'm coming in there to get you.

KEITH: OK.

Keith appears. As he passes through the family room, he looks at the television program his mother and sister are watching, and it takes more threats by Father to get him finally to the table.

FATHER: All right. What's the history assignment for tonight?

KEITH: Huh?

FATHER: I said, what's the history assignment for tonight? Joyce, please turn that television set down.

KEITH (shuffling through a mass of scrawled notebooks and scraps of paper): It was here somewhere.

FATHER: Keith, you have to be more orderly. Let me look. Is this it?

KEITH: No, that was the one we did last night.

FATHER: Then where the hell is tonight's assignment?

MOTHER: Al, don't lose your temper. Swearing isn't going to . . .

FATHER: Would you like to take over here?

Mother declines. She's been through it many times and dreads the prospect.

KEITH: I can't find it. I think I left it in school.

FATHER: Then call Sally Morgan and get it.

KEITH: OK.

It takes five minutes to find Sally Morgan's telephone number and get the history assignment. The first inning of tonight's session of Tug-of-War is over, and so far Keith is ahead.

127

FATHER: Now, here we are. The War with Mexico. Read pages one hundred sixty-two to one hundred sixty-five. Read them.

KEITH: OK. [He reads them.]

FATHER: Now we'll do the exercises. There are five questions. Put "The War with Mexico" and your name at the top of the page.

KEITH: OK.

FATHER: It's Mexico, not Maxico.

KEITH: Oh, I forgot [Spends one and a half minutes rubbing out Maxico and putting down Mexico.]

FATHER: First question. Why did President Polk want a war with Mexico?

KEITH: To fight the Mexicans.

FATHER: No, no, that's not what the book said. What did the book say?

This continues for forty minutes. Then they get on to the "new math," and there's still the geography scrapbook to do. Keith's yawning routs Father completely, and the geography scrapbook doesn't get done.

By the end of the school year Father and Keith are in the bottom quarter of the class. Their relationship has deteriorated into disgust and revulsion on both sides, and this extends into all their activities with each other. School stretches out another seven years ahead of them. Moreover, how good a preparation is this for what Keith will do when he goes away to college?

Let us examine two ways in which this game of Tug-of-War can be broken up.

Method Number One:

KEITH: I have a lot of homework to do.

FATHER: Do it then.

KEITH: I can't.

FATHER: Have you tried?

KEITH: Well . . .

FATHER: I'm reading. I suggest you try. However, I'm through struggling with you. You and I fight so much over homework that it's ruining our relationship. We're both mad at each other all the time. That's not as it should be. I'm your father, not your schoolteacher.

KEITH: You mean I don't have to do homework anymore?

FATHER: I mean that you have to spend two hours at the dining-room table with your books every night. What you do there is your problem. I'll give you occasional, brief help if you come here and ask, but only that.

KEITH: I may flunk the fifth grade.

FATHER: In that case, you'll repeat it. You have good intelligence, as we know from your IQ tests. You'll stay in the fifth grade until you decide to buckle down and pass it.

KEITH: When did all this start?

FATHER: Right now.

Method Number Two:

KEITH: I have a lot of homework to do.

FATHER: Donna Jensen will be here in a few minutes.

KEITH: What?

FATHER: I said, Donna Jensen will be here in a few minutes.

KEITH: What does she have to do with it?

FATHER: I made a deal with her.

KEITH: I don't get it.

FATHER: Donna baby-sits for everybody in the neighborhood to make money for all the special clothes she likes to wear in high school. Well, instead of baby-sitting she's going to get paid the same rate per hour for tutoring you in your homework. From now on, I'm out of it. I'm going to be your father, not your slave driver.

KEITH: What'll the other kids say when they hear that Donna Jensen is baby-sitting with me for my homework?

FATHER: That's your problem, not mine. Maybe in time you can improve and get rid of her.

KEITH: This costs money.

FATHER: I'm aware of that. However, I figure that the savings on my tranquilizer pills will cover at least half of it.

The doorbell rings. Donna Jensen enters.

FATHER: There he is, Donna. Take him to the kitchen where we can't hear what goes on. I've explained the

129

problem to you. If it gets too rough, I'll give you an extra fifty cents an hour hardship pay.

DONNA: Yes, Mr. Loomis. All right, Keith, pick up the other half of the books and let's go to the kitchen and get at it.

Hidden Words

Damaging interpersonal relationships in the early years of life occasionally produce a condition that deceptively resembles mental retardation; it is called *pseudoretardation*. Hidden within the pseudoretarded child are average or above-average intellectual abilities, but painful interpersonal events have unconsciously caused him to retreat behind a façade of apparent mental dullness. He has retired into a less involved way of life by appearing to be of low intelligence.

This withdrawal into pseudoretardation may be so pervasive that the child scores in the mentally retarded range on intelligence tests. However, in most cases a clinical psychologist can detect evidence in the intelligence testing of a pseudoretarded child that his IQ score may be falsely low because of emotional turmoil. Careful study of the child and in many cases follow-up observation over a period of a few months or two or three years may be necessary to decide the question.

Various kinds of emotional damage in the first several years of life can produce pseudoretardation. Parental brutality (which may be emotional or physical), frequent changes of home because of broken marriages, neglect, isolation, a barren cultural environment in which no value is placed on learning and no incentives for it are apparent, and other things can cause pseudoretardation. Some psychiatrists feel that sexual traumas during the first two or three years of life, such as repeatedly observing parents or other adults in sexual intercourse or being menaced with physical deformities of the genitals if the child is caught masturbating, can cause a stifling not only of sexual curiosity but of *all* curiosity, thus creating a block in school education.

The eventual adjustment of pseudoretarded children in adulthood is not clear. No research team has ever followed a large number of these children for twenty years or more to find out what happens to them. However, the general impression of psychiatrists and clinical psychologists is that they go through life labeled as mentally retarded. Pseudoretardation probably is more common in socially and economically deprived groups, but it can occur in any level of society. I had one pseudoretarded patient who lived in a twenty-four-room villa and his father had a six-figure income.

If recognized early, or even during adolescence, psychiatric treatment improves some pseudoretarded children a great deal. I have seen children and adolescents whose IQ scores rose as much as 40 points over a three-year period of treatment. In some cases the child's home environment is so unfavorable and the parents are so uninterested in his treatment that improvement occurs only if the child can be removed from the home for two years or more and put in a therapeutic residential school or a well-supervised foster home.

Let us consider a child whose game was pseudoretardation.

Wendy was born into a dissolving home. Each of her parents had been unfaithful during their brief, brawling marriage, and each had a paramour waiting for a second marriage when their divorce was final. When she was two months old, Wendy was sent to her maternal grandmother, a thrice-married woman in her middle forties who did not want her. The grandmother tried to reject this unwelcome burden from her screaming, demanding daughter but finally took her. During the two years Wendy was with her grandmother, she was shunted from one negligent maid to another.

Then her father, now remarried, quarreled with his former mother-in-law and took Wendy to live with him. He was by now a successful salesman, with a large income and a suburban house. His wife and he got along badly, but the marriage survived because they saw little of each other. He had his business and she had her boyfriends. When Wendy was three, she was twice driven from her stepmother's bedroom into which she had wandered while the stepmother was having sex with a lover. When she was four Wendy was sent to live with her father's mother, an arthritic semi-invalid who accepted her only because she was accompanied by a sizable monthly check from Wendy's father. Here Wendy was simply ignored. She got her food from the refrigerator or a pantry shelf and spent much time watching television alone. When Wendy was five, her grandmother entered a nursing home, and Wendy was sent to live with her mother, who now worked outside the home to supplement her husband's salary. Wendy was placed in school and was given a door key to get herself in when she got home from school.

Wendy had been slow in walking, talking, toilet training and other aspects of her development, and her slowness in learning followed her into school. In the first grade she was given a routine intelligence test, and her score was 61, which placed her in the range of marked mental retardation. Later in the year she was more carefully tested. On some parts of the test she scored very low, but on others she bordered on normality. However, when the various parts of the test were averaged, she had an IQ of 67, and she was therefore put in a special class for mentally retarded children and remained there for five years. By the end of that time she read, wrote, spelled and did arithmetic at the level of a second-grade child.

When Wendy was eleven, her mother and her current husband got divorced; her mother moved to a distant state, and Wendy was sent to live with her father, who in the intervening years had obtained a divorce and remarried. This time in his game of marital roulette Wendy's father had married an emotionally stable woman, who brought with her two children from a former marriage and was willing to put up with Wendy's father's personality problems because of the economic security and educational opportunities his large income gave her and her children. The marriage was successful because she made it so.

Wendy's new stepmother accepted her as a mentally

retarded burden from one of her husband's former marriages and felt sorry for her, and for the first time in her life Wendy received some affection. Wendy was put in a special day school for mentally retarded children, and as part of the admission routine she was retested by a clincial psychologist, who reported the same things the others had. In time a simplified form of the report arrived in the stepmother's hands. She read it and decided to go to the school and talk to the psychologist. He said that Wendy was probably mentally retarded but that there were many aspects of the test that suggested that her true potential might be higher than the test indicated. He used the word "pseudoretarded," the stepmother asked what that meant, and he explained. She then asked how they could find out if Wendy was retarded or pseudoretarded, and the psychologist suggested interview treatment for Wendy, perhaps beginning with special play materials and toys, and counseling for the parents.

The stepmother (whom, for adequate interpersonal reasons and literary convenience, we shall hereafter call Mother) talked to Father about it. Sure, sure, he replied, whatever the kid needed was fine with him. She knew him well enough to know that suggesting that he participate in the treatment would only rock the boat and accomplish nothing.

For the next three years Wendy was seen in therapy by a child psychiatrist, and Mother saw the school's psychologist twice monthly to adapt the home environment to Wendy's needs. Mother oriented her other two children to ways they could help Wendy. Father was informed from time to time that Wendy was doing better in school, and he said that was "great, great, I always said there was nothing wrong with the kid," and let the matter drop at that.

By the time Wendy was fifteen her IQ score was 108. When she was sixteen, she entered a private school for girls of normal intelligence where, with some special tutoring, she was able to make average grades. She is still somewhat shy, but she is developing new social capacities. When she graduates from high school, she will go to a small liberal arts college, which one of Mother's older daughters attends, and the older daughter is sure she can arrange for Wendy to enter her sorority and live there. Wendy has a boyfriend.

The Expert

The intellectually gifted child (whom we shall define as one with an IQ of more than 150) should throughout his academic career remain with children of his own age. He may be given special studies in music, art, science, mathematics and other fields in addition to his regular studies, but when the bell rings for recess, he should go out and play baseball or hopscotch with the others. The theme of the parents and teachers of the gifted child should be: "You are very bright and your special abilities should be developed, but you must also learn to live comfortably with people." He cannot do this if he is pushed too fast; a thirteen-year-old is not ready to associate healthily with college men and women.

Various factors tempt parents and teachers to push the gifted child too fast and to treat them in special ways interpersonally. In addition to the vanity of having a distinguished child or student, parents and teachers may feel they have a duty to society to develop his talents to the utmost. In other instances parents and teachers simply do not know what to do with him and let him go pell-mell through grade school and high school and arrive in college before he is emotionally ready.

Moreover, in some instances the gifted child is reared in unhealthy ways within his family. Because of his intellectual distinction he may be considered exempt from the ordinary restrictions and obligations that his siblings have. This is poor preparation for social living, for people outside the family will not treat him similarly and he will emerge into adolescence and adulthood poorly equipped for effective interpersonal life.

One of the games to which the gifted child is vulnerable is The Expert. Let us consider a typical case of it.

Quentin, with a little help from his mother and older

sister, learned to read when he was four. At this age he began piano lessons, and his phenomenal progress encouraged his teacher to envision her name in a footnote to musical history as the first instructor of another Mozart. Quentin learned chess, and by the age of seven he was making the semifinals in tournaments in his city. By making economic sacrifices, his father, who was the assistant manager of a supermarket, placed Quentin in an expensive private school; the first year he was admitted to the second grade, and it was expected that he would complete the work of two or three grades each calendar year.

Although Quentin's intellectual career was coming along well, his personality development was not. He soon discovered that he could get out of emptying the trash, weeding the garden, cleaning his room, running errands and all other household chores by stating that he was busy with piano practice or the current book he was reading, so all household tasks descended on his grumbling older sister and younger brother. Mother arranged whatever Quentin wanted and daydreamed of one day receiving the congratulations of neighbors when Quentin's Nobel Prize was announced. Father was pleased to have a bright son, but he also wanted a boy to go fishing with. Moreover, he felt that his son was developing into a vain, self-centered person and that Mother's partiality was bad for the other two children. However, Father was paralyzed by the feeling that if he obstructed Quentin in any way, he would be depriving humanity of a future benefactor. When Father occasionally tried to intervene, Mother inquired, "How do you expect a child with his potential to be interested in fishing?" or "Why should a boy with his intelligence help you mow the lawn?" By the time Quentin was seven Father disliked his son and felt guilty about it; Quentin's brother and sister openly resented him and did not feel guilty about it.

A sample interchange after dinner went as follows:

MOTHER: Sarah and Billy, clean off the table, put the dishes in the dishwasher, and tidy up the kitchen. I have some things to get ready for the club luncheon tomorrow.
BILLY: Why can't Quentin help?

QUENTIN: I'm reading.

SARAH: So what? This kitchen is a mess and . . .

QUENTIN: Don't bother me. I can't concentrate with you two yelling at me.

SARAH: I'm not yelling at you, you little . . .

MOTHER: Now stop that, Sarah. Quentin is busy reading and his reading is very important.

BILLY: It sure is. It gets him out of all the work around here.

FATHER: Ingrid, maybe Quentin should pitch in once in a while and help the other kids. I'm not so sure that . . .

MOTHER: Maybe you'd like to put down that sports page and read something else so you can give Quentin a little of the intellectual stimulation he needs?

FATHER (crushed): I was just trying to suggest that . . .

MOTHER: Sarah and Billy, get to work. Go on with your reading, Quentin.

QUENTIN: (rubbing it in, with obvious satisfaction): You two try not to make so much noise. Besides, if you knew how to organize the job, it would be over in two minutes.

SARAH (seething): Yes, Dr. Einstein.

Billy manages to express a little of his hostility by breaking a plate.

When Quentin was seven and a half, his parents received a call from the manager of a neighborhood drugstore saying that Quentin had been caught stealing. A family scene followed in which Mother told Father that if he were a district supervisor instead of an assistant store manager, Quentin wouldn't be forced to take things that they couldn't afford to buy him. Billy and Sarah repeatedly inquired in loud voices if he was "going to get away with this." Quentin howled that he couldn't study with so much noise.

However, fueled by his hostility toward his son, his competition with his wife, and a real concern for the whole family's welfare, Father didn't let the matter drop. He said he was going to do something about it and told Mother that it was better to have "a law-abiding average citizen in the family than an intelligent thief." He said that it was time to crack down on Quentin. However, he needed somebody to back him up, and Billy and Sarah were not enough.

One of the checkout girls at Father's supermarket had taken her child to the branch of the Family and Children's Service Agency in their suburb, and she reported that after a few months of counseling things were better in their home. Father dragged Mother to the same counseling service, they were seen in two interviews by a psychiatric social worker, and Quentin was examined by the staff's psychologist. The case was discussed with the clinic's consulting psychiatrist in one of his twice-weekly meetings with the staff. After that the psychiatric social worker spent three sessions showing Mother and Father how Quentin's game of Expert was malforming his personality, poisoning his relationship with his brother and sister, and putting a dangerous strain on their marriage.

Mother and Father then had weekly conferences with the psychiatric social worker for four months and once-monthly conferences for six months after that. The clinic's psychologist had several conferences with the teachers and principal at Quentin's school to suggest ways in which his intellectual capacities could be developed while remaining in classes with children of his own age. In time Quentin's game of Expert was broken up, but it involved many scenes such as the following:

FATHER: All right. This morning everybody is going to pitch in, and we're going to clean up the garage and the storage room. Billy, Sarah, and Quentin, up and at it!

BILLY: Quentin?

SARAH: Him?

FATHER: All of us—you two, Quentin and I.

SARAH: I'll have to see this to believe it.

BILLY: He'll get out of it somehow.

FATHER: I don't think so. Sarah and Billy, start hauling everything out of the garage. Come on, Quentin.

QUENTIN: I'm busy.

FATHER: Come on. This business of you being something special around here has to stop. You may be bright, but you have to learn to live the way everybody else does.

QUENTIN: Can't you see I'm busy reading? Sarah and Billy can take care of the garage.

MOTHER: Your father's right, Quentin. Put your book down and go to work.

QUENTIN: Garage cleaning is not *my* kind of work.

FATHER: Come on. [Since Quentin does not move, Father takes the book from him and pulls him along.]

SARAH (gleefully): Come on, little genius.

BILLY: Let's go, Superboy.

FATHER: You two stop that. You're all going to be treated equally from now on.

QUENTIN: But I'm—

FATHER: No "buts" about it. Get moving.

QUENTIN: I suppose this is what that dumb social worker told you to do.

FATHER: Precisely.

MOTHER: And it's long overdue.

Quentin is bright enough to know that he is beaten and that his game is over, but it still took two years to get the job done.

6

BODY GAMES

In this chapter we shall discuss games which cause dysfunctions of some part of the child's body; such disorders include stomach ulcers, enuresis, stuttering, and many others. A body game involves three levels of closely interwoven disturbances: (1.) interpersonal difficulties, (2.) emotional turmoil in the child, and (3.) a body dysfunction. These three aspects of a body game are illustrated in Figure 1.

Many physicians employ the words "psychosomatic" and "psychophysiologic" in talking about these disorders.

We are using the term "body game" to include not only the problems usually labeled psychosomatic but also other kinds of body difficulties such as stuttering and obesity.

However, the terms "body game" and "psychosomatic" can also be used in a broader sense. Many games of children and adolescents can have marked effects on the *courses and outcomes* of diseases that are *not caused* by interpersonal disturbances and emotional turmoil. For example, lobar pneumonia is caused by bacteria that invade the lung, and emotional factors play no part in producing the disease. However, disturbed interpersonal patterns, or games, can affect the outcome of the disease. Thus, an adolescent with sound interpersonal relationships stays in bed, takes his penicillin or other antibiotic, and recovers from lobar pneumonia. On the other hand, an adolescent in wild rebellion against his parents and society may reject treatment, ride his motorcycle in the cold night air while he

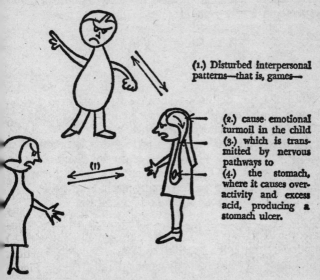

(1.) Disturbed interpersonal patterns—that is, games—

(2.) cause emotional turmoil in the child (3.) which is transmitted by nervous pathways to (4.) the stomach, where it causes overactivity and excess acid, producing a stomach ulcer.

FIGURE 1. AN EXAMPLE OF HOW A BODY GAME WORKS

has a fever of 103 degrees, dull the distress of his disease by marijuana and other drugs, and die from lobar pneumonia. In such a case, even though the patient's game did not cause his disease, it determined its outcome. *Interpersonal relationships and body functioning form one indivisible process, and when we discuss them separately, we are adopting an artificial device for convenience in talking about them.*

Parents and children who *understand* body games often can deal with them more effectively. For example, when a child and his parents see the child's stomach ulcer (ulcers are more common in children than was formerly recognized) as the end point of a chain of interpersonal and emotional causes, as outlined in Figure 1, their attempt to cure the ulcer becomes more than a search for the right pill. It is broadened to include an inventory of the child's relationships and his emotional state, and if the child's games are not too severe, his parents and he can often do useful things not only to heal his ulcer but also to improve his interpersonal life in general.

A Game to Play in Bed

The most common body game of small children is enuresis, or bed-wetting. Bed-wetting is common, and it occurs in many children who must be considered "within normal limits" emotionally. In such children it is caused by minor stresses of interpersonal life.

In other children, however, bed-wetting is produced by deeper difficulties. It may be the way in which a passive child unconsciously expresses some of his pent-up hostility. He has been made to feel guilty each time he is assertive, and in time some of his bottled-up turmoil comes out as loss of bladder control while sleeping. Some psychiatrists feel that children who have been made to feel guilty about masturbation or playing with their genitals may become enuretic. Enuresis may also be associated with anxiety and emotional insecurity caused by various kinds of interpersonal stresses.

When a child has no obvious physical abnormalities

and there are no signs of infection in his urine, the chances are 99 percent that his bed-wetting is caused by emotional tension. In the absence of obvious physical disease the odds are so great that bed-wetting is caused by emotional factors that most child psychiatrists feel that elaborate work-ups by urologists not only are unnecessary but make subsequent psychological treatment more difficult.

Although most children have achieved bladder control by the age of three, a wide margin for error is allowed, and a child is not considered enuretic until the age of four or so. Bed-wetting usually ends spontaneously by the age of ten or twelve, but in 10 to 15 percent of the cases it continues into adolescence and even young adulthood. After the age of twenty-five it is very rare. Most enuresis occurs only during sleep, but in a few cases it occurs during the day.

Bed-wetting is so common that each decade produces a new group of techniques, gadgets, medications and psychological measures to treat it. Most enuretic children are successfully managed by the joint efforts of parents and family doctors or pediatricians. Only those children with severe personality problems in addition to their enuresis need treatment in child guidance clinics.

The following case illustrates how interpersonal factors caused A Game to Play in Bed and how modifications of parental attitudes and the use of a time-tested psychological technique, which can be employed by either physicians or parents, broke it up.

Janice's mother was an affectionate but domineering woman who ran her husband's life with a loving but firm hand, and since he was seeking a mother-figure as much as a wife, their marriage went well. She made all the decisions, but her decisions carefully took into account his comfort and welfare. When she gave sharp reminders to her husband, she always did it when they were alone, and she never humiliated him in front of others. She was prudent with money, saw that the house was well run, entertained gracefully, and did not interfere in her husband's business activities. It was a happy marriage, and since she needed a passive husband and he needed a dominant wife, it could not be called a sick one.

141

Janice was reared along the same lines; Mother was affectionate but controlling, and Janice got along fairly well. She could be affectionate, but she was more comfortable in expressing affection toward her father than toward her mother. She was well behaved, but there was something cold and mechanical in her deportment. She could stick up for her rights but only *outside* the home. Mother read books on how to rear children, and she knew that they should be allowed to express a moderate amount of anger, and Mother allowed this but *not toward herself*. However, she encouraged Janice to defend her rights with other children and to blow off steam toward her dolls. Janice's brother Craig, who was two years younger, was being reared in the same manner.

When Janice was four, her long-suppressed hostility toward her mother led to A Game to Play in Bed. At first she wet the bed only once a week or so, but as she sensed that wet sheets and blankets upset her mother, a subtle battle between them began. Janice had accidentally found a way in which she could unconsciously express toward her mother some of her pent-up resentment. Mother tried prizes for "dry nights," limiting fluid intake after 6 P.M., getting Janice up to urinate at 11 P.M., having Janice change the wet sheets and hang out the blankets to dry, and many other things. Everything failed. By the time she was five Janice wet the bed every night and Mother anxiously noted that Craig was still wetting the bed at three. Despite her dislike of airing her family problems to anyone, Mother decided to talk to their pediatrician about this difficulty on Janice's next visit.

In addition to taking care of Janice and Craig, Dr. Crawford knew Mother and Father socially and understood the family fairly well. In as tactful a manner as possible he explained that enuresis is caused by "the little emotional tensions of life" and tends to be more common in "kids who keep too much bottled up inside themselves and don't blow off enough steam." He suggested that children should "be allowed to blow off a little steam *even around the house* once in a while."

After making this brief stab into psychotherapy, which is

142

about all that a busy pediatrician's schedule will allow and which actually did cause Mother to let Janice be a bit more assertive with her at times, Dr. Crawford said he was going to teach Janice a way to break up her Bed Game. He said that the mother-daughter aggravation over wet sheets and blankets each morning only increased "whatever little tensions there might be" and that getting rid of bed-wetting would be a small contribution to "better relationships" in the home.

Then, while Mother sat a little way off, he drew Janice close to his desk and put a piece of paper and a pencil in front of the two of them. He asked Janice very seriously if she "really wanted to lick this bed-wetting problem." Janice stared at him and said nothing. Success with this approach depends on a cooperative effort by the child and the doctor; it cannot be just one more thing an adult shoves down the child's throat. So, after a moment's pause Dr. Crawford said again, "You know, Janice, you and I can lick this thing if you want to."

She "bit" and asked, "How?"

"Well," said Dr. Crawford, "I'll show you how." Then, while Janice watched, he drew the diagram shown in figure 2.

"Here," he said, "is the place inside you, shaped more or less like a balloon, where the urine is stored before you urinate. When you are ready to urinate, you go to the toilet and it comes out here. Now, surrounding this tube where the urine comes out is a round muscle; it is shaped like a doughnut, and so we can call it the doughnut muscle. When you are not urinating, the doughnut muscle is closed tight and there is no hole in the center. When you urinate, the doughnut muscle opens the hole and lets the urine come out." Dr. Crawford illustrated this by making a doughnut-shaped figure with his clasped hands and opening and closing the central hole.

He then said, "Janice, do you want to know what your trouble is?"

Janice "bit" again and asked, "What?"

"Your trouble," he replied, "is that you have a weak doughnut muscle. Our problem is to strengthen that

143

doughnut muscle so that it won't accidentally open up
when you're asleep and cause you to wet the bed. Do you
know how to strengthen a muscle?" Janice wasn't sure.

"Well," he said, "we exercise it. For instance, [here he
demonstrates by raising his arms and pointing to his

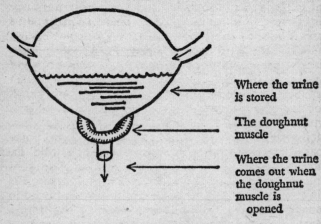

Where the urine
is stored

The doughnut
muscle

Where the urine
comes out when
the doughnut
muscle is
opened

FIGURE 2.

biceps muscle] if we had a weak arm muscle, how would
we strengthen it? We'd exercise it." He flexed his arm up
and down. "After a while the muscle becomes strong. We
must strengthen your doughnut muscle. Do you know how
we do that?" Janice, who was fascinated by this time, indicated that she didn't know.

"I'll tell you how," the doctor said. "Every morning
when you get up you immediately drink a big glass of
water, or maybe two. Pretty soon you have to urinate, and
so you go to the toilet. When you begin to urinate, you let
just a little out and clamp it off again. Then you let a little
more out and clamp it off again. You keep this up until you
finish urinating. In this way you are opening and closing
the doughnut muscle and exercising it. You do this every
time you go to the toilet, every day. Then, after a while the
bed-wetting stops. This is your project and mine. We'll do
it, won't we?" Janice said she would, and she did. When

144

he returned for a brief visit with **Dr. Crawford** four weeks later, she was beginning to have some "dry nights." and eight weeks after that her enuresis stopped. Her Bed Game was over.

Why did this approach work? By letting Janice express a little more anger around the house, Mother contributed, but the "doughnut muscle technique" probably was more important. This technique works in about 50 percent of the cases, even if no attention is paid to the emotional tensions in the child's life, and some pediatricians and family physicians with special knacks for talking with children report cure rates of up to 75 percent. Unlike many other psychiatric symptoms, removal of enuresis without attention to its emotional roots usually does not cause another type of symptom, such as a phobia, to take its place. Moreover, terminating the morning upset over urine-soaked bedding stops a chronic irritation between the mother and the child. In addition, removal of enuresis broadens the child's social opportunities, for he can spend nights at the homes of relatives and friends and can go to summer camp without the embarrassment of bed-wetting. Many enuretic children have relatively minor emotional problems that do not merit child guidance clinic treatment, and removal of the symptom is a worthwhile goal in itself.

In Europe some psychiatrists feel that this technique has a physiological basis and that muscle training actually occurs. However, most American psychiatrists and pediatricians feel that it works because (1.) it is a cooperative effort between an enthusiastic adult and a willing child, (2.) it helps the child become more comfortable emotionally with his genitals and their functions, and (3.) it includes suggestion, a poorly understood process which is probably involved in the success of more medical procedures than scientists are willing to admit.

Janice's mother was a quick study. Six months after Janice's bed-wetting ended, she sat her son Craig down at the kitchen table and, after sending Janice out of the room, imitated Dr. Crawford's procedure. Fortunately, Craig also fell into the group of 50 percent or more in which this approach works.

Obesity is rarely caused by endocrine disturbances and other physical disorders. In the majority of cases it is caused by overeating, which may be produced by family eating patterns, social customs and dietary carelessness. However, in some cases overeating is the result of emotional tensions and interpersonal problems.

Obesity is more likely to be caused by unhealthy interpersonal patterns and thus constitutes a body game that distorts social development. Thus, it is more often an emotionally caused disorder in children and adolescents than in middle-aged and elderly persons. In children and adolescents obesity interferes with social acceptance, athletic activities and dating, and it subjects them to ridicule by their equals; whereas obesity, though unhealthy, does not cause social problems in older age groups. A child or adolescent may overeat to assuage anxiety, to cling to an immature role, or to achieve some other unhealthy interpersonal goal. As in all body games, this is an unconscious process; the person knows that he overeats, but he does not know why.

For example, obesity may occur when a mother has a sick need to keep her child tied to her. By encouraging overeating she produces a grossly obese child who is ridiculed by his classmates, excluded from their activities, and shunned in dating. In other instances the child or adolescent is uncomfortable with persons of his own age group and unconsciously finds in obesity an avenue to social isolation. For some children and adolescents overeating diminishes feelings of anxiety, depressiveness and loneliness.

In adolescence obesity may be the means by which a teenager, usually a girl, flees the challenges of adjusting to the opposite sex. Marked obesity is a form of ugliness that is under the control of the person. In such cases overeating usually is a solitary process; the adolescent munches between meals and at bedtime, often hiding his overeating from his nagging parents and disapproving siblings. Let us consider a fairly typical game of Solitaire.

Olivia was by eight years the youngest of three sisters. She was reared in comfortable circumstances in a well-to-do suburb of a large city, but when she was fourteen, her father lost his money in a business disaster and became a minor employee with a small salary in the firm of one of his former competitors. He saved his home and its contents, but little else. Olivia's two sisters were married when this occurred and escaped its interpersonal consequences. Olivia did not. She abruptly found herself unable to compete economically and socially with the other girls in high school. The country club membership, the second car, the modish clothing, the special recreational activities, the out-of-town summer vacations and all the other things that were accepted as routine in her neighborhood were gone, and the snobbish cruelty of her girlfriends made her shabbiness all the more painful. Her well-married sisters, one of whom now lived in a distant city, showed little compassion for the family misfortune and mild irritability that their father had "made such a mess of things." College loomed a few years ahead for Olivia. Going away to one of the "right schools" was now impossible, and commuting the long distance into the city to attend a state school would be difficult.

If Olivia had been a different kind of person, she might have become a defiant rebel; she might have made a virtue of the drab life that had been forced on her and might have flaunted it to her classmates as more honest than their snobbishness. However, even before her father's financial decline, she had been somewhat shy and had felt inferior to her handsome, fashionably married sisters. Instead of rebelling, she retreated into a game of Solitaire. Olivia's story illustrates how personality structure, economic factors and social forces may combine to produce a game.

During a ten-month period between the ages of fourteen and fifteen Olivia put on 45 pounds, and her obesity made her ugly. It made the expenses of fashionable clothing, fine cosmetics and beauty shops—which she could not af-

ford—pointless. Shunned by both boys and girls, she use
the excuse of her obesity to retreat into the life of a bookish
recluse. In Solitaire she found a sick solution to her in
terpersonal crisis.

Her parents were too preoccupied with their ow
problems to pay much attention to what was happening t
Olivia, but from time to time they aggravated her game b
haranguing her about her obesity.

FATHER: Olivia, how much do you weigh now?

OLIVIA: I haven't weighed myself lately.

MOTHER: You've put on at least forty pounds in th
last year, and you look awful.

FATHER: Boys never call here the way they did whe
your sisters were your age.

OLIVIA: I don't care. I'm too busy with my studies.

MOTHER: You eat all the time. You're getting so fa
the other boys and girls your age won't want to be aroun
you.

OLIVIA: It doesn't bother me.

FATHER: Well, it should. You should go on a diet.

MOTHER: Yes, you must cut out all this eating betwee
meals and at bedtime. You don't want to be a hermit, d
you?

Not only did Olivia's game solve *her* problem in a sic
way, but it also enabled her parents to avoid facing th
painful fact that their economic decline had been a soci
disaster for their daughter. At her parents' insistence Olivi
started on several diets but did not stick to them, and an
minor weight losses were soon regained.

At eighteen Olivia entered a nursing school in a larg
hospital in the center of the city. After receiving her nur
ing diploma, she went to work on night duty, attended co
lege during the day, and in time got her bachelor's an
master's degrees in nursing. By the time she was in her la
twenties she held a responsible administrative position in
large university nursing school and was accumulatir
credits for her doctorate. When she was twenty-nine, Oliv
no longer needed her game, went on a diet, and over

period of several months lost forty pounds. Cinderella became a beautiful woman, and the young resident physicians in the hospital where she worked soon became interested. At twenty-nine she had her first date, and she realized she needed help in adjusting to a new world. From an interpersonal point of view she had not gone through adolescence and early adulthood. For a year and a half she had counseling from a psychiatrist, and during this time she ended her long game of Solitaire.

Tongue Twisters

Various aspects of stuttering have long suggested that emotional factors play a large role in causing it. For example, most stutterers can whistle well, and many of them are free of stuttering while singing. Stuttering in both children and adults may entirely disappear for several days or more in a new environment, such as a summer camp or a vacation resort in a distant state, but it begins again when the stutterer returns to his usual surroundings. Stuttering often is noticeably worse when the stutterer is under emotional stress, and some stutter only when they are under stress. In many cases stuttering gradually improves over long periods of time, and it is more common in children than in adults.

There is much controversy about the causes of stuttering. Some speech therapists feel that it is produced by faulty training in breathing and speech articulation and that the stutterer needs careful training and reeducation in the relaxed formation of sounds. Other investigators feel that mixed cerebral dominance (which is discussed in Chapter 5 under the game of Mirror, Mirror on the Wall) plays a role in stuttering. In former times, when many left-handed children were forcibly shifted to right-handedness by parents and teachers, the incidence of stuttering was much higher in such children than in the general population. Today, most parents and teachers know that forced changing of handedness is unwise, and only a small percentage of stutterers have such a history. However, some clinicians feel that mild mixed cerebral dominance of unclear origin exists in many stutterers but is difficult to

149

identify because of our relatively crude ways of testing for it.

Many psychiatrists and speech therapists believe that interpersonal stresses are the main causes of stuttering. Psychiatrists who have investigated stuttering feel that in many cases a child releases much pent-up hostility through this symptom and that in other cases stuttering is produced by diffuse anxiety and insecurity. Moreover, stuttering is a provocative symptom. It annoys the hearer. He fidgets impatiently while the stutterer struggles to get his words out, and he wants to finish his words and sentences for him. Parents in particular tend to be upset by stuttering in their children. Brief periods of stuttering are common in the speech development of many children, but when the child with a poor relationship with his parents senses that his stuttering infuriates them, he may unconsciously adopt it as a way of retaliating for their lovelessness or harshness. Thus, what might have been a minor speech difficulty for a few weeks or months becomes an ingrained interpersonal game of Tongue Twisters.

Various types of treatment are used for stuttering. Many speech therapists use techniques that train children to form sounds in a relaxed manner, and many children get over their stuttering in a few months to two or three years with such treatment. However, these results are hard to evaluate because a large number of children in time recover spontaneously from stuttering and it is difficult to know whether a child's stuttering cleared *because* of speech therapy or merely *during* it. Moreover, the psychological impact of speech therapy may be as important as the retraining techniques. Prolonged cooperative work between the child and an interested adult may be an important ingredient in the speech therapist's success. Many speech therapists recognize this and cultivate warm relationships with their patients and also include in some cases a certain amount of counseling with parents on ways any obvious tensions in the home can be corrected. When the tensions in the home are major or when the speech therapist's efforts are unsuccessful, stutterers and their parents are sometimes referred to child guidance clinics.

Let us examine a case of stuttering in which emotional factors played an important role.

Kevin was the only child of a strong-willed mother and a domineering father, each of whom wanted to control the marriage. Such a couple may get along fairly well during courtship, when their relationship is diluted by continual associations with others at cocktail parties, poolside gatherings and other social occasions; but when they marry and must live together, their bickering, which before marriage was mild, becomes severe. The marriage of Kevin's parents hung together because of the pressure of their two families and because they did not spend a great deal of time alone together; they entertained frequently and often spent evenings and weekends with friends and relatives. However, after Kevin was born, they spent more time at home and the intensity of their fighting increased. By the time he was three Kevin had become a frequent pawn in their quarrels, and their chronic irritability spilled over into their handling of him. He got little love and emotional security from either of them.

When he was three, Kevin began to stutter. At first his stuttering was infrequent and mild, but he unconsciously grasped that it infuriated his parents. They fidgeted as he struggled to get his words out and irritably ended his sentences for him. Thus Kevin found a way to retaliate for the loneliness and turmoil in which he was being reared, and his parents could do nothing about it; they could neither punish nor criticize him for a problem he could not control. By the time he was four his stuttering was severe.

A typical family dialogue went as follows:

FATHER: Come on, let's go. My foursome tees off at eight thirty, and you and Kevin want to get to the pool before it gets too hot. Where are the car keys?

MOTHER: I saw Kevin playing with them ten minutes ago.

FATHER: Kevin, what did you do with the car keys?

KEVIN: I th-th-th-th-th-th-think I p-p-p-p-p-put th-th-th-th-th-them on-n-n-n-n th-th-th-th——

151

FATHER: Where?

KEVIN: On-n-n-n-n th-th-th-th-th—

FATHER: Oh, hell, just tell me where you put the car keys.

MOTHER: Shut up, Henry, and let the boy talk.

FATHER: You stay out of this.

KVEIN: I'm-m-m-m-m-m n-n-n-n-not s-s-s-s-sure i-i i-if I if i h-h-h-h-h-h—

FATHER: Kevin, just one word. Please, just one word. Where are the keys?

MOTHER: Don't blow up at the kid over something he can't control. He can't help it if he stutters.

FATHER: Oh, damn, where are the car keys?

KEVIN: Y-y-y-y-you h-h-h-h-had th-th-th-th-th—[He gives up—unable to get it out].

FATHER: (Controlling his irritability with great effort): Yes, Kevin, now take it easy, boy, and just tell me where the keys are.

MOTHER: Hell, you're not even sure he knows where they are.

FATHER: Oh, damn!

MOTHER: Kevin dear, now think and say it slowly. Where are the keys?

KEVIN: Wh-wh-wh-wh-wh-when I w-w-w-w-w-was g-g-g-g-going in th-th-th-th-th-th—

MOTHER: Oh, Kevin, don't say anything. Just point.

KEVIN: I c-c-c-c-c-can't d-d-d-d-d-do th-th-th-th-th—

MOTHER: Oh, Lord, Kevin, just relax and get it out. Where are the keys?

The more upset his parents became, the more Kevin's speech deteriorated and he slowly turned them on a spit over a low fire. Ten minutes later the keys were found between two cushions on the couch.

When Kevin was four and a half, at his grandparents' insistence his parents took him to a speech therapist who treated Kevin and sent the parents to a psychiatrist for marriage counseling. The speech therapist was a warm, insightful person, and for the first time in his life Kevin had a good relationship with an interested adult who was not upset by his stuttering but instead tried to help him get his words out with deliberate ease. The psychiatrist made limited progress with the parents' marital problems, but he was able to get them to treat the boy with more interest and less irritability; he also helped them tolerate Kevin's stuttering with less annoyance. By the time he was six Kevin's game of Tongue Twisters was over, although the future of his parents' marriage was still uncertain.

Holdout

Constipation is one of the most common complaints for which the public seeks medical advice. A large number of people devoutly believe the myth of the necessity of the daily bowel movement and dread a pseudodisease called irregularity. They are convinced that lack of daily defecation causes bloating, gas, headaches, dizziness, irritability, depressiveness, childhood cantankerousness, vocational spats and many other physical and emotional difficulties. These beliefs are strenuously fostered by the advertisements of the cathartic manufacturers, who have a large vested interest in them, since the truth would drive them out of business. Although such advertisements vary from the absurd to the revolting, they have a large impact on Americans' bowel habits.

Extensive medical studies have shown that if left alone, the normal human colon is very irregular in many people. Some perfectly healthy people go two or three days without having bowel movements. Others may defecate once or twice a day for three days, then skip two or three days, and so on. A few healthy people, including children, go for four to seven days or more without bowel movements. The various physical and emotional symptoms some people develop when they do not defecate are caused by their anxiety about not defecating, not by any physiological process.

Some mothers afflict their children with barrages of laxatives, rectal suppositories and enemas in determined searches for the elusive goal of "regularity," and they attribute any misbehavior, fearfulness and crying spells of their children to "sluggishness." From this interpersonal struggle, based on false ideas about bowel functioning, a game of Holdout may arise.

The alleged disorder of constipation is usually an *interpersonal* problem caused by the parents' obsessive concern, which is gradually transmitted to children. Bowel overconcern, once established in childhood and early adolescence, often becomes a lifelong pattern, and the struggle to void the daily quota of feces goes on for decades. Ideas about bowel functioning are often shared by an entire family and are passed on from one generation to another. I have known families in which the morning "results" were routinely discussed at the breakfast table. The gastrointestinal tract is the one body system whose intake and output are available to the scrutiny of the public; they can choose what goes in and inspect what comes out, and they may attempt to regulate their general health by dietary and excretory regimens.

Hemorrhoids in many instances are the product of a prolonged game of Holdout. After years of straining for long periods each morning to void the daily minimum of feces, the rectal veins become distended and hemorrhoids develop. In such cases the hemorrhoids often are difficult to cure; they return after an operation because the person's ideas about bowel functioning have not changed.

Thus, in most cases constipation is caused by *unhealthy patterns of family communication* and hence may be labeled a body game of Holdout. Except in physically ill persons and in immobilized, debilitated and elderly people, constipation usually is a disease of the brain, not the colon. The cure is education, not laxatives. Let us consider a scene in a typical *family game* of Holdout.

Scene: The breakfast table where Mother, Father, and five-year-old Donald are seated. Prunes and some variety of bran flakes are on the table, since they are touted as aides to regularity.

MOTHER: Pass the coffee, Herb. [Turns to Donald.] How did things go this morning?

DONALD: I didn't do anything.

154

FATHER: Nothing at all?

DONALD: I tried hard.

MOTHER: This is the second morning you haven't had
results. Did you have one of your headaches yester-
?

DONALD: I think so. I didn't feel so good.

FATHER: How do you feel this morning?

DONALD: OK. Well, I guess I feel a little sluggish [He
already begun to pick up the jargon, as well as the
ptoms, that go along with a game of Holdout.]

MOTHER: Maybe I'll give you a couple of Res-Lax
lets after breakfast.

FATHER: If you didn't go yesterday, what time was it
t you went the day before?

DONALD: In the morning.

MOTHER: That's forty-eight hours since his last move-
nt.

DONALD: I don't feel like eating anymore.

FATHER: If the Res-Lax doesn't work, it will be three
's by tomorrow morning.

MOTHER: I'll give him the Res-Lax, and if he doesn't
ve any results by this afternoon, I'll give him an enema.

FATHER: Maybe you ought to talk to Dr. Novak about
s the next time Donald goes in for his shots.

When Mother consulted Dr. Novak, he spent ten
nutes carefully explaining the points outlined earlier in
s section on Holdout. He spent most of the time assuag-
 Mother's anxiety over the possible consequences of
nald's not defecating. He urged her *never* to give
nald another enema, cathartic tablet or laxative sup-
sitory. In front of Donald and as reassuringly as possi-
, he told her that irregularity is normal and not a di-
se. He told her to telephone him for brief reassurances if
 couldn't stand waiting for Donald to defecate spon-
eously.

Mother told Father. He was doubtful but said they
uld try. During the next two months Mother and Dr.
vak had many brief telephone conversations, such as the
owing:

MOTHER: Dr. Novak, it's been three days since Donald went to the toilet.

DR. NOVAK: Don't worry, Mrs. Greenberg. He's had a lot of laxatives and enemas the last couple of years, and it will take a little while for him to even out. But nothing bad will happen. He's just fine.

MOTHER: He has a headache and he's very irritable.

DR. NOVAK: These things have nothing to do with whether or not he moves his bowels, I assure you. Send him next door to play with the neighbor kids and his headache and irritability may go away.

MOTHER: My mother-in-law says that a woman in her neighborhood had to be operated on for "locked bowels."

DR. NOVAK: Well, I'm not sure what she meant by "locked bowels." That's not a term we doctors use. But I assure you that Donald will suffer no ill effects from not moving his bowels for a few days.

MOTHER: What will we do tomorrow if Donald doesn't go?

DR. NOVACK: Call me again. The problem is your worry, not Donald's bowels.

The next day Dr. Novak got another call.

MOTHER: Good news, Doctor. Donald had a movement.

DR. NOVAK: That's fine. However, let's accept it in a matter-of-fact way and not make a big deal out of it, just as we're not going to be upset if he skips another day or two.

MOTHER: But, Doctor, it was sort of hard and dark.

DR. NOVAK: Mrs. Greenberg, such things are of no importance, and they just give you more to worry about. Why don't we just tell Donald to flush the toilet and not inspect his bowel movements? I assure you it will all turn out all right.

It did. Mother and Father were brave, Dr. Novak was patient, and Donald was saved from a lifelong game of Holdout. Moreover, since Holdout is often passed from

156

one generation to another, Dr. Novak may have also helped Donald's children.

A Game with Many Names

The ways in which emotional turmoil may affect the body are legion. The anxiety-ridden child or adolescent may at times have an accelerated heart rate, rapid respirations, diarrhea, intestinal cramping, stomach pain, frequent urination, headaches, facial pain, fatigue, nausea, vomiting, skin rashes and many other symptoms. These symptoms are caused by interpersonal stress that produces emotional turmoil, which leads to body changes, as illustrated in Figure 1 at the beginning of this chapter. Body games arising from anxiety are so diverse that we label them only as A Game with Many Names.

These body games may be minor and brief or major and long-lasting. For example, a five-year-old who is frightened by a midnight brawl of his parents may have mild stomach cramps that last an hour or two, or, depending on the nature of his interpersonal stresses, he may have painful gastrointestinal symptoms for weeks, months or years. Mild muscle-tension headaches caused by day-to-day problems are so common that about 20 percent of children and more than 60 percent of adolescents and adults have them occasionally. An adolescent facing important university examinations may have urinary frequency, diarrhea, or perhaps a brief return of asthma that has not bothered him since childhood, and his symptoms usually clear when he sees a passing grade posted on his instructor's office door.

Most of the people whom we label "within normal limits" have some of these symptoms once in a while. The manner in which they and the persons around them react to such symptoms is important. If, for example, parents shrug off such a difficulty, reassure the child that he is "only upset because you're worried," and send him off to play, the child views his symptom without alarm and often it soon subsides. However, physicians' waiting rooms and hospital rosters are crowded with people whose symptoms precipitate alarm, which in turn increases their severity.

157

For example, if a child becomes upset in an argument with his father and vomits, his mother may calm them down and the vomiting soon passes. Another mother under similar circumstances may call the doctor or take the child to a hospital emergency room and may hover over him; in this case his vomiting often gets worse and persists for a day or two. Furthermore, the chance is increased that he will vomit the next time he faces interpersonal stress.

The term "body overconcern" is sometimes applied to this process. Years of parental worry focus a child's attention on his body reactions to stress, and his resultant gastrointestinal complaints, or "pounding heart," fatigue, muscle-tension headaches, or other symptoms become fixed. Some pediatricians state that 25 percent of their time is devoted to these body games, and many interns estimate that half their working hours are spent dealing with such problems. Body games often begin in childhood and early adolescence and are firmly rooted by the time the patient is an adult.

There is a cultural factor in body games. Campaigns to inform people about the early signs of heart disease, cancer and other illnesses, publicity about possible rare side reactions to medications, mental health programs and other public education on medical matters have made the American public very health conscious. However, a health-conscious public is also a disease-conscious public. A public that knows much about disease also tends to worry a great deal about minor alterations in body functions. For example, physicians have learned to their dismay that the public is now so well instructed on the signs of heart disease that doctors are often consulted by people with strained left-shoulder and arm muscles who are convinced they are having heart attacks; electrocardiograms and physical examinations may not completely convince them otherwise. Similarly, many mothers insist on batteries of laboratory tests for their children to rule out rare diseases, and often they buttress their demands with newspaper clippings or citations from television programs.

If carefully analyzed, most public education on physical and mental health is based on fear. Parents are admonished do this or that or their children will be neurotic, and the public is threatened with cancer if each new body sensation is not checked by a physician. To ignore a body change or to minimize its importance is taboo. Although enthusiasts may proclaim that we are becoming the most health-conscious public in history, many physicians wonder if we are becoming the most hypochondriacal.

Let us examine how these unhealthy patterns, or A Game with Many Names, begin in childhood:

MOTHER: Yvonne, what's the matter?

YVONNE: I have a headache.

FATHER: Eight-year-old girls shouldn't have headaches as much as you do.

YVONNE: I don't have so many of them.

MOTHER: Where does your head hurt?

YVONNE: I don't know. It's not too bad.

FATHER: Answer your mother's question, Yvonne. Point to where your head hurts.

YVONNE: Here and here.

MOTHER: It may be sinus.

FATHER: Has she been checked to see if she needs glasses?

MOTHER: I'll take her to Dr. Robinson tomorrow.

YVONNE: I'm going out to play.

FATHER: I think you should stay in the house until you're better. Lie down for a while.

MOTHER: I'll give you an aspirin.

FATHER: How does your head feel now?

YVONNE: I don't know. Maybe a little worse.

FATHER: I'll look up headaches in the index of *The Home Medical Adviser*. Let's see now . . . Headaches, causes of . . . allergy . . . aneurysm of blood vessel, rupture of. . . brain tumor, early signs of . . . migraine . . . Does your headache throb, or does it feel like there's a heavy weight pushing down, or is the pain sharp?

YVONNE: Well, I guess it sort of throbs.

FATHER: That's probably vascular. Be sure to tell Dr. Robinson that tomorrow.

YVONNE: I'm beginning to get sick to my stomach.

Let us examine how a less alarmed mother and father might have handled Yvonne's headache:

MOTHER: Yvonne, what's the matter?

YVONNE: I have a headache.

MOTHER: Where?

YVONNE: In my forehead and the back of my neck.

MOTHER: I have the same thing once in a while when I'm upset about something. Dr. Robinson told me that it's due to tension in the thin muscle layer in the scalp and in the thick muscles at the back of the neck. He said that ninety percent of the headaches people have are caused by that and it's nothing to worry about.

FATHER: Many people get little headaches once in a while when they're tense about things.

MOTHER: You probably got the headache because you and Harry have been fighting over that new game in the family room.

YVONNE: Harry's a rat.

FATHER: You're mad at Harry. Why don't you go next door and play with the Miller kids for a while?

YVONNE: What about my headache?

MOTHER: When you get over your upset with Harry, it will probably go away. If not, I'll give you an aspirin.

LUST AND COUNTERLUST

During the age period of about nine through eleven a new kind of interpersonal need emerges: the need for intimate relationships *outside the family* with persons of one's own group. This need first finds expression in close relation ships with individuals of the same sex. Boys group together in gangs and clubs, and girls have favorite girlfriends and small cliques. Lust (a term employed by Harry Stack Sullivan to indicate genitally directed sexuality) usually does not play a significant role in these relationships. Lust becomes a powerful factor during puberty, which runs from twelve through thirteen, and in most cases it turns much of the person's interpersonal interest from persons of his own sex toward those of the opposite sex.

The close relationships that a person has *outside the family* from late childhood onward may have corrective effects on previously formed personality problems. In these extrafamilial intimate relationships the person has opportunities to see himself and others in new ways, and if his personality warps are mild and moderate, he may develop new viewpoints about relationships with others.

For example, outside the family the unloved child may find affection and thus develop better capacities to give and receive warmth. The rejected child may find acceptance and then be able to bridge the gap between himself and others. The scorned child may discover prestige and be able to form close bonds with both children and adults. However, the child who has undergone marked emotional damage usually does not improve during this period. His severe games prevent him from engaging in the corrective relationships that might help him.

Lust and Counterlust

Lust is the interpersonal force that draws a person toward relationships in which genital sexuality is a possible result. It begins to emerge as a strong drive at about the age of twelve or thirteen, and by the age of fifteen or sixteen it has acquired the prominence it will continue to have for most of one's life. The term "lust" is somewhat equivalent to the genital aspects of the Freudian term "libido."

An individual's lust may be directed toward persons of the opposite sex, toward those of the same sex, or, in masturbation, toward himself. In the transitional periods of late childhood and puberty (age nine through thirteen) there is sometimes a limited amount of homosexual play. Mutual masturbation among boys is fairly common at this time. In most persons such homosexual experimentation is brief, and their lustful drives soon become riveted on the opposite sex.

An emotionally healthy person is able to achieve comfortable intimacy (friendships) with persons of both sexes independent of his lustful drives. Thus a well-adjusted man is able to have good relationships with both men and women without the interference of lust, and a well-adjusted woman has similar capacities. However, in addition the individual should be able to combine both *intimacy* and *lust* in special relationships with those of the opposite sex. Between late childhood and middle adolescence these capacities emerge, are tested, and assume the form they will have for the rest of the person's life. Hence, what goes on in the child's interpersonal life between the ages of nine and sixteen has lasting importance; it is not merely a reflection of what has gone on before. The events of the first nine years, which we discussed in previous chapters, are important; but the things that occur in late childhood, puberty and early adolescence, which are to a large extent *extrafamilial,* also play significant roles in personality development.

Counterlust. A person's adjustment to his lustful feelings may be disturbed by various forces that can be grouped under the general term "counterlust." Anxiety, hostility, competitiveness with persons of the opposite sex, and dread of genital intimacy with others are examples of counterlust. For instance, a boy may have had such a traumatic relationship with his mother that he has developed a profound fear of close relationships with women and he is panicked by his lustful feelings. Throughout his adult life he may be unable to form prolonged lustful relationships with women; he may be sexually impotent, or he may go through a series of turbulent marriages and divorces, or he may flee from women into homosexuality.

The direction of a person's lustful drives is greatly

fluenced by the relationships he had with his parents during his formative years. The person who identified with his parent of the same sex and had a sound relationship with is parent of the opposite sex establishes a heterosexual orientation. For example, the girl who made a good idenfication with her mother and had a sound relationship with her father assumes the feminine attitudes implied in her mother's role and seeks in boyfriends the manly qualities she found in her father. On the other hand, a boy who had a poor relationship with his father and did not identify with him, but instead identified with his overprotective mother, may in adolescence and adulthood seek as sexual partners the persons whom a woman would seek—men—and develops a homosexual way of life.

However, in some cases the individual has undergone marked trauma in his relationships with his parents and other close persons, and tendencies toward both heterosexuality and homosexuality (as well as other kinds of sexual difficulties) waver in him. In such cases *accidental* factors in late childhood, puberty and adolescence may determine the final form of his lustful drives. For example, a boy who because of poor relationships with his parents teeters between a heterosexual and a homosexual orientation may be decisively inclined in a homosexual direction by a close friendship with an older homosexual adolescent during puberty and early adolescence. But the same boy may be directed into a firm heterosexual pattern by good relationships with heterosexually oriented individuals. The role of such *accidental* associations (*accidental* in the sense that they are the results of chance meetings and various other unpredictable human situations) has probably not received sufficient emphasis by psychiatrists and social scientists.

The counterlust forces include many kinds of personality problems. We shall cover a few of them, for counterlust forces produce some of the unhealthy interpersonal patterns, or games, that may arise during late childhood and early adolescence.

A person's emotional maturity may be evaluated in terms of his capacity to adjust comfortably in ever-widening circles of interpersonal life.

At each point in a person's development his degree of emotional maturity may be evaluated by examining his interpersonal circle and how he is adjusting in it. For example, if a sixteen-year-old boy does well in his studies and in athletics, but his major emotional investment is still in his parents, he is not emotionally mature for his age. His interpersonal circle is still that of a five-year-old, although he may do well in other aspects. Similarly, an eighteen year-old girl who is panicked by the forces of lust within her and dreads any kind of closeness with a boy is immaturely fixed at the level of a ten-year-old. In later years she may go on to a distinguished professional career, but if she makes no progress in widening her circle of comfortable interpersonal activity, she is still immature from this point of view. There are various ways of attempting to measure maturity, but many psychiatrists feel this is the most valid and practical one.

Emotional health does not require the expression of lust in genital sexual activity. Sexually continent clergy and many other persons may be emotionally healthy, while sexually active men and women may be very ill psychiatrically. *It is important, however, that a person is comfortable with his lustful feelings—that he is neither panicked nor stampeded by them—and that he has freedom of choice as to whether he wishes to give them genital expression.* The concept that genital sexual activity is necessary for emotional health, or can be used as a means of evaluating it, is often based on a misinterpretation of Freudian theory. Social customs, religious beliefs, family attitudes and many other things, in addition to personality structure and games, affect what a person does with his lustful drives.

A Little Game to Play Alone

Occasional masturbation may occur in some infants and small children. They may rub their genitals against bedclothes or rhythmically play with them, but curious exploration or aimless play with genitals—similar to exploration or play with other body parts such as toes and navels—is more common in small children than true masturbation. Masturbation in small children does not have the sensual intensity of masturbation in adolescents, and it is rarely accompanied by daydreams of genital activity with other persons. Probably about 10 percent of small children engage in true masturbation, but 50 percent of adolescent girls and almost 100 percent of adolescent boys masturbate at times.

At first glance it may seem that since masturbation is a solitary activity, rather than an interpersonal one, it cannot be considered a game or a contributor to games. However, masturbation has significant interpersonal aspects. It usually involves a fantasied, or daydreamed, sexual partner, and in this sense it is interpersonal. Moreover, masturbation is a substitute for an interpersonal relationship, since lustful drives arise in puberty and early adolescence before the individual has socially acceptable interpersonal outlets for them. Also, most adolescents feel uncomfortable about their masturbation. They fear discovery by parents or others, with consequent ridicule or disapproval; the scowling unseen spectator haunts most people during masturbation. The adolescent says, "I know most kids do it, *but* . . . ," and he winces, and the parent says, "I know it is normal and we shouldn't disapprove, *but* . . . ," and he frowns.

The main disadvantage of masturbation is that it is a *non-interpersonal* release for drives that are basically *interpersonal*. The individual is substituting manipulation of his own body for activities with others. Social customs conspire to force him into such a course, but he nevertheless feels anxious and guilty about the small fraud he is engaged in. He is somewhat angry that he is forced to seek this subterfuge, and he feels inadequate that he gratifies in this way drives that older and bolder people gratify interpersonally. Hence, although so common a thing as masturbation is normal, the anxiety and guilt about it sometimes give it an unhealthy coloring.

The frequency of masturbation also influences our opinion of it. A fifteen-year-old boy who cannot concentrate on his studies because of distracting sexual daydreams may find relief by masturbating once or twice a week; he accepts it as a poor substitute, about which he feels slightly uncomfortable, for interpersonal sexual outlets that are not yet open to him. However, a fifteen-year-old boy who spends hours in the bathroom masturbating several times a day, and who is substituting much solitary activity for association with girls, is following an undesirable pattern. Moreover, the guilt and anxiety adolescents feel about intensive masturbation occasionally contributes to later sexual maladjustments such as impotence or frigidity. Hence, simply telling pubertal children and adolescents that masturbation is normal is not enough; it should be pointed out that it is normal only if it is seen as a temporary measure and that it should not become so absorbing that it blocks interpersonal development. Also, they must learn that the traces of guilt and anxiety they feel about it should be cast off with a shrug.

In terms of *lust* and *counterlust,* masturbation is both. It is an expression of lust, but it may also block or distort the interpersonal expression of sexuality. For example, giving a shy adolescent a solitary form of sexual release may retard his social development and give him a lifelong *noninterpersonal* pattern of sexual activity. Masturbation by married persons (among whom it is more common than is generally recognized) may allow them to avoid problems of sexual adjustment, which should be solved in the bedroom rather than eluded in the bathroom; as such, it may contribute to the deterioration of a marriage.

What does a parent do when he discovers his child masturbating? Let us examine two ways in which it can be handled.

Scene: Father opens the bathroom door, which fourteen-year-old Floyd forgot to lock, and finds him masturbating.

FATHER: What the hell are you doing?

FLOYD: Uh . . . er . . . I was just . . .

FATHER (Knowing full well, but pursuing the point anyway): You were just doing what?

FLOYD: Just putting this towel away.

FATHER: You're lying. You were masturbating.

FLOYD: Well, every kid does it . . . a little . . .

FATHER: It seems to me you spend half your time in here. How many times a day do you do it?

FLOYD: Well, not too many.

FATHER: That probably means a lot. That's why you just drag around all the time, never have any energy, don't do well in school, and are such a mess in athletics. You waste all your energy and time doing this.

FLOYD: I'll stop it.

FATHER: A *real* man doesn't do this. He works his energy off in sports and he has a girlfriend. But you're not to have any sex with girls at your age, do you hear?

FLOYD: OK.

FATHER: You're turning into an introvert, a slinky kid who will never amount to anything unless you stop this.

MOTHER (coming in): What's the matter?

FATHER: Nothing.

MOTHER: Was Floyd doing something he shouldn't? [She has now grasped the situation, and Floyd knows it and cringes.]

FATHER: It's just between Floyd and me.

MOTHER: All right.

FLOYD: I'm going now.

FATHER: All right, but you remember what I said.

Healthy Way

Scene: Same as above.

FATHER: Oops, it looks like I walked in on something I wasn't supposed to see.

FLOYD: Yeah . . . well . . . er . . .

FATHER: I'm leaving. Lock the door. I don't thin
you'd want your mother or sister to walk in on this litt
scene. [Father leaves and the click of the lock is imm
diately heard.]

Later in the day, when Mother and Sister have gone o
shopping, Father calls Floyd to the family room.

FATHER: Instead of slinking around and avoiding eac
other for a few days, I suppose we ought to have a bri
chat about the bathroom episode this morning.

FLOYD: I can explain everything.

FATHER: Don't try. You may end up telling a few litt
fibs. Let's just admit that you were masturbating—jackir
off, or whatever it's called in the slang of your generation.

FLOYD: Well, I guess so.

FATHER: Most boys your age masturbate once in
while. You get to feeling real sexy, don't have any oth
way to work it off, and so you masturbate.

FLOYD: Yeah . . . .

FATHER: The important thing is not to feel guilty ar
scared about it.

FLOYD: I don't . . . not very much.

FATHER: And remember, it's just a tempora
substitute until something better comes along.

FLOYD: I read some books. It really doesn't do ar
harm.

FATHER: No, it doesn't. However, it shouldn't be s
frequent and important to you that you get all tied up in
and it stunts your social life, your school life, and your i
terest in girls.

FLOYD (grinning): I have plenty of interest in girls.

FATHER: Glad to hear it.

FLOYD: Is that all?

FATHER: Just one more thing.

FLOYD: What's that?

FATHER: Next time, lock the bathroom door. Yo
mother or your sister may not be as understanding as I ar

Beauty and the Beast

A sexually developing adolescent girl may arouse unconscious sexual excitement in her father, and this is particularly apt to occur when, as in the case of a stepfather, there is no blood bond between them. Since divorce and remarriage are common and the children usually remain with the mother, adolescent girls and their fathers in several million American homes are not blood relatives. The father's unconscious sexual excitement by the sexual maturation of the daughter may lead to various kinds of games. We shall describe the two most common ones, Brawler and Protector.

Brawler. In order to defend himself against his unconscious lustful feelings, the father may pick continual arguments with the girl and incessantly nag her about minor things; he thus creates a chronic quarrel that alienates them from each other and enables them to avoid facing the flickerings of sexual attraction between them. The girl may unconsciously cooperate in a game of Brawler, for she too may feel sexual attraction toward him, and constant feuding serves an identical purpose for her. Such chronic fighting often goes on until the girl leaves home to go to college, or to work in another city, or to be married. Once the girl is removed from daily close contact with the father, the game of Brawler in most cases halts abruptly. Changed circumstances protect them from each other, and they no longer need their game.

An intense game of Brawler often has secondary effects on the mother. She frequently becomes involved as defender of the girl or ally of the husband, or she may vacillate as she helplessly tries to be a peacemaker. If she remains uninvolved, she may preserve reasonably good relationships with both of them, although she is often accused by each of callous indifference to "all the problems she [or he] is causing me." Regardless of what she does, however, the sexual adjustment between the mother and father often deteriorates to some extent during the game of Brawler, but it usually improves again when the game terminates with the daughter's departure from the home.

Few games of Brawler end in rupture of the family, although crises are frequent. Like all games, Brawler may be mild or severe. In severe cases the turmoil may eventually precipitate a divorce or may cause the girl to leave home and live with relatives. Also, Brawler sometimes exacerbates the normal parent-adolescent tensions, and an adolescent who might otherwise have had mild adolescent rebelliousness may undergo marked rebellion because of the added stress of this game. However, mild and moderate games of Brawler are more common, and after several years of shouting, sobbing and pouting, the game ends spontaneously without serious consequences.

Let us examine a typical scene in the game of Brawler. Trudie is fifteen, and her stepfather, who married her mother when Trudie was three, is thirty-six.

FATHER: Trudie, turn that damn stereo set down. We're not all deaf in this house.

TRUDIE: If you don't like music, shut the door.

FATHER: I said, turn that damn thing down. Closing the door doesn't do any good. You just turn it higher.

TRUDIE: Maybe you'd like me to move out to the garage?

FATHER: And let you bring that crew of teen-age hoodlums in there to wreck the car?

TRUDIE: You and your precious car. I'm ashamed to be seen in the thing. It has dents all over and is four years old.

FATHER: If you think it's so damn easy to make enough money to keep up with the way you, your mother, Lowell and Johnny spend it, you can just get off your butt and make a little money baby-sitting the way every other girl in the neighborhood does.

MOTHER: Oh, Mack, lay off Trudie. Trudie, close the door and . . .

FATHER: You stay out of this. If you hadn't spoiled her, she wouldn't be the impossible mess she is.

TRUDIE: Look who's talking. Old man Temper Tantrum himself.

MOTHER: Trudie, please.

FATHER: And I'm the one who bought you the damn stereo set to begin with.

TRUDIE: Big deal! So I'm supposed to kiss the ground in front of you because of that? I'm getting out of this place. I'll be at Rhonda's, Mom.

FATHER: Don't hurry back.

TRUDIE: You needn't worry about that.

Protector. In the game of Protector the father becomes the vigilant defender of his daughter's virginity against what he views as the horde of lascivious boys who are assailing the citadel of her purity. He disapproves of all her boyfriends and repeatedly warns her that "they're only out for one thing. They're a bunch of bums." He raises a storm about each date, scowls at each boy who comes to the house, and accuses the mother of stupidity for not supporting him in these actions.

Unconsciously he is saying, "If I can't have her, no one will," and he sees in each boyfriend the sexual excitement toward her that he cannot recognize in himself. He throws himself into the virtuous role of her Protector to avoid facing his own unconscious lust toward her. A hard game of Protector usually forces the girl into secret dating or open rebellion. The mother sometimes conspires to hide her dating, and when the father discovers their complicity, as he usually does in time, stormy scenes follow in which he often accuses the mother of encouraging her daughter's delinquency. Protector may grind on for several years, and it sometimes precipitates an ill-considered early marriage by the girl to get away from home. Then the father proclaims, "I told you so. Look at the bum she married. If you had listened to me. . . ." However, in most cases Protector jolts along from one minor crisis to another until the girl leaves home for college, or work, or marriage.

Let us consider an episode in a game of Protector. Frieda is sixteen and her stepfather is forty-three.

FATHER: It's ten forty-five. Where have you been all evening?

FRIEDA: I've been studying at Jenny Norton's.

171

FATHER: And Jenny walked you home and kissed you down at the corner?

FRIEDA: I came home alone.

FATHER: You're lying. I was sitting here at the front window, and I saw you coming around the corner with some bum and he kissed you.

FRIEDA: You're imagining things. You have rocks in your head.

FATHER: You're a lying little tramp. You're sneaking out of here to meet those guys who just want to get their hands all over you, and probably more than that.

FRIEDA: I was at Jenny Norton's.

FATHER: Fine. I'll call her and check that. I'll just say you're not home yet and ask her what time you left.

FRIEDA: Go ahead and call her.

FATHER: So, you have it all worked out with her to lie and say you were there?

MOTHER: Maybe she just met a boy on the way home.

FATHER: You approve of all her running around in the middle of the night, I suppose?

MOTHER: Well, she's going on seventeen and it's only ten forty-five and . . .

FATHER: Then you have no more brains than she does. Those guys are after only one thing, and if Frieda gets in trouble, you'll be to blame as much as she will.

MOTHER: Oh, Ted, Frieda's a good girl and so far . . .

FATHER: So far! So far nothing has happened because I've been keeping an eye on her and getting rid of all those teen-age hoodlums she brings around here.

FRIEDA: I'm going to my room.

FATHER: I don't want to see any more of this.

FRIEDA: I'll make sure that you don't.

A Two-Handed Game

As mentioned briefly in the introductory paragraphs of this chapter, a limited amount of homosexual experimentation, particularly in boys, is common in late childhood (ages nine through eleven) and puberty (twelve through thirteen). Crushes on favorite friends of the same sex are common. Mutual masturbation may occur among boys, but genital sex play between girls is rare. After puberty and early adolescence this type of sexual expression disappears in the vast majority of cases, and the individual's orientation stabilizes into a heterosexual path.

Most psychiatrists feel that genital play (as in mutual masturbation between two boys or by one lying on top of the other and rubbing their genitals together) is usually harmless, though undesirable, *if it occurs for only a few months or so between boys of the same age.* However, several years of it—especially if it occurs between an older, admired adolescent or adult and an impressionable boy between nine and fourteen—may shunt the boy into homosexuality, or bisexuality, particularly when marked emotional trauma in his earlier years makes him vulnerable to homosexual development.

A related subject is the homosexual exploitation of a young child by an adolescent or an adult. In such a case a homosexual adolescent or adult sucks the penis of or masturbates a three- or four-year-old boy, and when parents are not vigilant, this may go on intermittently for several months to two or three years. Equivalent homosexual exploitation of young girls may occur but seems to be less common than in boys. Does this early homosexual stimulation tend to produce homosexuality in adolescence and adulthood? Probably not, if the child has sound relationships with both his parents. However, such seduction of children is unhealthy and should be guarded against, and it probably is more common than is recognized.

Let us consider unhealthy and healthy ways to deal with A Two-Handed Game.

Unhealthy Way

Scene: Mother walks into eleven-year-old Phillip's bedroom and finds him and eleven-year-old Howard, a neighbor boy, lying side by side on the bed masturbating each other.

MOTHER: Phillip! Howard! What's going on here?

PHILLIP: We were just . . .

MOTHER: What a horrid, filty business!

173

HOWARD: We were just seeing if . . .

MOTHER: I saw what you were doing. What are you, a couple of perverts?

PHILLIP: Howard started it.

HOWARD: I did not.

MOTHER: Well, this awful business has to stop. Howard, go home at once, and I never want to see you in this house again.

Howard leaves quickly.

MOTHER: How long has this been going on?

PHILLIP: Not long.

MOTHER: How long?

FATHER (entering): What's the matter?

MOTHER: You may as well know. I came in here to put some clothing away and found Phillip and Howard lying on the bed playing with each other's penis.

FATHER: My Lord!

MOTHER: And they seemed to be enjoying it.

FATHER: What the hell are you—a queer?

PHILLIP: I'm sorry. I won't do it again.

FATHER: If you do, you'll end up a damn fairy.

MOTHER: You're never to go to Howard's house again or to have anything to do with him, and you're grounded for two weeks. Except for school, you're not to leave this house.

SISTER (age sixteen, entering): What's all the uproar about? Howard Davis left here like he'd been shot out of a cannon.

MOTHER: It has nothing to do with you.

SISTER: What's the trouble, Phil? [Phillip has been tattling to their parents about her and her boyfriend, and though Sister hadn't yet grasped entirely what is going on, she senses she is about to get both revenge and a whip to hold Phillip in check.]

FATHER: Get out of here, Lisa.

SISTER: See you later, Phil boy.

FATHER: Now close that door and we're going to straighten this out.

The straightening out consists of a forty-minute rehash of what everybody has already said.

Healthy Way

Scene: Same as above.

MOTHER: Phillip and Howard, stop this. Howard, zipper up your trousers. I think it's time for you to go home.

HOWARD: Yes, Mrs. Harris [He leaves abruptly.]

MOTHER: Phillip, we ought to talk about this. I'm going to call your father, and we'll have a little conference. [Father comes in, and after the door is shut, she tells him what she saw.]

FATHER: Phillip, was this the first time, or has it occurred before?

PHILLIP: A couple of times.

FATHER: Phil, this sort of thing happens to boys your age once in a while. You're beginning to grow up sexually, and you have a lot of new sex urges. You don't quite know what to do with them and so this kind of experiment occurs.

PHILLIP: I won't do it again.

FATHER: It's best not to. It's like playing ball in the middle of the street. Kids do it, but it's not a good idea; they can get hurt that way.

PHILLIP: OK.

FATHER: It's better to get interested in walking a girl home from school, or something like that. Girls are a lot more fun in the long run, anyway.

PHILLIP: OK, Dad.

FATHER: So let's not do this anymore.

MOTHER: What about Howard?

FATHER: Until further notice from me, you and Howard play together only outside. You are not to go into his house, and he's not to come in here. And you're not to play behind the garage, either.

PHILLIP: OK. Is that all?

FATHER: That's all.

PHILLIP: Can I go?

FATHER: Sure.

Should Mother and Father tell Howard's parents? That depends on how well they know Howard's parents and what kind of people they are. If Howard's parents are sensible and will handle the matter as Mother and Father have, I feel they should be told. If Howard's parents do not meet these criteria, it is probably best not to tell them, since they may deal with the situation in a way that is more likely to harm Howard than help him.

Should Mother and Father be vigilant about future associations of Phillip and Howard? In my opinion, yes. As outlined earlier, A Two-Handed Game is usually harmless, but not always so.

I Spy

Parents occasionally encounter pornographic booklets, pictures and records that their pubertal and adolescent children bring into the home, and at times adolescents flaunt obscene talk before them. A variety of games may arise in connection with these things.

The argument is sometimes advanced that pornography does no harm and is a healthy release for sexual feelings that, if not given expression, might cause neurotic problems. This point of view is often based on a misunderstanding of Freudian theory. Except in a few of his early writings, which he later rejected, Freud did not believe that sexual feelings must be physically or verbally expressed to maintain mental health. On the contrary, in his article "Observations of 'Wild' Psychoanalysis" he warned against encouraging sexual licentiousness as a cure, or preventive, for psychiatric troubles. He felt that people should be comfortable with their sexual feelings and that children should be instructed about normal sexual behavior, but he believed that most sexual feelings were sublimated in socially acceptable ways. Careful examination of Ernest Jones's definitive three-volume biography of Freud reveals that he reared his own children in ways that would today be considered conservative in many American homes.

Much confusion arises from the way Freud's word *Trieb*

176

is translated into English. It is usually translated as "instinct," but *Trieb* is far more than that. *Trieb* implies a force that is produced in a person by an interaction between his environment and him. Thus, *Trieb* (or in this case, "sexual instinct") is produced by (1.) the physical nature of the person and (2.) his interpersonal experiences. Viewed in this light, pornographic literature not only releases sexual forces, but also stimulates and molds them.

Sexual drives cannot simply be likened to accumulating quantities of energy that must be released once in a while; they are increased by stimulation from the environment.

An emotionally healthy person is comfortable with sexually stimulating literature, pictures and films. Such material neither pushes him into licentiousness nor shocks him into prudishness. He should be sufficiently at ease with pornography to enjoy a little of it and to be disgusted by a great deal of it.

A person should not be exposed to sexually stimulating material until he is mature enough to handle it comfortably. For example, homosexual pornography does little or no harm to an eighteen-year-old whose heterosexual orientation is already well established, but it may damage an eleven- or twelve-year-old who is still struggling to establish a secure heterosexual role. Pornography can be a harmless, though perhaps tasteless, pastime for middle-aged men at conventions, but it may stimulate fifteen- and sixteen-year-olds into sexual excitement that they handle neither wisely nor well. Middle-aged businessmen do not get pregnant, and they have simple, discreet ways to consult physicians if they contract venereal disease.

Also, it is important to consider the interpersonal settings in which people are exposed to pornography. When those of the same age read pornographic literature and look at pornographic pictures, it often is harmless; but when an older person introduces a younger one to it, it may be damaging. For example, a couple of twelve-year-old boys giggling over pictures of heterosexual intercourse are engaged in an activity that probably is harmless. However, when a twenty-one-year-old youth excites a fifteen-year-old girl with pornographic pictures, she may engage in sexual acts that she might otherwise not have participated in. Pornography between persons of widely different ages is often used more for seduction than amusement.

Is pornography educational? Hardly. That is not its goal. A sexually excited person is not in a condition to analyze and assimilate facts and opinions, which is what education consists of. Sex education tries to instruct a person about sex with a minimum of sexual arousal. Is pornography art? Rarely. It usually is tasteless and badly done. Art may have erotic features, but to arouse eroticism is not its major goal. Chaucer and Boccaccio may somewhat titillate us by the erotic aspects of their stories, but that is not their main aim or effect.

Pornography probably does no harm to the vast majority of pubertal children and adolescents who are exposed to it. However, it may stimulate a small percentage of them into sexual imprudences, pregnancies and venereal disease, and in medical practice a several-percent rate of complications is considered high enough to merit concern. Then why have pornography at all? If outlawed, it merely goes underground and becomes more fascinating. Moreover, in a free society it is difficult to draw easily applied legal guidelines on such matters. Pornographic booklets, pictures and records, legal or illegal, are here to stay, and parents should be able to deal with them in reasonable ways when they encounter them in the hands of their children. They should steer a middle course between priggishness and blanket approval.

Let us consider how a parent might handle such a situation.

MOTHER (walking into thirteen-year-old Julie's room and finding Julie and her girlfriend Christine hurriedly hiding a magazine under the bed): What's that you're so eager for me not to see?

JULIE: Nothing.

MOTHER: Well, if it's nothing, I'm all the more interested in seeing it. Get it out and let me take a look at it.

Julie reluctantly gets it from under the bed and hands it to Mother.

MOTHER: Well, this magazine has some interesting ctures. However, I think they're a little exaggerated. Sex- l intercourse isn't quite that big a deal.

CHRISTINE: We were just looking at it a little bit, Mrs. rummond.

MOTHER: No, you probably were looking a lot. I sup- se you find this stuff more fascinating than what they ach you in your sex education classes at school.

JULIE: Well . . . er . . . sort of . . .

MOTHER: At school and in what I've told you, we tell as it is. These magazines make more exciting reading, but ey are about as realistic as Donald Duck and Mickey ouse. The people who publish them are out to make oney, not to educate you.

JULIE: All the girls at school read them, Mom.

MOTHER: I'm sure they do. The question is: Do they elieve all they read?

JULIE: Uh . . . I don't know.

MOTHER: Do *you* believe all this?

JULIE: Well . . . er . . . I guess not . . .

MOTHER: If you don't take this junk seriously, it prob- bly won't do you any harm. However, it's bad taste and out as realistic as Batman.

JULIE: We'll throw it away and never do this again.

MOTHER: Don't make promises you may find hard to ep.

JULIE: You're not going to take it away from us?

MOTHER: Why should I? You undoubtedly know here to get another one for fifty cents. However, don't ake a collection of this stuff. I don't want your ten-year- d sister seeing it. She's too young. When you're through ping and giggling, get rid of it somehow. [Mother turns leave.]

JULIE: Mom?

MOTHER: What?

JULIE: Are you going to tell Dad?

MOTHER: I'll mention it to him, but I'll tell him I ready talked to you about it. He won't make a fuss.

CHRISTINE: Are you going to tell my parents?

MOTHER: I may tell your mother in a month or so, but

I'll break the news in such a way that it ought not to caus
you too much trouble.

CHRISTINE: OK.

What happens when parents do not handle pornographi
material in the manner outlined above? Two commo
results are games of Hide-and-Seek and Bait the Bear.

Hide-and-Seek. In this game an adolescent and hi
parents engage in a chronic war of evasion and detection
The adolescent hides pornographic material under the lin
ings of drawers, beneath carpets, in the bottoms of sho
boxes and in the garage, and the parents conduct frequen
raids to free the house of this "pollution." The contest soo
becomes more fun for the adolescent than the pornogra
phy. However, the struggle may contribute to deterioratio
of the parent-adolescent relationship and a breakdown o
communication between them. Then, when the adolescen
has a big problem to talk over, his relationship with hi
parents may be so bad that he cannot come to them fo
help.

A sample exchange of Hide-and-Seek runs as follows
Maxine is fifteen.

MAXINE: Who's been going through my dresse
drawers and closet? Everything is out of place. [She know
the answer, but this is her opening move in a wel
entrenched game of Hide-and-Seek.]

MOTHER: I was arranging some things.

MAXINE: You mean you were looking for dirty pic
tures and sexy magazines. Why not tell the truth, Mon
like you always tell me to do?

MOTHER: Your morals are important, and that trash i
not going to be brought into this house.

MAXINE: Talking about morals, Mommy, does tha
include lying? Like when you tell me you were "just ar
ranging a few things" in my drawers when you actuall
were ransacking my room?

MOTHER: I was *not* lying.

180

MAXINE: Of course not. And you also trust me completely, don't you?

MOTHER: Do you deserve it?

MAXINE: Wouldn't you like to know? Anyway, you didn't find anything in your big hunt around here.

MOTHER: Then you admit you're still reading that filthy trash?

MAXINE: Didn't you read it when you were my age? Remember now, Mommy dear, let's always tell the truth, like you tell me to.

MOTHER: Well . . . er . . .

MAXINE: Never mind, Mom, it's all right. Hypocrisy is fashionable in your generation. Keep up the good work! I'm going out for a while.

Bait the Bear. Parental storming about obscenity sometimes leads the adolescent to flaunt it openly in a game of Bait the Bear. A sample of this game is given below. Yvette is sixteen; the game has been going on for a year and a half; and she is an expert at it.

YVETTE: Where the hell is my raincoat?

FATHER: "Hell" is not an acceptable word for a young lady.

YVETTE: I think I remember that a fellow named Dante wrote a book called *The Inferno,* and *inferno* is merely Italian for "hell." Have you read it, Daddy?

FATHER: That has nothing to do with it. It's not ladylike.

YVETTE: I don't give a shit whether it's ladylike or not.

FATHER: Stop that!

YVETTE: Stop what?

FATHER: That word.

YVETTE (innocently): What word?

FATHER (controlling himself with difficulty): That, that—that toilet word.

YVETTE: Oh, you mean "shit."

FATHER: Yes. I mean that.

YVETTE: But, Daddy, "shit" is in Chaucer's *Can-*

terbury Tales. That's one of the great classics. We read part of it in high school. Don't you like Chaucer?

FATHER: I don't give a damn what Chaucer says. You're not to use that word.

YVETTE: Well, there's one I can use—"damn." My parents are my models. Since you can use it, so can I.

FATHER: You're impossible.

YVETTE: What's so fucking impossible about me?

FATHER: That does it! Never let me hear you use that word again.

YVETTE: You mean "fucking"?

FATHER: Stop that!

YVETTE: But that word is often used in *Portnoy's Complaint,* which was praised by the New York *Times* and *The New Yorker* magazine. Don't you approve of those periodicals?

FATHER: Oh, hell! What have I done to deserve all this?

YVETTE: "Hell"? That's the word you just said I shouldn't use. This is where I came in. So long, Daddy-o.

Secrets

In a game of Secrets heterosexual activity, usually consisting of some form of mutual masturbation, occurs between an adolescent boy and a prepubertal girl. We shall examine this problem from the viewpoint first of the boy and then of the girl.

When forces of counterlust prevent one from showing sexual expression in the usual channels, lust may be distorted into abnormal ones. This is the basic mechanism of most sexual perversions. For example, dread of sexual intimacy with girls may cause an adolescent boy to be blocked in approaching them. He becomes fixated at the level of spying on other people during their sexual activity or when they are naked, and he thus becomes a voyeur, or Peeping Tom. He retreats to one of the early stages of sexual excitement—looking at a stimulating sexual object. His fear of sexual intimacy prevents him from going further.

Other sexual perversions are produced by variations of

his basic process. For example, an exhibitionist has a dread of sexuality (which may consist of fear of intimacy with women, or of sexual inadequacy, or of other things) and is fixated at the level of an initial step in sexual intercourse, exhibiting his body; he gets sexual gratification by briefly exhibiting his genitals to women and girls in public places such as parks. The fetishist is similarly blocked in sexual expression and gets orgasms by lavishing attention on a woman's scarf, shoe, lock of hair, or some other article that is symbolic of her. One of the factors that contributes to homosexuality is profound discomfort with genital intimacy with persons of the opposite sex, and this tends to shunt his sexual drives toward persons of the same sex.

In some instances an adolescent boy who dreads sexuality with girls his own age (because of feelings of inadequacy or other emotional problems) may direct his sexual impulses toward girls between the ages of three and nine. Since they are obviously his inferiors in all respects, he can be sexually comfortable with them. He gets sexual orgasms by touching their genitals or by having them stroke his penis. He may also rub his genitals against the girl's, but complete sexual intercourse is uncommon. If this type of perversion is undetected and untreated, it may become a fixed pattern of sexual expression that lasts throughout adult life; psychiatrically it is called pedophilia. In many instances the man eventually overcomes his sexual discomfort with women sufficiently to marry, but sexual activity with small girls nevertheless may continue to crop up sporadically throughout his adult life.

The adolescent boy usually lures the girl into a game of Secrets as a kind of play, and he frequently gives her candy, toys and money to secure her compliance. Once she has become involved, the adolescent uses various threats to dissuade her from telling her parents. He may say that her parents and everyone else will not want to have anything to do with her and will send her away to live in an awful place if they find out. He may threaten her with physical violence if she tells, and he may state that he will say she is lying if she discloses their sexual activity. Also, he often points out that her acceptance of his gifts makes her a collaborator and that they are equally responsible.

How often is the adolescent boy successful in silencing the girl by such threats? Most psychiatrists feel he is successful in a large percentage of cases, for they hear such stories from time to time in psychotherapy from adult women who are often telling someone for the first time. How damaging are games of Secrets to girls? This question cannot be statistically answered. Psychiatrists hear of such sexual traumas only from women who have psychiatric problems, but they do not know how many girls have such experiences and do not suffer emotional damage. Of 100 girls who become involved in a game of Secrets, do 3 or 30 of them have persistent emotional problems because of it? Moreover, if only 3 or 5 percent of them eventually see psychiatrists, is this ratio any higher than the incidence of psychiatric problems in the general female population? There are no reliable answers to these questions.

However, most psychiatrists feel that a game of Secrets often damages the girl. It is not the physical sexual play that upsets her, but the anxiety, guilt and shame she feels about it and the fact that she carries this burden alone; for months or years she may dread discovery, disgrace and parental rejection because of it. Also, in some instances she fears that she has suffered irreparable physical damage because of her sex play and that she is now "different" and will never be able to marry. In rare instances she worries that she is pregnant, even though the boy's penis did not enter her. All her fears are greatly alleviated if she can eventually tell her parents and receive reassurance. When parents discover a game of Secrets that has been going on a short time, they may be able to handle the situation by talking with their daughter and reassuring her. If the game has been going on for a long time and the child seems quite upset about it, the parents should have her evaluated at a child guidance clinic.

In any case, the parents can do useful "first aid" when such a situation is encountered. The child can rarely put into words the things that are really upsetting her, and the parents must know what to ask and how to reassure her

Let us examine how a well-informed mother and father can handle a game of Secrets.

Scene: Mother and Father are talking with seven-year-old Laurie, whom earlier in the day Mother surprised in the front seat of their car in the garage in mutual masturbation with a fourteen-year-old neighbor boy, Allen.

MOTHER: Laurie, Daddy and I want to talk with you about what we today found out was happening between you and Allen.

LAURIE: I'm sorry.

FATHER: We feel that you did nothing to be punished for. However, it is not healthy because little girls often feel very upset about it. Sometimes they're even relieved to share their secret with their parents.

LAURIE: You mean that other girls get mixed up in things like this?

MOTHER: Yes, boys with Allen's kind of problem are fairly common.

LAURIE: I feel awful about it.

FATHER: What did Allen do to get you not to tell us? Did he threaten you? [Leading questions are necessary in this type of discussion. Otherwise, the child can rarely talk about what is bothering her.]

LAURIE: He said that if you found out, you wouldn't love me anymore and that you would send me to live somewhere else and that no one would want to have anything to do with me.

MOTHER: Allen lied. All that is not true. He told you those things to get you not to talk.

LAURIE: And he said that no one would want to marry me when I grew up and that he'd say I was lying if I said anything. And he said he'd beat me up some dark night.

FATHER: All that is not true. Allen is a coward and a liar. However, all these threats must have frightened and worried you a lot.

LAURIE: I was awfully scared.

MOTHER: I suppose maybe you felt guilty and ashamed about it, too.

185

LAURIE: Yeah.

FATHER: Did he give you any presents to keep you quiet?

LAURIE: He gave me candy and a bracelet and three dollars.

FATHER: And I guess that you felt that after you accepted these, you were caught in his little game?

LAURIE: I'll give the money and bracelet back.

MOTHER: Don't worry about it. Later you give me the bracelet and any money that is left. Keeping them will only remind you of all this upsetting business.

FATHER: Did you have any other fears?

LAURIE: Noooo . . . I guess not.

MOTHER: Did you worry that this experience might damage you in some way and that you might not grow up to be a normal girl and woman?

LAURIE: Yes. Something like that.

MOTHER: It did not harm your body in any way, and the only upset it gave you is your worry about it, which I hope we're getting rid of by talking about it.

LAURIE: I feel better.

MOTHER: Did you worry that in some way you might get pregnant or get a disease from this?

LAURIE: Not too much.

MOTHER: Then you did worry about it to some extent. Neither of those things can happen.

FATHER: It goes without saying that you and Allen will not see each other anymore. He is not to come here. You're not to go to his house, and you're not to meet him anywhere else.

LAURIE: I never want to see him again.

MOTHER: Is there anything else you want to say?

LAURIE: I don't think so.

FATHER: All right. Go on into the family room. Your brother and sister are watching television there.

Should Mother and Father tell Allen's parents? In my opinion, yes. It will be awkward, but it should be done. If Allen's parents are conscientious, they will take him for evaluation and counseling at a child guidance clinic. Timely

186

reatment may break up Allen's game, which otherwise could become a lifelong pattern. Also, if nothing is done, Laurie may have many successors in later years, and their parents may not be able to help them as Laurie's parents have helped her.

8

GAMES FOR ADOLESCENTS

By the time a person reaches adolescence a great deal of personality formation has occurred. However, personality structure never becomes static; an individual is constantly influenced by what is going on between him and the people around him, and during adolescence a person's interpersonal capacities are either enlarged or stunted by these relationships.

However, a person's capacity for personality growth during adolescence is greatly affected by what has gone on during the preceding years.

At the beginning of adolescence the individual is emotionally and socially dependent on his parents, and his major emotional attachments are still in his parents' home. At the end of adolescence he is emotionally and socially independent, and although he retains affection and respect for his parents and his siblings, his main emotional investments are in *extrafamilial* persons of his own age. During adolescence more changes occur in the life pattern of a person than in any subsequent period of his life. Step by step the parents relinquish the authority that the adolescent takes over, and frequently there are disagreements about how much autonomy an adolescent should have at any particular point. At what age should he, or she, begin to date, and at what hour should he come home? At what age should he, or she, be allowed to choose his social crowd, his hairstyle, his clothing, his reading material, his vocabulary of obscene expletives, his sexual patterns, and many other things? Moreover, the parents' role in controlling all these things when he is fifteen is different from a scant three years later when he is eighteen. This is the stuff of which family crises are made.

The progressive social independence that adolescents develop can have both healthy and unhealthy consequences. Some adolescents with mild or moderate personality difficulties develop healthier interpersonal capacities in their new *extrafamilial* circles. For example, the rejected adolescent who emerged from childhood feeling unlovable and inferior may find affection and esteem in a broader interpersonal environment, and he may grow emotionally. An indulged, demanding adolescent may grasp that the world does not cater to him as his parents did, and he may develop more self-control than he brought out of childhood. *Thus, if personality warps are mild or moderate, and if interpersonal games are not severely etched in his personality, the adolescent may grow into a better-adjusted person.* However, when his games are deeply engraved and his personality structure is badly damaged, the adolescent's capacity to benefit from extrafamilial influences is small; he carries his problems into each new social situation and repeats old dramas with new casts.

The Isolation of Adolescents

To the casual observer it might seem that the average American adolescent is anything but isolated. Adolescents congregate in spontaneous groups that range from half a dozen in a drive-in parking lot to several hundred thousand at a music festival. They wear distinctive clothing and insignia, and they unite in their special social and political causes. Viewed from a distance, adolescents seem a tightly knit group.

However, closer scrutiny of adolescents reveals a profound sense of isolation and rootlessness that the so-called adolescent subculture rarely satisfies, for in it adolescents find little of the interpersonal security and intimacy they long for. Moreover, they are haunted by the briefness of adolescence and the fact that whatever small comfort they have found in its special groups will soon slip from their grasp. Few of them can put this into words, but it gnaws at them.

The feelings of isolation that trouble modern adolescents are to a large extent caused by the dissolution of American family life. Divorce destroys between one-fourth and one-third of American families, and many children are reared in homes in which one parent is not a blood relative. Twenty percent of American familes, an estimated 40,000,000 people, change residence every year. Job transfers, changing economic opportunities, mass racial migrations and vast changes in municipal zoning and building codes throw many adolescents into neighborhoods where they have no long-term ties. Many of them scarcely know their uncles, cousins and grandparents, and their longest friendships may stretch back only a few months or two or three years.

Moreover, in many families affluence and automobiles have made home more a base of operations than an emotionally close group. It is a place where people shave, store their clothing, and eat hurried meals. In one-third of American homes both parents work, and the children are away at school and other activities most of the daylight hours. For recreation the family scatters to bowling alleys, cocktail parties, clubs and many other nonfamilial settings. As a result, the adolescent, with his special needs for intimacy with people, has an acute sense of isolation, and he seeks closeness in his fellow adolescents. However, they are ill-equipped for meeting such emotional needs. They are all ships struggling in heavy seas, and although they may haphazardly group together in convoys, they are incapable of guiding and aiding each other.

The adolescent subculture is so weak that it must invent special customs and regalia to give it a semblance of unity. It must have its own clothing, hairstyles, jargon and insignia, and it must find special missions to give it the appearance of social and political cohesiveness. Moreover, adolescents feel they must justify their special groupings on moral grounds. They maintain that they are honest and society is hypocritical, that they are generous and society is selfish, that they are tolerant and society is bigoted, and that they are loving and society is hostile.

Of course, real differences of opinion on social, political and economic issues exist between the young and the not-so-young. However, underlying and fueling the adolescent's bitterness are their feelings of emotional isolation from adults and their anger about the closeness they needed so much and never got at home. There is much truth in what they proclaim, but their emotional turmoil makes them what they most condemn—extremists—and they know not why.

All these characteristics vary a great deal from one adolescent to another, and the traditional customs still are dominant in a significant number of them. However, the general sweep of the adolescent current is toward rejection of the standards of their parents' generation and the substitution of new patterns, often poorly defined and thought out, of their own creation. Adolescents who deviate too much from the adolescent mainstream tend to be drawn into it by the ridicule or ostracism of their peers.

The games adolescents play, more than those of any other age group, differ in degree rather than nature from the patterns we label "within normal limits." For example, the adolescent who is in a delinquent rebellion against his family is merely carrying to an extreme the normal rebelliousness of most adolescents. The girl who uses sexual promiscuity as a tool to defy society is different in degree rather than nature from the girl who hotly argues with her parents over the merits of a boyfriend of whom they disapprove. In adolescence the line between health and sickness, between normality and games, is often hard to draw. Extremes are obvious, but there is a broad middle ground in which decisions are hard to make, and some adolescents rampage into every nook and cranny of this middle ground before they emerge into adulthood. The weary parent, the perplexed educator and the troubled citizen may find scant solace in the cynical psychiatric adage: Adolescence is not a stage of life, but a psychiatric diagnosis.

We shall examine a few of the games of adolescence and the ways in which they may be handled.

Shadowboxing

In many families an adolescent and his parents can find little to talk about unless they are quarreling. The adolescent finds his parents' concerns outdated, and they find his interests ridiculous or repulsive. The parents are not interested in the latest popular music, the current adolescent social or political crusade, or the details of teen-age romances. On the other hand, the adolescent is not interested in what is going on at the office, the company's new product, mother's club activities, or the upcoming golf or bridge tournament. Friendly communication collapses.

Hence, the most intense contacts between many adolescents and their parents occur during bickering, and since adolescents have an intense need for contact and intimacy, they may promote chronic quarreling into a game. Brawling is a defective kind of communication, but for many adolescents it is better than none at all. The adolescent and his parents are unaware of the true motivations of their constant battles, the fighting is obvious, but its causes are unconscious.

Shadowboxing has certain telltale signs that distinguish it from more malignant types of parent-adolescent fighting. A primary feature is that, despite his continual quarrels and ostensible rejection of everything his parents stand for, the adolescent continues to conform basically to their way of life. His rebellion is only clothes deep; he may wear beads and a headband to school, but he makes passable or good grades. He rants about social injustice and his parents' hypocrisy, but he does not throw rocks at the police. His parents, who do not see his need for closeness behind his defiance, are alternately furious and alarmed.

Another characteristic of Shadowboxing is that no issue is too trivial or too large to be a source of conflict. The food of the evening meal, the state of the nation, the value of a particular television program, and the future of mankind serve equally well for the evening's brawl. Moreover, the adolescent readily shifts his position when necessary to keep the conflict going. If the parent surrenders and agrees with him to get some peace, the adolescent may go over to the other side and attack the parent from the same position he was assailing half an hour before. A further aspect of Shadowboxing is that the brawling goes on mainly, or only, with the parents. The parents are puzzled when neighbors, friends and teachers comment that "Barry is such a nice young man," or "I'm so glad when Elsa comes to our house; she's a good influence on our daughter."

Another feature of Shadowboxing is the endlessness and pointlessness of the quarrels and the impossibility of resolving them by any means. Compromise, capitulation and evasion are futile, and flight by the parent from one room to another does not work. The adolescent sits on the edge of his parents' bed to continue a quarrel that started earlier in the family room.

Shadowboxing has a good prognosis. When the adolescent's needs for interpersonal closeness are eventually met in college associations, marriage and a family of his own, the game ends, and then the parents and their child may get along fairly well. The parents conclude that "he grew out of it," and the adult child states that he "broadened their vision a little, and now they're not as unreasonable as they used to be."

Let us examine a brief sample of Shadowboxing. This is an excerpt from a two-hour argument between seventeen-year-old Tony and his father.

TONY: I see in the paper that that company you slave for has been given two years to stop polluting the air and killing the citizens of this town.

FATHER: We didn't kill anybody, and that stupid issue is all settled. By next April the things that damn commission insisted on will be done.

TONY: I'll believe it when I see it. All you guys are out

for is to make a buck, and how much you damage everybody else doesn't mean much so long as the grass on your golf greens is pretty.

FATHER: Now look here, that issue is dead. We've been over it a dozen times. The company is spending four million dollars to end that so-called pollution. Drop the subject.

TONY: And when are you going to stop polluting the air around this house by stopping smoking? It's giving me sinus trouble and bronchitis. [Coughs to prove it.]

FATHER: Oh, Lord, if it's not one thing with you, it's another. If I want to smoke and die at sixty-five instead of seventy-five, that's my business, and nobody else complains about the air in this house. Besides that, I shifted to cigars, and all the medics say they're not as bad as cigarettes.

TONY: Those cigars foul the air worse than the cigarettes did. You're always in such a cloud of smoke that you didn't notice the murk around here.

FATHER: Don't you have any studying to do? Why don't you go somewhere else? I'm reading.

TONY: Is that what you call it? It's just propaganda, but I suppose that kind of pap keeps you happy.

FATHER: Damn it, for a kid who's never done a full day's work in his life and never had to pay any bills, you sure are cocky. If you don't like it here, go somewhere else. You're a lazy bum.

TONY: Yeah? Last month you told me I'm making better grades in high school than you did. Since I'm so lazy and you're such an eager beaver, I must be a hell of a lot more intelligent than you are. Thanks for the buildup, Pop.

FATHER: You're impossible. I had to work after school when I was your age.

TONY: But you tell me you don't want me to work after school so I can make good grades, and then you tell me I'm lazy because I don't have a part-time job. I don't get it.

FATHER: I didn't say that at all.

TONY: Then explain it to me, Daddy. I'd like to understand just what goes on inside the heads of people like you.

To deal with a game of Shadowboxing, the parent first must grasp that behind the bickering lies a desperate bid for contact and closeness. Then the parent has two possible courses. He can patiently engage in Shadowboxing and recognize it for what it is—communication on the level of a chronic debate. The second course is to establish a certain amount of comradeship and closeness with the adolescent so that Shadowboxing is not necessary. This requires weekend hunting and fishing trips, talking about pop music and social injustice, tinkering with secondhand cars, and many other things. Some parents can do this and others cannot. For the latter group of parents the best course is a compromise—a certain amount of Shadowboxing and some flexible comradeship.

In any event, there is no time-saving way out of Shadowboxing. Once this game is well established in a family, the parents are compelled to spend a fair amount of time with their teen-ager, in one way or another.

Two Against One

During a tug-of-war between an adolescent and his parents over his increasing independence, one parent sometimes becomes the adolescent's defender and the other his critic. The adolescent is quick to grasp the situation and to play his parents off against each other, and he usually gets whatever he wants and has little true affection or respect for either of them.

Various emotional factors may cause a parent to abet an adolescent in this manner. In some cases the parent's early steps in this direction are justifiable. For example, a father may encourage his son to be more independent of the unhealthy possessiveness of a fearful or controlling mother; however, the adolescent may use his parents' divergent views to pit them against each other and race too fast toward autonomy. In other cases a parental struggle over the adolescent unmasks latent marital discords or exaggerates existing ones. In still other instances a parent identifies with the adolescent and gets a feeling of

outhfulness by mimicking the teen-ager's customs and
rebelliousness, and the other parent is cast into the role of
the "repressive older generation."

In yet other cases a parent reenacts the unsolved problems of his own adolescence in a game of Two Against
One. A parent whose independence was stifled during
adolescence may relive these problems in his own child. He
may get unconscious gratification in the taunts the adolescent hurls at the other parent, the freedom the teen-ager
recklessly seizes, and the sexual liberties he has.

A game of Two Against One is unhealthy both for the
parents and for the teen-ager. A vicious circle is often set
up in which the parents' quarrels increase the teen-ager's
misbehavior and his misbehavior provides more fodder for
their quarrels. One parent defends the adolescent's "independent strivings," while the other condemns his "delinquency." Under such stress the parents' marriage may
badly deteriorate, and in occasional cases this game may
contribute to their divorce.

Two Against One is easy to slip into and hard to get out
of. As the adolescent exploits it, the vicious circle spins
faster, and after a year or two the parents are entrenched in
their roles as the teen-ager's ally and enemy. Parents who
are caught in this game should seek counseling with a
Family and Children's Service Agency, a psychiatrist or
a clinical psychologist. Group psychotherapy sessions for
parents of adolescents often are useful in breaking up this
game. These groups contain six to eight couples and meet
once a week for sessions of two hours or so to exchange
views on the problems the group members are having with
their adolescents; a professional therapist sits in to
moderate the discussions.

Let us consider a typical dialogue in Two Against One.
Vickie's ally is her mother, and the antagonist is her father.

FATHER: Where are you going, Vickie?
VICKIE (ignoring Father's question): Ray will be by in
a few minutes, Mom. I'm taking the door key.
MOTHER: All right, dear. Have a good time.
FATHER: It's nine thirty. The last time you went out

with that boy you didn't get home until two. That's too late for a fifteen-year-old girl, and this is a school night. You're not leaving this house.

MOTHER: Don't pay any attention to him, Vickie. It's all right.

FATHER: You have as little sense as that kid does. You're both acting like a couple of teen-age delinquents.

MOTHER: Oh, shut up, Dean. Your ideas went out of style thirty years ago. Things have changed, and Vickie is no different from any other girl her age.

FATHER: I don't like Ray. He's not attending school, he's nineteen, and he doesn't have a job. He's no good for Vickie.

VICKIE: He has a job now, and he's going back to school in September. You never like any boy I date.

MOTHER: Ray is all right. You don't like him because he doesn't come in here and tell you what a great, big, important man you are, like that Harrison kid did.

VICKIE: Harrison was a square—a total loss.

FATHER: In my opinion he was the only decent one you ever brought home.

MOTHER: He was a mama's boy. I sometimes wonder if he wasn't a queer. Ray is a real man.

FATHER: Ray is a bum, and Lord only knows what he does with our daughter when they're out until all hours of the morning.

VICKIE: Don't you trust me?

FATHER: Not with him.

MOTHER: You have a filthy mind. Vicki wouldn't do anything wrong, but you'll drive her into trouble if you keep on accusing her of such things.

FATHER: Neither of you has any judgment at all.

MOTHER: Maybe you don't trust me either.

FATHER: I didn't say that.

MOTHER: You meant it.

FATHER: You're putting words in my mouth. We're talking about Vickie.

VICKIE: There's Ray's car. So long, Mom.

She leaves, and Mother and Father go for another half hour playing out this session of Two Against One.

Let us examine how Mother and Father might handle the same situation after gaining insight into their game during six months of group therapy for parents of teen-agers.

FATHER: Where are you going, Vickie?

VICKIE (ignoring Father's question): Ray will be by in a few minutes, Mom. I'm taking the door key.

MOTHER: I think your father asked you a question, dear.

VICKIE: Huh?

FATHER: I said, where are you going?

VICKIE: I'm going out with Ray.

FATHER: I don't think that's a good idea.

VICKIE: Tell him what the score is, Mom.

MOTHER: Well, Vickie, your father and I have had a few talks. We're not sure Ray is the right boy for you, and we think you stay out too late.

VICKIE: What's going on? Are you getting a lot of kooky ideas at those psycho sessions you and Dad are attending?

MOTHER: Well, frankly our opinions have changed somewhat.

VICKIE: Well, mine haven't. Ray will be here in a couple of minutes, and I'm going out with him.

FATHER: We're not much impressed with Ray. He's nineteen. He has dropped out of high school, and he never holds a job more than six weeks. He's been arrested half a dozen times for speeding. I think you've had your last date with him.

VICKIE: Says you.

MOTHER: Says *we*.

VICKIE: We? You're not going to let Dad do this to me, are you? He's still back in the Dark Ages.

MOTHER: I agree that Ray is no good for you.

VICKIE: Try and make it stick.

FATHER: We're going to try to do that.

VICKIE: How? Are you going to chain me to the fireplace?

FATHER: No, but when Ray gets here, I'm going out and tell him you have a headache . . .

VICKIE: That's a lie.

FATHER: A small one. And then I'm going to tell him that I think he's a little too old to be dating you. You can come out and hear this if you want to. If you do come, your mother will come with you to back me up.

VICKIE: Oh, Mom, you wouldn't. You couldn't. I could never look Ray in the face again.

MOTHER: Your Dad is telling it the way it is, Vickie. He'll handle it in a nice way; he won't embarrass you.

VICKIE: You can't stop me. I'll see Ray without you knowing it.

MOTHER: That's possible. But at least you won't be playing your father and me off against each other in the process, and I hope that in time you get interested in a boy with a better future, and also a better past and present, than Ray.

FATHER: There's his car now. I'm going out and talk to him. I'll handle it in a very quiet, polite manner, Vickie.

VICKIE: You're cruel. You both hate me. [She runs sobbing to her room.]

The troubles between Vickie and her parents probably are not over, but their game of Two Against One is. The outlook for healthier interpersonal lives for all of them is distinctly improved.

Quiz Game

An adolescent continually wants more things. He wants more liberty, more money, special clothing, the latest records and cassettes and many other things. His demands often strain the family budget and go beyond his parents' ideas of prudence, and the parents frequently find themselves trapped into endless haggling.

In some cases an adolescent uses demands to express hostility toward parents, since by escalating them he can sually precipitate an argument. A teen-ager may also use emands to belittle his parents: "Why don't you make nough money to buy me the things the other kids have?" n addition, demands may be employed to box parents into orners: "If you don't give me the freedom I deserve, I'll it the road and find it for myself" and "If you can't give ie the clothes I need, I'll drop out of school." Demands an develop into a Quiz Game that dominates the parent-dolescent relationship.

In a well-established Quiz Game the relationship of the een-ager and his parents degenerates into chronic bar-aining. The parent who gives in too much often finds iat the adolescent's demands outstrip his ability to pay for hem, and he usually gives the teen-ager more freedom han he can handle well. Moreover, a decade of indulgence s poor preparation for adult life. On the other hand, the arent who refuses too many of the adolescent's requests inds himself in constant battle with him.

There are a few general rules that help parents avoid)uiz Games, or at least keep them within reasonable)ounds. These rules are most applicable in early and mid-lle adolescence; by late adolescence the teen-ager has ac-uired so much autonomy that they should be less iecessary.

1. *Link a liberty to a responsibility.* For example, if a)oy or girl wants to use the family car, couple this privilege vith the responsibility of cleaning it once a week and, if he has a part-time job, of paying for the gasoline he uses. If a girl wants extra nights for dating, couple them with the responsibility of babysitting with her younger brother and sister one or two nights a week so her parents can go out. Thus, if an adolescent complains, "Why can't I have the car this afternoon?" the parent can reply, "Why haven't you washed it and vacuumed the upholstery in the last two weeks? That was our deal. We're doing our part. Are you doing yours?"

2. *Link a restriction to a privilege.* Parents must fre-quently deny adolescents' requests; tying such refusals to alternative privileges helps avoid arguments. For example, if a teen-ager wants the car to go to a late-night party,

which the parent considers unwise, the parent may say "It's too late tonight, but you can have it all afternoc: tomorrow." If a girl wants to date a boy whom her parent consider undesirable, they should couple their refusal wit a list of half a dozen boys (such lists sometimes can b culled from the telephone calls she receives) who they thin are better. If the teen-ager tries to box his parents into corner, they may counter with "We gave you reasonable al ternatives that we think are a lot healthier for you."

3. *Tie some of an adolescent's demands to his earnin; capacity.* Instead of chronically turning down an adoles cent's demands for things, a parent can often couple them with his ability to pay for them. For example, if an adoles cent says, "All the other kids' parents give them the money to buy the discs and cassettes they want, and you don't,' the parent may reply, "I'm paying twenty-five dollars a month to that yard service company to cut the grass, trin the bushes, dig up the ground around the roses, and rak the leaves. The money is yours if you take over the same work and do it well." If a girl asks why she can't have al the currently fashionable clothes, cosmetics and costume jewelry, her mother may reply, "Rita [the maid] comes i once a week to wash and clean. Half that money is yours i: you take over half her work and I'll have her come in once every two weeks. Besides that, you're going to get marriec someday, and I doubt your husband will be able to afford a Rita for the first ten years of your marriage, and it will b good training for you." In such discussions it is best to avoid the phrase "When I was your age . . ."; this waves a red flag in front of adolescents.

4. *Turn aside some requests with praise ane reassurance.* Many parents are afraid to praise ane reassure their teen-age children for fear they will become more rash and willful. Not so. Behind all their brashness usually are feelings of insecurity and inadequacy. Adoles cents are frequently worried about how attractive they are how loved they are, how talented they are, and how worth while they are. Many of their bold exploits are attempts to reassure themselves of their value, attractiveness and importance, and praise and reassurance often decrease their

200

needs for such acts. Of course, the teen-ager frequently responds with "I suppose you read that in some book on how to handle kids," or "Knock it off. You don't really mean that," or "What do you want now?" However, despite his protests the praise and reassurance sink in.

Some parents reply that they find it difficult to find anything praiseworthy in their adolescent, but every teen-ager has at least a few qualities he can be complimented on. Thus, the brash adolescent may be told, "Well, at least you're an individualist and there's something to be said for that." The adolescent who is a fairly good student but who takes baths so infrequently that dinner is a trying experience (which may be why he doesn't take baths) may be told, "You make better grades in school than I did. You have a head for math and I never did well at it." A handsome adolescent should be told so, even though his parents wince at his clothing, his amount of hair, and the ornaments that adorn him.

5. *Admit ignorance occasionally.* Many parents find it difficult to say to a teen-ager "I don't know" and "I don't understand that." They bristle at each adolescent challenge. An admission of ignorance frequently stuns an adolescent, and after recovery from his initial surprise he may begin to expound his views. The parent should listen. Even if he doesn't agree, he can say, "Well, that's one side of it I haven't thought much about" or "Where did you learn all this?" One of Newton's laws of mechanics states that every force is met by an equal and opposing force, and this is particularly true of parent-adolescent relationships.

An admission of ignorance may be met by "Then why do you argue with me so much?" or "Then why don't you wake up and find out what's going on in the world?" To this the parent may then reply, "Explain it to me if you're so anxious for me to understand," and the adolescent may respond with a digusted "What's the use?" or a two-hour lecture. The parent should listen to the lecture; even though the communication is one-way, it is a beginning.

6. *When in doubt or at an impasse, reflect feeling tones and listen to what follows.* The technique of reflection of feeling tones, which is discussed in Chapter 1, is par-

ticularly useful with adolescents. When he cannot think of anything else to do, the parent can say, "Well, I guess you're pretty disgusted with this situation"; however, he should be prepared to listen afterward to a half hour's outpouring of the disgust. On other occasions the parent may say, "You're rather angry with us because of that," or "You're disappointed because of this," or "You're pretty fond of that boy [or girl]." Reflection of feeling tones often opens the gates of communication, and in the process the parents and the teen-ager may become better friends.

Masquerade

The expression of sexual feelings may serve emotional ends other than sexual ones. For example, sexual promiscuity may be motivated mainly by hostility against parents who are embarrassed by the open delinquency of their son or daughter; the sexual activity of the teen-ager is produced more by antagonism toward his parents than passion for his lovers. In other instances sexuality is an avenue for establishing independence; the adolescent is unconsciously saying, "I *am* a free person—I can prove it by my sexual liberty." In still other cases sexual license is part of a general rebellion against social standards. In each case the adolescent and his parents battle about the teenager's sexuality and do not realize that it is a means to an end, not an end in itself.

A game of Masquerade may be mild or severe. In mild cases the adolescent frequently restricts his sexual rebellion to talk. He proclaims to his parents that "sex is normal between kids who like each other" and patronizingly torments his parents about their "hypocritical attitude toward sex." He praises sexual promiscuity as a means of "establishing communication" and chides his parents for their "pathological inhibitedness." In such a case Masquerade is a parlor game; the teen-ager preaches "the modern view of sex," but his pattern of sexual behavior may be little different from that of his parents when they were his age.

In the following scene fifteen-year-old Theresa and her parents are engaged in a session of Masquerade:

MOTHER: Mrs. Thompson told me that Cynthia Palmer is pregnant.

THERESA: What's so wrong with that?

FATHER: My Lord! What's so wrong with that? She's sixteen and she's not married. What do you mean, what's so wrong with that?

THERESA: She just had a little bad luck. She should have been more careful about taking her pills.

FATHER: Pills? She should have been more careful about something else.

THERESA: You mean in her sexual intercourse with her boyfriend?

FATHER: Er . . . uh . . . yes.

THERESA: I agree. It's inconvenient to get pregnant when you're in high school.

MOTHER: Inconvenient? It's immoral! It's . . . well . . . uh . . . it's awful.

THERESA: Oh, Mother, you and Daddy have such stuffy, old-fashioned ideas about sex. After all, sex is just like kissing only more so.

FATHER: A hell of a lot more so.

THERESA: Oh, Daddy, your ideas are so quaint.

FATHER: My Lord, I hope we've been able to teach you the right way to act.

THERESA (who, despite some heavy petting, is still a virgin but would lose her game of Masquerade by admitting it): Daddy, things have changed. Kids today are not all hung up with the hypocritical, neurotic, sick ideas of your generation.

MOTHER: Theresa, we've tried so hard to make you a good girl.

THERESA: "Good" is a value-judgment word and—

FATHER: A what?

THERESA: Oh, never mind. Anyway, you don't have to worry about my getting pregnant. I'm not stupid. I can take care of myself.

FATHER: Just what do you mean by that?

THERESA: Oh, Daddy, don't be so naïve. I have to go

study now. I have a history exam tomorrow. [Leaves the room.]

MOTHER: Ben, do you think she's doing anything she shouldn't do with that Simpson boy she's dating?

FATHER: I don't know. All you can do with these kids nowadays is pray and hope for the best. Give me a couple of my ulcer tablets.

Theresa's game of Masquerade is well under control (Theresa's control, not her parents'), and if she gets around to sex with the Simpson boy or one of his successors, it will probably be two or three years later and with contraceptive precautions.

However, other games of Masquerade are malignant. The teen-ager's hostility against parental standards leads him into sexual imprudences that involve pregnancy, social scandal, or a turbulent, brief marriage that scars his adolescent years. In the severe games of Masquerade the adolescent's rebellious use of sex is in action rather than talk.

Let us outline briefly a severe game of Masquerade. Hollie was by eight years the younger of two sisters. She saw little of her parents during her growing years; her father was building a law firm and dabbling in politics, and her mother was busy scrambling up the paths of social prominence. Hollie's older sister had been reared at a time when her parents had time for her; she had identified with her parents, had married a boy they approved of, and had accepted their way of life. Hollie, on the other hand, was reared by a series of middle-aged housekeepers who were supplemented by expensive nursery schools and day schools; her parents were vague figures on the periphery of her life. To save themselves trouble, the housekeepers let her do as she wanted and hid her temper tantrums and misbehavior from her parents.

Hollie emerged into adolescence a demanding, affection-hungry girl with a deep bitterness about the loneliness of her childhood. When she was fifteen, her hostility against her parents and all they represented broke out in a malignant game of Masquerade. She dated the most disreputable boys of her own social group and soon afterward began to associate with delinquent boys from slum districts; she often came home at daybreak. Her parents complained, threatened and pleaded, but the fury of Hollie's game swept everything before her.

She responded to her parents' complaints with shrieking temper tantrums and threatened suicide if they tried to stop her. She refused to see the psychiatrist as they urged, saying, "You're the one who needs a shrink, not me." When she was sixteen, she began to date petty criminals much older than herself and at seventeen became pregnant by one of them. For three months she and her parents argued over an abortion, and she told them that she was going to have the baby and rear it in their home. However, Hollie's demands carried over into her relationships with her lovers, and one night she came home with her face badly beaten and her body bruised. A few days later she agreed to an abortion, and shortly after that she consented to see the psychiatrist. In him she found the first parent she knew, and during a two-year period of intensive psychotherapy she emerged from her game of Masquerade.

The principles of child rearing outlined in the early chapters of this book can prevent malignant games on Masquerade from starting; however, once they occur, they are professional matters.

Rule Book

In the games previously discussed in this chapter we dealt with adolescents who were rebelling against parental restrictions. However, in some instances an adolescent is so uncomfortable with his sexual feelings and independent urges that he retreats into rigid conformity. He sticks to the rules laid down by his parents and society and presents a façade of flawless behavior.

The interpersonal relationships of such adolescents have a spiritless, passionless quality; they have *pseudo relationships* rather than true ones, and there is no intimacy in them. Their dating is colorless, and their involvement with other adolescents is cautious and superficial. Often they retreat into studiousness and hobbies, and they spend more time with adults than with teen-agers.

Because of moral convictions some adolescents follow restrained codes of sexual behavior and conform to traditional customs. For example, a girl who intends to become a nun would find it incompatible with her goals to fight chronically with her parents and to be sexually promiscuous during adolescence. She is preparing to enter a life in which obedience to authority and chastity are prominent features. A devout boy may behave similarly because of moral convictions. However, in each of these cases the adolescent is following a restrained pattern of behavior *because he chooses to do so. He is not driven to it by fear of being independent of his parents and their way of life.* A healthy adolescent should be emotionally comfortable with his urges and thus have the capacity to choose whether he wishes to follow his parents' way of life or find a new one.

An adolescent who fearfully clings to a restrained role gives his parents less trouble than one who chronically hammers the limits they allow. Hence, the parents of a socially inhibited Rule Book adolescent may see him as "mature" and "serious about the things that count in life," and they may consider him superior to the teen-age sons and daughters of their friends. They do not grasp that his inhibited behavior is caused by terror rather than virtue.

A game of Rule Book may be mild or severe. When mild it may sometimes be broken up by parents who understand it and encourage in their child more social independence and perhaps even a certain amount of rebelliousness. However, severe games of Rule Book require professional help to decrease the anxiety and guilt that chain the adolescent to conformity, isolation and pseudo relationships.

Let us consider a family in which Rule Book is being played. The family consists of sixteen-year-old Owen, the Rule Book player, his seventeen-year-old sister Pattie, who sees the game and objects to it, and Mother and Father, who find Owen a much more satisfactory child than Pattie. The family is finishing lunch.

MOTHER: Pattie, where are you going?

PATTIE: Brian is coming by, and we're going to his ouse and listen to records with some other kids. We may at at a drive-in.

MOTHER: I think you'd better eat here.

PATTIE: I'll call you if I go to the drive-in.

FATHER: You never do what we think best. When I vas your age. . . .

PATTIE: Oh, Dad, I don't want to hear all that again.

FATHER: Why can't you be like Owen? He doesn't run all over town with a bunch of wild teen-agers. He has his aam radio set and his. . . .

PATTIE: You keep Owen here with a ball and chain. The only girls he ever talks to are in Bangkok and Honolulu. Come with me, Owen. Brian's sister Stephanie is ifteen, and she told me she thinks you're cute.

OWEN: I'm too busy.

MOTHER: Owen has *worthwhile* things to do.

PATTIE: Owen isn't in this world.

MOTHER: You leave Owen alone. Stephanie is prob-ably a little hussy. Owen is not interested in girls like that.

PATTIE: There's Brian honking now. Come on, Owen.

OWEN: Uh . . . no . . .

PATTIE: Come on, Owie, you have nothing to lose but your chains.

FATHER: Owen has *mature* interests. He doesn't play all the time and. . . .

PATTIE: So long, then. I'm off.

Father was a well-intentioned man, but for twenty years he had been climbing the ladder in his company and had seen little of Owen. However, in time he noted Owen's isolation and discomfort with other adolescents, and he told Mother that they ought to "take inventory about what s going on with Owen." They did. Mother was a reasonable woman, but Owen was so convenient that she had found it easy to accept his social isolation as "seriousness," his docility as "respect," and his fear of girls as "waiting for the right one to come along." In brief, this was a relatively mild game of Rule Book because Owen's parents were sufficiently healthy to grasp it and to take action. Owen's breaking out began a few weeks later as the family was finishing dinner.

MOTHER: Where are you going tonight, Pattie?

PATTIE: I'm going over to Brian's. Some of the kids will be there. We'll probably dance and then go out for pizzas. I'll be in a little after midnight. It's like I do every Saturday night. You know that.

FATHER: Will Stella be there?

PATTIE: Who?

FATHER: Stella, or whatever her name is—that sister of Brian's who thinks Owen is cute?

PATTIE: You mean Stephanie? Yeah, she'll be there. She's only fifteen, and her folks don't let her solo date. She always makes the parties.

FATHER: Why don't you go, Owen? It sounds like fun.

OWEN: What?

PATTIE: What's that?

MOTHER: Owen, your father and I have been talking about you. We think you see too much of us and not enough of kids your own age.

OWEN: I'm all right. I have studying to do.

FATHER: On Saturday night? It can be done tomorrow.

PATTIE: Come on, Owen, break out. Grab it before they change their minds.

OWEN: I'm not dressed to go.

PATTIE: Don't be such a square. You look better than most of the kids who will be there.

OWEN: Well . . . uh . . .

FATHER: Fine. That settles it. Have a good time and Pattie, smooth the way for him a little. It's a new crowd for him.

PATTIE: There's Brian honking. Come on, Owen.
They leave.

MOTHER: Do you think he'll get along all right?

FATHER: I think Pattie and Stephanie will arrange it.

9

THE DREAM GAMES

In this chapter we shall cover a further aspect of adolescent life that became prominent during the 1960's and 1970's; the use of marijuana, hallucinogenic drugs such as LSD, amphetamines, sedatives, and narcotics.

With the exception of marijuana, all these drugs can cause body damage. However, the main objection of psychiatrists to them is that *they can harm a person's interpersonal adjustment*. The user is attempting to solve by chemical means emotional problems (such as anxiety, insecurity and feelings of inadequacy) that should be interpersonally solved. Instead of working out his problems with his parents, friends, teachers and others, he is fleeing into the sensuous relaxation that drugs can give. In place of "people and I" he substitutes "the drug and I," and if his emotional difficulties are marked, the drug can become a seductive alternative to struggling with them.

Those who defend the use of drugs, especially marijuana, overlook three important points. First, emotional turmoil, though distressing, has some useful functions. Pain is a warning. The pain of a broken ankle warns a person that he should not walk on it until an orthopedist has put it in a cast, and the pain of a stomach ulcer warns a person that he should start taking appropriate medications and should try to reduce some of his tensions. In a similar way, anxiety should alert a person to search for sounder ways of living.

Second, all these drugs can contribute to the social, scholastic and economic deterioration of the user, although they vary a great deal from one to another in this respect.

In addition, the ways in which most of them can cause body dysfunctions and psychotic disorders will be covered later in this chapter.

The third factor that defenders of drug usage overlook is that, historically, no creative, progressive society has ever existed in which the use of these drugs was widespread. Extensive use of marijuana, opiates, cocaine and other drugs has occurred only in civilizations that were stagnant or deteriorating. For example, marijuana was heavily used in Arabian countries only during their decline, not during their golden period, and cocaine usage has been widespread only in stagnant Andean cultures. Scholars may debate whether extensive use of drugs is a cause or a symptom of social decline, or both, but the unhealthiness of them on both individuals and society as a whole is apparent to all neutral observers. These arguments against drug usage do not imply support of harsh laws against people who take them. There is much doubt that such laws are effective, and they may even encourage drug usage by making illicit traffic in them a highly lucrative business.

Drugs and Games

Slightly more than half the games previously discussed in this book, if severe and unsolved, can cause the anxiety, insecurity, depressiveness, rebellion and defective self-images that make drug abuse an attractive escape. The child who carries into adolescence a severe game of King on the Mountain, or Ready or Not, Here I Come, or Throwing Mud Pies is ill prepared to make emotional adjustments, and he may try to assuage his panic and fury by drugs that offer a chemical, not an interpersonal, solution to his distress. The child who has much unresolved parent-directed hostility from a game of Carrousel or Two Against One may use drugs as tools in a rebellion against his parents and the standards they represent. Ugly Duckling, Baa, Baa, Black Sheep, A Game with Many Names and others, when severe and uncorrected, can predispose one to drug abuse.

Our main emphasis in this chapter is not to explore the

omplex issue of drug usage but to deal with ways in which
arents and other adults can talk to adolescents about it.
Ve shall approach this subject in four parent-adolescent
ialogues.

Pot

FATHER: Let's talk about pot.

HAL: Huh?

FATHER: Pot, marijuana, reefers, grass—whatever you
ids call it.

HAL: Oh, it's pot.

FATHER: I've been doing my homework.

HAL: What?

FATHER: I've been reading a book about pot and a lot
f other drugs.

HAL: Who put it out—the Salvation Army?

FATHER: Not exactly. It was put out by a doctor.

HAL: Yeah? Probably some shrink who says that it
urns kids into criminals and sex fiends and dries up their
rains.

FATHER: No, not at all. He says it really doesn't do
ny physical harm and that criminal and sexual acts while
nder its influence are no more common than at other
mes.

HAL: I could have told you that.

FATHER: Why didn't you?

HAL: Well . . . er . . .

FATHER: That means you've experimented with pot.

HAL: All kids do.

FATHER: Not quite. The figures show . . .

HAL: What figures?

FATHER: Lots of people's figures. About twenty dif-
rent research teams have interviewed kids in various
ays and places, and they all come up with about the same
sults. About thirty-five percent of kids experiment with
ot at some time.

HAL: It's more than that.

FATHER: Only among special small groups, such as

high school dropouts, wandering groups of hippies, and few others.

HAL: They're the crazies.

FATHER: Well, if I said that, you'd object. Anyway taking the nation's kids as a whole, the percentage who us a fair amount of pot over a long period of time may be n more than fifteen percent. Twenty percent is the top figure

HAL: It's higher than that.

FATHER: Read the book.

HAL: I'm too busy.

FATHER: O.K., but it's *not* "most kids" who use po The potheads are a minority, maybe a small one.

HAL: I'm no pothead. A few joints doesn't make a kid pothead.

FATHER: I'm glad to hear it.

HAL: But just the same, there's nothing wrong with i It's no worse than the martinis and old-fashioneds you an Mom drink.

FATHER: That's debatable. The medics think pot worse.

HAL: How come?

FATHER: Well, pot puts a person out of commissic for a while, in terms of doing things effectively with peopl

HAL: That's a lot of baloney. Pot is no worse tha booze.

FATHER: I can drink a cocktail at a business lunch an then, with my head clear and my judgment sound, hamm out a business deal or settle a problem with a customer. A ter a cigarette of pot you can't do that. The difference b tween pot and booze is that after mild use of booze you ca still function well as a person, but even a small amount pot leaves you unable to exercise good judgment and work well for one to six hours.

HAL: Kids don't hammer out business deals.

FATHER: No, but they have studies to do, cars to driv part-time jobs to hold, and lots of other things.

HAL: Most kids just smoke pot on weekends.

FATHER: Things can go wrong there, too.

HAL: Like what?

FATHER: Well, like sex, for instance.

HAL: You just said sex was no more common after pot than without it.

FATHER: That's right, but your judgment about what you do during sex is all fouled up after pot.

HAL: Since when do you need judgment to know what to do during sex? Sex is sex.

FATHER: Not quite. For example, when a fellow has sex, he ought to use a rubber in order not to get the girl pregnant or to pick up the syph or the clap from her. After pot he doesn't bother with such details. Sex is not just sex —there's more to it than that.

HAL: OK, that's for the guys, but girls . . .

FATHER: And girls, too. A girl who doesn't have rocks in her head won't have sex unless she's on the pill or insists that the boy uses a rubber. But after pot her judgment flies out the window and anything goes. She can get pregnant, and that's a little more complicated than the common cold.

HAL: Yeah, but the same thing can happen after booze. I've heard a lot of interesting stories from some of the kids about what goes on at their folks' parties after they and their friends get drunk.

FATHER: You're right. Too much booze can cause the same problems, but that's no defense of pot.

HAL: You sure got your lessons down pat from that book.

FATHER: I'm a quick study. I had to be, I worked my way through school during the tail end of the Depression.

HAL: Don't tell me that sad story again. I've heard it three hundred times.

FATHER: I don't think I could have done it smoking pot.

HAL: Things have changed. That was back in the Dark Ages.

FATHER: The book also says there are a few other things wrong with pot.

HAL: Like what?

FATHER: Well, it seems there are some sticky laws about it.

HAL: Those laws are barbaric.

FATHER: You may have a point. The book admits

that. However, the laws are still there.

HAL: The Supreme Court threw them out.

FATHER: I'm afraid not. They threw out a few provisions of them, but most of them are still intact.

HAL: They're still barbaric. Anyway, nobody enforces them.

FATHER: Well, for better or for worse, they sometimes do enforce them. They may give a kid a lecture, or a suspended sentence, or a year in jail. The funny thing is that judges usually are much more lenient than juries. A jury in Houston gave a man thirty years for having one cigarette of pot in his pocket; the prosecutor asked for much less and expected to get a fraction of what he asked for. Anyway you look at it, it's a risky game.

HAL: They ought to change those laws, and those juries are full of kooks.

FATHER: A lot of state laws are being made more lenient. Also, in a few years most of those juries are going to have members of your generation on them, and to convict a man, a jury's decision must be unanimous. So, things are going to loosen up. But that doesn't help a kid much right now.

HAL: I don't see why they make such a fuss about pot. There are a lot worse things. You can't get hooked on pot.

FATHER: No, you can't get physically addicted to it, but you can get to like it so much that you can become emotionally dependent on it. I got that phrase out of the book.

HAL: What does that double-talk mean?

FATHER: Well, pot is an escape, a way into a world of dreamy relaxation, and it's easy for some people with hang-ups to begin to smoke pot every time they face anything tense in life. And after a while they're smoking it every day and can't hold jobs, don't look after their children and homes, get pneumonia or diabetes and pay no attention to their diseases, and go down the drain, so to speak.

HAL: The same thing can happen with booze.

FATHER: Right. But, as I said, that's no defense of pot.

HAL: OK, OK. So you made a point. You can go to the head of the class.

FATHER: I have a few more points to make. Can I go on?

HAL: Who's stopping you?

FATHER: Pot causes a person to draw into himself. It slows down things that are going on between him and other people. When he's smoking pot, he's off on a cloud of his own.

HAL: So what's wrong with that?

FATHER: Everything. Doing things, producing things, and having fun with people is what life's all about.

HAL: You have to have some escape valve; you have to get away from it all once in a while.

FATHER: Yes, but it's better to do it with people. Pot is relaxation on the lowest possible level. There are other ways that involve people—talking, dancing, singing, games, sports and, if you're highbrow, art, theater and so forth. These are things that involve you with people while you're relaxing and getting away from it all. These ways are healthy. Pot isn't.

HAL: Kids have pot parties and some musicians use it.

FATHER: But if you watch what really goes on at a pot party, you will see that everyone sinks into himself, or at least has less contact with the people around him than if he hadn't smoked pot. Moreover, they've done some careful studies on those singers and musicians who use pot. They really don't do any better with pot than without it. They just think they do.

HAL: I still say there are worse things than pot.

FATHER: Yes, but there may be a little catch there.

HAL: What catch?

FATHER: Some people who study drugs feel that using pot may somewhat increase the percentage of kids who go on to experiment with heroin, cocaine and other narcotics. And they are bad, man, bad. Poison.

HAL: I know that.

FATHER: It's hard to be certain on this point. Many people who get hooked on heroin started out with pot.

Whether they would have gotten to the heroin without the pot is hard to tell. However, it's an ugly question. On the other hand, alcoholics rarely go on to heroin and other narcotics.

HAL: Even if pot's no good, you can't control the stuff. It grows everywhere. I know a kid who grows it in flowerpots on his window shelf.

FATHER: Right. The weed can be grown almost anywhere, and it's easy to make pot from it. So talking about it may be a better way to try to control it.

HAL: So that's why you've gone into this big spiel about pot with me?

FATHER: You catch on fast. Anyway, here we are at the football field. We'll have just enough time to park and get to our seats before the game begins.

HAL: You sure picked a smart time to open up on this. I was a captive audience.

FATHER: Why start a discussion if you can't hold the customer until you finish your pitch? Lock the door on your side as you get out.

Acid

During the 1960's and 1970's some adolescents and young adults have used a variety of drugs that are psychiatrically referred to as *hallucinogenic substances*. The most common of them is lysergic acid diethylamide popularly called LSD or acid. Various other drugs produce similar effects but are less frequently employed; they include mescaline, psilocybin, morning-glory seeds and others. Somewhat similar sensations can be felt by inhaling the fumes of various kinds of aromatic chemicals such as some types of glue and benzine derivatives. The word "psychedelic" is sometimes applied to these substances and the sensations they produce, but this term may also be used in a broader sense.

WANDA: Where have you been all afternoon? You look like you've been through a wringer.

MOTHER: I've had a bad afternoon.

WANDA: What happened?

MOTHER: Irma Johnson called me and asked me to drive her to the hospital. She was so nervous she was afraid to drive. Also, I think she wanted somebody to go with her. Her husband is out of town on business.

WANDA: Is she sick?

MOTHER: It's her daughter Cheryl.

WANDA: What's wrong with Cheryl? I noticed she wasn't at school today.

MOTHER: Well, late last night, or early this morning, she ended up in the St. Mary's Hospital emergency room. She didn't have her wallet or a purse, and they couldn't find out who she was until about noon today. The kids who took her there just dumped her and scrammed. They finally found out who she was and called her home, and Irma asked me to drive her down there.

WANDA: My Lord, what's wrong with Cheryl?

MOTHER: She's as nutty as a fruitcake. It was awful. She's hearing voices, seeing people walking around with bloody knives, and just huddles in the corner like a scared rabbit.

WANDA: My Lord, what happened to her?

MOTHER: She's been taking some of that stuff you read about in the newspapers—lyserol acid, or something like that. I think you kids call it acid or LSD.

WANDA: It's acid.

MOTHER: She was still in the emergency room suite when Irma and I got there. After we arrived, they got Irma's persmission to admit her to the psycho ward, and Dr. Oldham is going to take care of her.

WANDA: Did you see him?

MOTHER: No, but there was an intern on duty, a Dr. Levy. He arranged everything once Irma arrived and gave her an OK. He seems very young, but apparently he knows a lot about this LSD stuff. He says they get two or three cases a month like that.

WANDA: Acid is not all that bad.

MOTHER: Yeah? Well, you go down and take a look at Cheryl. It's bad enough for me. Anyway, this intern spent half an hour talking to Irma and me and gave Irma a copy of a booklet put out by the Mental Health Society. It seems he's going into psychiatry when he finishes his internship, and he knows a lot about this stuff. Do you know anything about this LSD?

WANDA: Well . . . uh . . .

MOTHER: My Lord, I hope you haven't been using it.

WANDA: No . . . well, only once.

MOTHER: Good grief, honey, don't ever use it again.

WANDA: Lots of kids do.

MOTHER: Not according to this booklet. The top figure for kids who use it a few times is ten percent, and those who use a lot of it are two or three percent, or less. It's poison.

WANDA: The people who write those books don't know much about kids, and that doctor is only an intern.

MOTHER: Let me fill you in, kid. I got a liberal education on LSD this afternoon.

WANDA: How do they know so much? Acid is new. It's just been out a few years.

MOTHER: No, it's been around for quite a while. It's just the kids who discovered it a few years ago. Thirty years ago psychiatrists were using it in research because they thought it produced something that looked like schizophrenia.

WANDA: What's that?

MOTHER: It's that mental illness they call split personality. Anyway, this LSD can produce something like that, apparently.

WANDA: That's only when a kid has a bad trip.

MOTHER: "Bad trip." That's the term Dr. Levy used. Sometimes these so-called bad trips last for only a few hours, but in other cases they go on for days, or weeks, or months. You can call it a bad trip, but after seeing Cheryl, it looks like plain insanity to me.

WANDA: Poor kid. She had a tough break.

MOTHER: The people who say that this stuff is "mind-expanding" and "mind-blasting" are talking nonsense. All it does is to produce a chemical change in the brain that makes you see everything different and goofed up for a few hours or more.

WANDA: It makes everything look beautiful and wonerful, and you feel you're suddenly seeing the world as it eally is for the first time.

MOTHER: That's a lot of rot. It makes everything you ee and feel seem like a technicolor dream, but the world is ot a technicolor dream. At other times it makes the world eem terrifying and weird. It's no more mind-blasting than he delirium tremens of some drunk who's seeing snakes nd purple bugs on the wall. It also fouls up your sense of ime and space, and you can't do anything reasonable or vorthwhile when you're under the influence of the stuff.

WANDA: The Indians in New Mexico have been using t for centuries, and they're still around.

MOTHER: They use something else. LSD was invented y a Swiss chemical company as a research tool in psychia-ry. I wish the damn Swiss would stick to their watches and hocolate bars. They certainly haven't done Cheryl John-on any good.

WANDA: Not many kids have bad trips.

MOTHER: You're wrong there. Apparently they're airly common. LSD breaks down the barriers between ormality and being nuts. You cross over the line for a vhile, and some people have trouble getting back. A few of hem never get entirely back or weave back and forth for rears, especially if they go on taking the stuff. I'd like to ake you down to that psycho ward and show you Cheryl.

WANDA: I'd rather not.

MOTHER: I looked through this booklet. LSD is not hysically addicting, but some kids get to like it so much hat they take a lot of it. Then they don't study, or hold egular jobs, or do anything else they're supposed to do.

WANDA: Those kids probably would have gone to ieces even if they hadn't found acid.

MOTHER: It seems there's some question about that. A ot of medics think that acid pushes some people into the utter who wouldn't have gotten there without this extra hove. On top of that, there's a big question about how of-en LSD leads people into experimenting with even worse tuff like heroin. And that's bad trouble.

WANDA: That Dr. Levy seems to be quite a salesman.

MOTHER: He didn't have to sell me anything. After five minutes in that room with Cheryl Johnson he couldn't say anything to scare me more than that.

WANDA: I know some kids at school who use acid once in a while and still make good grades and are tops in everything else.

MOTHER: Just because you speed through a red light and don't have a wreck is no argument in favor of going through red lights.

WANDA: You have all the answers, don't you?

MOTHER: I graduated from an intensive course on this subject this afternoon, and Cheryl Johnson was a very effective professor.

WANDA: She'll come out of it.

MOTHER: Dr. Levy says she probably will, and maybe within a few days or less. However, there are other problems with this junk. It may change your chromosomes.

WANDA: Your what?

MOTHER: Chromosomes, genes, the stuff that makes heredity.

WANDA: Oh, yeah, I studied that in biology.

MOTHER: Well, some scientists think that LSD sometimes changes chromosomes, and then if a person later has a kid, the kid can be born mentally or physically damaged. Apparently, this is not entirely certain yet. However, they think it may be particularly bad if a girl takes LSD while she's pregnant.

WANDA: Cheryl's not pregnant.

MOTHER: No, but if she got to like the stuff, she might go on taking it at some time when she was pregnant.

WANDA: Are you trying to scare me?

MOTHER: I had the hell scared out of me this afternoon.

WANDA: Well, I'm no idiot. I only took it once and I don't intend to take it anymore.

MOTHER: I'm glad to hear that.

WANDA: Can the police do anything against Cheryl?

MOTHER: I don't think so. Most states don't have laws against LSD, but some of them are beginning to pass them. I don't think they can do anything in this state.

WANDA: Then why did those kids just drop Cheryl at St. Mary's emergency room and run?

MOTHER: They were just thinking of their own skins. They didn't want to get in trouble with their own parents.

WANDA: They were lousy to treat her that way.

MOTHER: I agree. Now help me get dinner. It's six thirty. Your father will be home any minute, and he'll want to know why dinner wasn't started an hour ago.

WANDA: Are you going to tell him about Cheryl?

MOTHER: Of course. If there was poison lying around in the neighborhood, don't you think everybody should know about it?

WANDA: I guess so.

Speed and Goofball

Two other groups of drugs that sometimes are misused by adolescents are amphetamines and barbiturates and similar sedatives. Amphetamines are central nervous system stimulants whose commercial names include Benzedrine, Dexedrine, Desoxyn, Methedrine and others, but they are called speed, bennies, and many other things in adolescent jargon. Barbiturates and other sedatives depress the activity of the brain, and in small doses they may give feelings of euphoric giddiness to which the terms "jag" and "kick" are sometimes applied by adolescent users. Barbiturates and other sedatives have slang names that vary from one part of the country to another and from one year to the next; "goofball" is a popular one.

Let us examine how Gene's father went about talking to his son about them:

FATHER: I've been playing Perry Mason.

GENE: What's that?

FATHER: Detective. I've been watching you.

GENE: What have I done now?

FATHER: I don't think you slept very much, or maybe not at all, during the semester exams last week. You were awake studying for seventy-two hours straight.

GENE: I passed, didn't I?

FATHER: You did, and I'm glad you did.

GENE: So what's your gripe?

FATHER: After the exams you slept almost all the time for three days and walked around like you were in a fog.

GENE: A kid is entitled to rest after exams, isn't he?

FATHER: Yes, but I think you had a little help.

GENE: What do you mean?

FATHER: I mean that a kid couldn't stay up for seventy-two hours and end up with trembling hands and as edgy as you were unless he was taking pills of some kind.

GENE: I drank black coffee.

FATHER: I suspect you took something more than that.

GENE: Like what?

FATHER: Speed.

GENE: Who told you?

FATHER: Nobody. I just guessed it. It wasn't too hard. Joe McKinley at the plant found his kid was doing the same thing—staying up for three or four days running at exam time and becoming a nervous wreck, and he found speed pills in the kid's room. So, I put two and two together and came up with four. At any rate, you admit you've been taking speed?

GENE: OK, but I passed at school. So you have no gripe coming.

FATHER: About your grades, no. About how you got them, maybe so. I read up on speed.

GENE: Where?

FATHER: Well, the public library has a couple of shelves of books for parents whose kids use speed and stuff like that. I got a couple of books and read a chapter or two.

GENE: That's probably the first time you've been in a library since we got the color TV set.

FATHER: I must admit that I had to get a new card to get the books out.

GENE: Did you learn anything interesting?

FATHER: Well, yes. Speed is not the best thing in the world for your health.

GENE: Lots of kids use it, and some of them don't just use it for exams.

FATHER: Not "lots of kids." They've interviewed thou-

222

sands of college students, high school students, Army draftees and other kids, and ten percent is about the top figure. The number of kids who use it a lot is no more than three percent.

GENE: So what? A little bit of speed doesn't hurt anybody.

FATHER: No, but a little sometimes leads to a lot.

GENE: You can't get physically addicted to it. You can stop it any time; so it's all right.

FATHER: Well, it's true it's not physically addicting, but a few kids get to like it so much that they feel they can't get along without it.

GENE: They're just the mixed-up ones.

FATHER: Yeah, but the line between the mixed-up ones and the not-so-mixed up ones is pretty thin in a lot of kids. The ones who lack self-confidence and get down in the dumps feel like they're on top of the world when they're taking speed, and they may get to like feeling that way.

GENE: I'm not one of them.

FATHER: I agree. But speed is still no good. Kids who take a lot of it lose weight, become flighty, can't stick to anything, sleep little, and tend to get diseases like pneumonia and other things. Once in a while they even die. Speed can kill.

GENE: That's only in the junkies. A little speed before exams doesn't hurt.

FATHER: The books disagree. They don't think it's a good idea to use it before exams.

GENE: Those books always exaggerate. Books are written to sell books.

FATHER: When they all say the same thing and are backed up by a lot of medical reports, they must have a point.

GENE: I still say that a little speed before exams doesn't hurt.

FATHER: Sometimes it does. After forty-eight to seventy-two hours on speed some kids begin to see things that aren't there, and they may think that people are trying to kill them; in short, they go nuts, and they may stay that way from a few hours to a few weeks, even after they stop speed.

GENE: Maybe that's what happened to Cliff O'Brien.

FATHER: Who?

GENE: Never mind. You don't know him.

FATHER: Furthermore, this stuff really doesn't increase your mental powers. It just keeps you awake.

GENE: Well, lots of kids take it and not many of them go goofy on it.

FATHER: Quite a few of them do. There are whole books written on this subject. "Amphetamine psychosis" is what it's called.

GENE: Those guys will write a book on anything. It gets them promoted at universities.

FATHER: To write a book, you have to fill up four hundred pages with something, and when they go looking for kids with bad reactions to speed, they apparently don't have much trouble finding them in hospitals and clinics.

GENE: I didn't take much of it.

FATHER: Where did you get it?

GENE: Uh . . . well . . . you can get it from lots of kids.

FATHER: I know it's easy to get. Reducing pills, allergy inhalers and so forth. Some kids even shoot it in their veins for thrills.

GENE: I just took a little to pass exams. Maybe you'd be happier if I flunked?

FATHER: No, I'm very happy you passed. Hugh Browning's kid flunked and he's quitting school; Hugh is having fits over it. It's just that I think there are better ways of passing.

GENE: Like what?

FATHER: Well, you might start studying three months or three weeks before exams instead of three days. Moreover, black coffee may not be as effective in keeping a kid awake as speed, but it's a hell of a lot safer.

GENE: All right, Billy Graham, is the sermon over?

FATHER: Not quite. And I don't view myself as Billy Graham. I'm more like Smoky the Bear.

GENE: How do you figure that, Smoky?

FATHER: If you see your kid playing with fire, you ought to tell him it can burn.

GENE: I think you've gotten your point across. I have things to do.

FATHER: Give me five minutes more.

GENE: Oh, hell! All right, Smoky, but I'm timing you. Five minutes.

FATHER: Thanks.

GENE: Don't mention it.

FATHER: After you finished your exams, you staggered around here like a zombie for three days.

GENE: I was pooped. I'd been up for three days straight.

FATHER: I think it was more than that.

GENE: You're imagining things.

FATHER: Well, I didn't have to Perry Mason it very much on this one. When your mother tried to wake you up for dinner, she found this red-and-blue capsule on the bedspread. It must have fallen out of your shirt pocket.

GENE: Oh.

FATHER: Is this what they call a goofball?

GENE: Did you show it to the guy at the drugstore to find out?

FATHER: No, I thought of that, but I thought it would be a little sneaky. I decided I'd just ask you.

GENE: I suppose it is. After the exams I was so keyed up and jumpy that I couldn't sit still or anything.

FATHER: That was the speed.

GENE: Don't rub it in. So I took a few goofballs to get some sleep and come out of it.

FATHER: Goofballs can be physically addicting.

GENE: I know.

FATHER: Also, they give some kids jags, or kicks, and kids can get to like that feeling. Goofballs dull anxiousness when a kid is tense over something. If a kid takes goofballs two or three times a day for a month or so, he can become physically addicted to them, and if he then stops taking them, he gets something that looks like the delirium tremens that alcoholics get, and in addition he can have convulsions. Are my five minutes up?

GENE: Almost, Smoky.

FATHER: Goofballs act mainly on the part of the brain you think with. They affect your judgment and physical coordination, and kids who take them have a lot of automobile accidents, surfboard accidents, and head conkings on bathroom floors. And in some circumstances they can get you into trouble with the law. I'm through.

GENE: OK. I'm going out. I have a date tonight.

FATHER: With whom?

GENE: Eleanor Wade.

FATHER: Here's five bucks. Have a good time.

GENE: How come the extra money?

FATHER: Well, down at the plant we call this the kick-in-the-ass-and-pat-on-the-shoulder approach. When we have to bawl out a man on the line or a foreman about something, we always mention something he does well after we tell him what he's lousing up. So you sat through my lecture—that was the kick in the ass—but I did get a few points over, I think. Also you passed your exams, even if I don't entirely approve of the way you did it. So, the five bucks is the pat on the shoulder.

Junk

What do you do with a kid who's addicted to heroin?

Only a fraction of one percent of American parents will ever face that question. Probably no more than 1.5 percent of adolescents and young adults experiment with heroin or other narcotics such as morphine and dilaudid. Moreover, most of the adolescents who take heroin use it only a few times and then desist for fear of its grave consequences. Only a very small percentage become addicted to heroin despite the widespread publicity it receives. In the argot of the addict world heroin is called junk, H, horse, and many other things.

A wide gulf separates heroin from pot, acid, speed and goofball. The outlook for an adolescent who has trouble with one of these other drugs is good; in time he usually stops taking it. Undesirable as they are, these drugs have a

226

much less profound effect on the person than heroin. The prognosis of heroin is grim.

Heroin addiction almost invariably is the end product of a severe game that begins in childhood and continues full-blown into adolescence and adulthood. The games mentioned in the early part of this chapter, and some of the others discussed in Chapters 1 through 8, may be the predecessors of narcotic adiction. Heroin decreases anguish and terror, and to some persons it offers an escape from painful interpersonal tensions into a world of sensuous relaxation. Narcotics give other disturbed adolescents a means of rebellion against their parents and society—an environment that did not meet their emotional needs and that they are now defying in self-destroying ways.

However, heroin and other narcotics do more than this. Physical addiction, which occurs after usage two or three times a day for a month or less, causes marked changes in the physiology of the brain and spinal cord. If a physically addicted person discontinues the drug, he undergoes an emotionally and physically painful ordeal that lasts for about two weeks. Rather than go through this agony, an addict will steal, prostitute herself, or do anything else to get money to buy drugs. Even after gradual withdrawal from the narcotic in a hospital, the addict has a restless craving for the drug for several months to a year. This yearning is probably caused by both physical and emotional factors. I recall one patient who six years after withdrawal from heroin (he was serving a long prison sentence for illegal possession of narcotics) would occasionally awake screaming after he had dreamed about taking drugs, and on physical examination at such times he had many of the typical physical symptoms that accompany withdrawal from narcotics. The person who has been addicted to heroin, morphine or other narcotics is a changed individual. The original game that led him into addiction has been greatly altered by the experience of being addicted.

Narcotic addiction almost invariably leads to severe social, economic and emotional deterioration. The addict is unable to study or work regularly because of the several hours of incapacitation he undergoes after intravenously injecting the drug two to four times each day. He frequently resorts to fraud, theft or prostitution to buy the illegal, expensive drugs he needs, and often he tries to get others addicted so he can make money by selling them drugs. The line which the courts try to draw between the "user" and the "pusher" is often a wavering one. The addict sinks into a hidden world of subterfuge with the continual menace of detection and imprisonment. He gradually loses most of his healthy interpersonal relationships, and his associates become other addicts whose talk is mainly of the sources and the quality of their drugs and the devices they use to get them.

To return to our original question: What do you do with a kid who's addicted to heroin? This is a medical matter, and the following dialogue therefore involves a physician. Since the answers to this question are controversial, I have used my own name as the physician's to emphasize that the answers are mine. Some psychiatrists would agree with them and some would not.

Scene: The home of the Kramers', eight thirty at night.

DR. CHAPMAN: Shirley, how long have you been hooked on H?

SHIRLEY: About a month, I guess.

DR. CHAPMAN: How long have you been taking it?

SHIRLEY: I popped off a few times a year ago, but I didn't really begin to shoot the stuff until about eight weeks ago.

DR. CHAPMAN: How many times a day?

SHIRLEY: Two or three. Lately it's been three.

DR. CHAPMAN: How did you get the money?

MR. KRAMER: What money?

DR. CHAPMAN: To support a habit like this costs about forty dollars a day.

MR. KRAMER: My God!

SHIRLEY: I sold one of Mom's rings and a few pieces of her costume jewelry.

MRS. KRAMER: Oh, Lord, I thought I lost that ring and yesterday I couldn't find my topaz broach.

DR. CHAPMAN: Anything else?

SHIRLEY: You seem to know the rest.

DR. CHAPMAN: I guess so.

MR. KRAMER: What does all that mean?

DR. CHAPMAN: Nothing important. Shirley, why did you tell your parents about this tonight?

SHIRLEY: I'm sick. I'm scared. The kid who supplied me with the junk kept raising the prices. Then he said he couldn't get it anymore. Now he's gone. They say the narcs picked him up and put him in jail. I had my last shot twelve hours ago. I'm getting sick. I need the stuff. I figured that Mom and Dad could get some from a doctor, or put me in a hospital where I could come off easy.

DR. CHAPMAN: We'll do something, but there's no easy way out of this.

SHIRLEY: Anything will be better than going off cold turkey.

MR. KRAMER: What hospital will we send her to?

DR. CHAPMAN: That's our first problem.

MRS. KRAMER: I read that the federal government runs a couple of hospitals for this kind of trouble—in Fort Worth and in Lexington, Kentucky. They ought to be good.

DR. CHAPMAN: I wouldn't recommend them for Shirley.

MR. KRAMER: Why not?

DR. CHAPMAN: I did my military service in the Public Health Service—half of it as a psychiatrist in the Coast Guard and the other half, fifteen months, at one of those hospitals. Almost all the patients in those hospitals are hardened addicts; many of them are there on jail sentences and many others are there because narcotic agents gave them the alternatives of hospitalization or prosecution. After spending four to six months, which is the minimum she needs, in a place like that, Shirley would come out worse than she went in. All she would hear from other patients the whole time would be talk about where to get drugs, the sensations they give, and ways of finding money to buy them. The motivation to get well among the patients in such hospitals is very poor. Even the government statistics show that almost ninety-nine percent of the patients who leave those hospitals are back on drugs in a few days to a few months.

MRS. KRAMER: Good grief!

MR. KRAMER: Doesn't the city or the state government have a special psychiatric division for adolescents who take drugs?

DR. CHAPMAN: The doctors I know who are familiar with those facilities say they all end up in about the same condition as the federal hospitals for addicts. I wouldn't send Shirley there.

MRS. KRAMER: I read about a group called Synanon in California and special outpatient clinics in some cities where they use a new drug.

DR. CHAPMAN: Both of these are experimental. If they work, about which there is a great deal of doubt, they work only for a small percentage of highly motivated addicts. The drug you're probably referring to is methadone which is a synthetic narcotic that's been around for twenty-five years or more. When it's made available in outpatient clinics for addicts, it decreases the amount of thefts they commit, but it's not at all clear that it decreases the amount of addiction.

MR. KRAMER: I have an insurance policy that covers everything. It's part of my company benefits. Can't you put her in the psychiatric ward at St. Mary's or Menorah?

DR. CHAPMAN: Yes, and that's probably what we're going to do tonight. However, you'll probably find that your insurance policy excludes narcotic addiction or limits coverage to emergency treatment for a week or so.

MRS. KRAMER: But isn't this a medical problem just like any other one?

DR. CHAPMAN: Yes, but I'm afraid that the general prognosis of narcotic addiction is so poor that insurance companies would rather give larger benefits for other kinds of medical and psychiatric problems. However, Shirley has a much better outlook than most addicts. She's young. She's been on the drug a relatively short time, and she had the courage to tell you about it, even though she did it under stress. In addition, she has not yet sunk into the addict underworld. The mere fact that she didn't know where to ook for more drugs when her supply was cut off shows that she's still in your world. Also, you have another factor working in your favor.

MR. KRAMER: What's that?

DR. CHAPMAN: Shirley is fifteen. When is your birthday, Shirley?

SHIRLEY: In August.

DR. CHAPMAN: That gives us about ten months before she's sixteen.

MR. KRAMER: What does that have to do with it?

DR. CHAPMAN: In this state until a person is sixteen, his parents can commit him to a psychiatric hopsital, whether he wants it or not, simply by signing papers. After sixteen he cannot be held against his wishes without a court hearing. And the way the law is written, it's difficult to get a commitment on the basis of addiction alone.

MR. KRAMER: Ten months? She doesn't have to be in the hospital for ten months, does she?

DR. CHAPMAN: Four months is the absolute minimum set by everyone who has long experience in this field, and most psychiatrists prefer six to eight months. An extra couple of months often is advisable. However, without some sort of legal restraint ninety-five percent or more of narcotic addicts sign out of the hospital a few days or a few weeks after entering.

MRS. KRAMER: Why does she have to stay so long?

DR. CHAPMAN: It will take about two weeks to get her gradually off the drug. The craving for it, which often is intense, then goes on for another four months or more. So hospitalization of six to ten months is more likely to have a lasting effect. Shirley needs a lot of talking with a psychotherapist to work out the emotional problems that made narcotics an attractive escape for her.

MR. KRAMER: All right, we'll put her in the psychiatric division of St. Mary's or Menorah under your care for six to eight months.

DR. CHAPMAN: Well, we'll put Shirley in one of those hospitals tonight and get her withdrawal started. However, as I said, Mr. Kramer, when you start reading the fine print in your insurance policy or talk to the girl at the insurance desk in your company tomorrow, and when you find out what hospitals cost without insurance coverage, I think you're in for a shock.

MR. KRAMER: Whatever it costs, I'll pay it. I can borrow on my insurance policies and refinance the house if necessary.

DR. CHAPMAN: Well, there's one other problem.

MR. KRAMER: What's that?

DR. CHAPMAN: It's me.

MR. KRAMER: You don't want to take care of Shirley?

DR. CHAPMAN: I would be happy to take care of her, but it's more complicated than that. How many kids do you have?

MR. KRAMER: Two are out of town at college, and there's one younger than Shirley.

DR. CHAPMAN: Well, it's a matter of medical philosophy. Keeping Shirley in a private psychiatric hospital for the better part of a year will make it difficult to keep two other kids in college and maybe to send them to professional schools after that. If I could guarantee a cure, or even give you a fifty percent or seventy percent prognosis for a cure, I might accept Shirley for long-term hospital care. But I can't. Even though Shirley's prognosis is better than that of most addicts, it's still an ugly problem. I hope Shirley does well, but you may be in for a difficult, long haul. So I can't accept Shirley for anything more than emergency hospital treatment, or until we get her off drugs during an initial two-week period. I have another suggestion to make.

MR. KRAMER: What?

DR. CHAPMAN: I suggest that after a few days at St. Mary's or Menorah Shirley be transferred to the Millbridge State Hospital at Littlefield. I know Dr. Jackson there. He was one of my students at the university years ago. I'll call him, and he'll take a special interest in her. He'll see that she gets individual psychotherapy with one of the staff psychiatrists or one of their experienced clinical psychologists. In addition, they'll probably put her in group psychotherapy. She will be in a ward with convalescent general psychiatric patients rather than in a ward with long-term, hardened narcotic addicts. They have good programs of occupational therapy, recreational therapy and other activities that are important in a psychiatric hospital. The buildings are old, but since Dr. Jackson and his colleagues took over at Millbridge a few years ago, the professional services are good. And that's what counts. Buildings don't cure people. People do.

MR. KRAMER: I don't like the idea of my daughter going to a state psychiatric hospital.

MRS. KRAMER: At fifteen she's too young to be in a state hospital.

DR. CHAPMAN: If she's old enough to become addicted and to find ways of supporting a habit at forty dollars a day, she's old enough to be in a state hospital.

MR. KRAMER: Aren't you being a little inflexible on this?

DR. CHAPMAN: You have a difficult problem on your hands.

MR. KRAMER: I thought psychiatrists were supposed to take a more hopeful attitude toward problems.

DR. CHAPMAN: Fortunately, we do pretty well with most of the difficulties we treat these days. Moreover, if this were a problem with marijuana, or LSD, or amphetamines, or addiction to barbiturates, it would be a different matter. I'd admit Shirley to the hospital for thirty days, start psychotherapy on an inpatient basis, and continue it on an outpatient basis afterward, and I'd have a good chance of getting the job done. Unfortunately, heroin is a very different matter. However, as I said, Shirley has a much better outlook than most kids who get addicted. Let's say that I'm optimistic about Shirley, who has a somewhat pessimistic problem. At any rate, in my opinion, Millbridge is the place for her.

MR. KRAMER: All right.

DR. CHAPMAN: I'll call the hospital now to get her a bed.

SHIRLEY: For God's sake, hurry. This is just plain hell.

10

AFTER THE GAME IS OVER

What happens to the children and adolescents who play the games discussed in this book? In this chapter we shall follow some of them into adulthood and trace the various courses they may take.

The Persistence of Games

A game that becomes ingrained during childhood and adolescence does not usually end when the person enters adulthood. The cast of characters changes, but the game goes on. For example, the person who throughout childhood and adolescence played a hard game of Ready or Not, Here I Come dominated his parents and others with aggressive, temper-tantrumish behavior and stampeded them into compliance with his wishes. Hence, in courtship he is demanding, in marriage he is bullying, in child rearing he is domineering, and in his work he must either have his way or he will bicker continually with his associates.

How successfully can such a person adjust in adult life? This depends on many variables. The main one is whether his game is mild or severe. If the game is mild and if he can be somewhat flexible, he may be able to adjust fairly well despite his personality handicap. People will say, "Ernie tends to be bossy, but he is not unreasonable and we can work [or live] with him." He tends to quarrel when he doesn't get his way, but he can give in, forget the issue, and go on. His game is a limp, but it does not cripple him.

However, when a person's game of Ready or Not, Here I Come is severe, he usually has continual marked difficulties in all his intimate, prolonged interpersonal relationships, and in some cases he is socially incapacitated. He must dominate his marriage or he brawls continually in it, and his marital history often consists of a series of brief courtships, stormy marriages and bitter divorces. He must control his children, and in doing so he drives them into either frightened submission or open rebellion. His job adjustment depends on the kind of work he does. If he works in an office or factory in which daily intimate contacts with people are necessary, he fights endlessly with them and often cannot hold any job long. On the other hand, if he does door-to-door or town-to-town sales work, in which his contacts with customers and sales supervisors are brief and superficial, he may do well. I have seen men who played marked games of Ready or Not, Here I Come and yet were very successful financially. Also, if such persons are self-employed in vocations in which contacts with people are short-lived, they may do well. If in their social life they move quickly from one group to another and never know anyone well, they may work out adjustments that on casual observation seem adequate, but such adjustments break down quickly when they have prolonged relationships.

Hard players of Ready or Not, Here I Come by trial and error unconsciously seek people with whom they can establish lasting relationships. These relationships are sick, but they may endure. For example, the player may go through a series of turbulent premarital realtionships until he encounters an insecure, passive person whom he can dominate. His aggressiveness and the other person's passivity, both of which are unhealthy, dovetail. Once married, even though the passive person suffers, he often does not have sufficient courage to extricate himself from the marriage, and, with temper tantrums on one side and frightened compliance on the other, the marriage may go on for decades. In a similar manner, a player who is a professional person or a businessman goes through a series of secretaries and office assistants until by trial and error he collects a small crew of passive people whom he can bully, and in this unhealthy manner he may run a successful office. In social situations the same process of unconscious selection goes on, and his interpersonal life in time is constricted to circles in which his domineering qualities are either tolerated or hidden.

Many other factors influence the life course of our Ready or Not, Here I Come player. If he is intelligent and talented, many people in business and professional groups may be willing to put up with his personality problems because of his abilities. If, on the other hand, he is mediocre, they are more likely to push him aside, and he may become a bitter misfit. Also, economic comfort gives him a small cushion; if he has money, he may be able to choose and manipulate his environment to a slightly greater extent, and this increases his chances of getting by without interpersonal disasters. In addition, accidental factors affect what happens to him. For example, if a passive wife in an unhealthy but workable marriage were to die unexpectedly, he then may go through two or three unhappy marriages in middle age and deteriorate into alcoholism and social isolation. Changing economic forces, such as the decline of an industry, may destroy a workable economic situation, and he may not be able to find another one in which he can adjust, despite his game.

Another variable that cannot be predicted is whether or not he will enter psychiatric treatment and how successful it may be. For example, faced with an impending divorce by his second wife, the alienation of his children, and a deteriorating job situation, even a hard player of Ready or Not, Here I Come may see that all his trouble is not caused by "the difficult people I've gotten mixed up with" and "bad luck." He may grasp that the basic causes of his difficulties are his own personality problems, and he may seek psychotherapy. Hard players of Ready or Not, Here I Come are difficult patients, but sometimes they improve. Mild players of this game have better chances of ending their game through psychotherapy.

Psychiatric treatment of another person may have a profound effect on the player's life. His wife may seek psychiatric treatment for the phobic neurosis or stomach ulcer to which her marital misery is a partial contributor. In psychotherapy she may gain insights into the personality structures of both herself and her husband, and she may lose the passivity and emotional insecurity that tied her to the marriage. Finding the marriage intolerable and having found the courage to leave it, she divorces him and takes the children with her. This usually is preceded by suggestions that the Ready or Not, Here I Come player try to change by seeing a psychiatrist, but he often refuses psychiatric help or, forced into it by his wife, cooperates poorly and gets nothing out of it.

In a similar manner we might trace into adulthood most of the games discussed in this book and outline the possible life histories of the players. The title of this chapter, "After the Game Is Over," has various twists. In many cases the severe games of childhood and adolescence are not over in adulthood; they last until death or senility terminates them. However, players often can diminish or annul mild or moderate games by gaining insight into them. Such insight sometimes comes in the course of day-to-day living with people; the players grasp what they are doing and change. Other players solve their games by help from psychiatrists, clinical psychologists, and members of the other mental health professions.

Game players tend to rear game players. Although the games of children often are different from the games of their parents, unsound homes tend to produce unhealthy children and the web of sick interpersonal relationships is spun from one generation to the next. Hence, any improvements in games, whether by spontaneous insights or by work with psychotherapists, help not only the players but also their children, and perhaps their children's children.

The Longitudinal View of Personality

The study of games emphasizes *the longitudinal view of personality,* which may be summarized as follows: *The personality structure of each adult is the product of all significant interpersonal relationships of his childhood, adolescence and adulthood.* Some relationships, especially the long-term close ones of the family, are more important than others, but all significant relationships contribute to personality structure and interpersonal functioning.

Freud wrote that the three sources of human misery are (1) man's struggle with difficulties in his physical environment, such as extremes of temperature, floods, drought and other natural phenomena; (2) the disease and decay of his own body; and (3) the problems he has with people. *The longitudinal view of personality* can decrease distress in this third category; the ability to see the child and adolescent in each adult and to define the games he plays helps an individual avoid much misery.

For example, a twenty-two-year-old girl may be considering marriage with a twenty-six-year-old man who played Throwing Mud Pies throughout his childhood and adolescence and has carried this game into adulthood. He is well educated, good looking, has a good job, and when things go his way, is a good companion. The girl is very fond of him, but as their courtship intensifies, she becomes aware of his game. She notes that each time a difference arises between them he begins to throw guilt at her in an attempt to control her. At first his guilt-throwing technique succeeds and she gives in, but she slowly realizes that this is a deeply ingrained pattern—a game. On a few occasions she sees him manipulate his parents and his sister by Throwing Mud Pies, and she sees that this began in childhood. She also recognizes that his game is so deeply entrenched that he is unconscious of the way he handles people.

If the girl understands games and *the longitudinal view of personality,* she does not fall into the common trap of assuming that his behavior will change in marriage. She does not accept the opinions of friends and relatives that he will "settle down and mature after marriage" or that "once you're married, it will be different." She knows that his game will probably be intensified by intimate living with him. If his game is mild, she may try to talk it over with him and may succeed in establishing their relationship on a new level. However, if his game is severe, such attempts will fail, and suggesting psychiatric treatment as a precondition for marriage is hazardous.

To cite another example, a businessman hires a promising man in his late twenties to work in his firm. The employee has excellent qualifications, makes a good impression in an interview, and comes with satisfactory recommendations from a previous job he held for a short time. However, as the months go by, the businessman realizes that each time a problem arises between the two of them, the younger man outmaneuvers him by manipulating other people in the firm. The new man plays the office manager off against the accountant and the production supervisor off against the merchandising chief in his efforts to dominate each situation. In brief, he is carrying a game of King on the Mountain into each interpersonal setting in the business firm.

If the businessman understands games and the longitudinal view of personality, he can speculate that this is a long-term problem in our game player. He assumes that during childhood the player used King on the Mountain to pit one parent against the other and thus dominated them both. The businessman knows, moreover, that the player probably carried this game into many interpersonal settings during adolescence and early adulthood and that "trying to talk this thing out" and "trying to explain to young Ainsworth that he shouldn't do this sort of thing" will not work. This is a deeply engraved personality pattern—a game—and the ordinary methods of solving business difficulties will accomplish nothing. A businessman cannot be both a therapist and an employer because he does not have enough time. Moreover, he should recognize that a King on the Mountain player can cause a great deal of trouble among people who were working harmoniously before he came.

The businessman may take one of several courses with our King on the Mountain player. If his game is mild and if he has proved himself highly capable in solving some long-standing technical problems in the firm, the businessman may decide to try to keep the game player in the firm despite his personality problems. He may give the player a sales district of his own, or a separate production unit, or some other clearly defined sphere of activities in which conflicts with other members of the firm can be kept to a minimum. However, in many cases the businessman will eventually conclude that the new man's game incapacitates him as an effective person in their business, and so he discharges him. A humanitarian businessman may have a final conference with the game player in which he tells him. "I think you have a few problems to solve in the ways you get along with people. In my opinion, you often tend to play your superiors off against each other when things don't go your way. That's one of the reasons we're letting you go. Maybe I'm wrong, but I have to call the shots the way I see them. Anyway, think it over." If the employee's game is mild, the boss's parting words may open his eyes a little. If his game is severe, he will merely say, "Old Patterson fired me because he didn't want any real progress in clearing up the mess this firm is in."

Understanding games and the longitudinal view of personality helps a parent rear children. For example, if the parent spots A Shell Game or Bang, Bang, You Shot Me Down when his child begins it, he can take steps to prevent it from becoming an ingrained personality problem. The informed parent can avoid such cliches as "It's only a stage she's going through," "He'll grow out of it," "All middle children are like that" and all the other evasions parents use to avoid dealing with serious problems when they are early and can still be corrected easily.

Lastly, understanding games and the longitudinal view of personality may help a person come to grips with some things about himself. If an individual's games are mild or moderate, he may be able to recognize how they began in childhood and have dogged him into his adult years. Such awareness may help him become a better-adjusted person. In other cases it may spur him to seek professional help.

The Doctor and I

We shall conclude our survey of the games of childhood and adolescence by outlining briefly the ways in which psychiatrists, clinical psychologists, and members of the other mental health professions work with parents and children to rid them of their games and to substitute healthy interpersonal relationships. Parents who understand games can frequently work out mild ones with their children, but severe ones can often be removed only with professional assistance.

The Child Guidance Clinic Approach

The basic model for treatment of children's emotional problems is the child guidance clinic. The first child guidance clinics were opened in the early 1920's, and during the past half century child guidance clinics have been organized in all major cities and many small ones. In addition, modified forms of the child guidance clinic approach are used in many other settings such as family and children's service agencies, juvenile courts and school systems.

A child guidance clinic operates on the basic principle that effective resolution of a child's games and the substitution of healthy interpersonal patterns requires treatment of both the child and his parents. The child's games to a large extent are arising from unhealthy interactions with his parents, and their relationship with him must be changed if he is to be helped. You cannot treat a child and ignore the environment in which he is being reared.

It is difficult for the same psychiatrist or clinical psychologist to treat both the child and his parents. If this is done, the child often feels that the therapist is relaying details of his treatment to his parents, and seeing the therapist as an agent of his parents, he becomes uncommunicative. In addition, the therapist who sees both the child and his parents runs the risk of becoming a pawn in their struggles with each other. Each party may try to win the therapist over as an ally and to maneuver him against the other side.

Hence, each child guidance clinic has a staff of psychiatrists, clinical psychologists and psychiatric social workers, and one member of the professional team works with the child and another works with the parents. The members of the clinical team operate flexibly. In some cases the child or adolescent is treated by a clinical psychologist and the parents attend group therapy sessions at which a psychiatrist or a psychiatric social worker is the moderator. The work of the various professional persons treating a particular family is coordinated in periodic case conferences.

Before treatment begins, the child and his parents are separately interviewed in several sessions by various members of the clinical team. A clinical psychologist gives the child several personality tests such as the Rorschach inkblot test. After this diagnostic work-up the members of the clinical team present their data in a case conference and discuss the child's problems and the ways they were developed in unhealthy family relationships. At the end of this conference, which may last up to two hours, treatment plans are formulated.

Play Therapy. A child under the age of eleven or twelve can rarely engage in the kinds of verbal interviews that are used with adolescents and adults. Therefore, play therapy has been evolved to meet the treatment needs of small children. In play therapy toys and other play materials are used to communicate with the child. A special room is equipped with blackboards, chalk, building blocks, toy cars, molding clay, paper and crayons, dolls, dollhouses, and many other things. In sessions of about fifty minutes each the therapist uses the child's play in the same way that he uses the words of an adult. For example, in play therapy the therapist may set up in a dollhouse a replica of the child's family, consisting of a mother, a father, a little brother, an older sister, and a doll who represents the patient (special dolls representing family figures in careful detail, even grandparent dolls, are commercially available). The therapist suggests that the child "show the things that happen in this family," and the child soon begins to act out with the dolls many of the problems and conflicts of his home. As the child plays, the therapist reflects feeling tones, helps the child express his feelings, and makes interpretations to aid the child in getting new insights.

In play therapy the therapist works with two main bodies of data: what the child does with the play materials and the kind of interpersonal relationship he sets up with the therapist. For example, the child who is caught in a hard game of Carrousel often expresses his hostility in destructive games with airplane crashes, automobile wrecks and bombardments of toy buildings, and the therapist, by the reflection of feeling tones and his interpretations, helps the child recognize his hostile feelings and grasp how they have arisen in unhealthy parent-child relationships.

In addition, the therapist uses the interpersonal relationship the child sets up with him, for the child tends to carry into the therapeutic situation the kind of relationship that he has with his parents and to play the same game. For example, when the child playing Ugly Duckling complains that he can't do something because of his limp or his defective hand and begins to cry to manipulate the therapist into doing it for him, the therapist says, "Terry, this is what you do with your father and mother. When you cry and say you can't do something, they rush in and do it for you. You boss them by crying. I understand how you feel, but I think we can find better ways for you to get along with people. I can't help you by doing as your parents do. However, perhaps I can help you by letting you tackle problems by yourself, with only a little assistance from me now and then." The therapist approaches the same interpersonal problem many times in different play situations until the child gradually ends his game and substitutes healthier interpersonal patterns. Meanwhile, his parents, in individual or group psychotherapy with another member of the clinic staff, are working to develop the capacity to do the same thing at home.

Group Therapy. Group psychotherapy is used a great deal in child guidance clinics. For example, a group of small children may meet once a week in two-hour sessions in a playroom that is equipped with toys and materials for various group games. The group usually contains from six to ten children of both sexes, and they are carefully selected for play therapy after their diagnostic work-ups. One or two therapists participate in their play, and by reflecting feeling tones and making occasional interpretations, they help the children work out interpersonal problems with each other. Such group psychotherapy is most useful for inhibited, shy children who need the active help of a therapist in breaking down the interpersonal barriers that separate them from comfortable interaction with others. For example, a child who is playing an Old Fashioned Game, or a child in the early stages of Rule Book often benefits from this kind of psychotherapy over a two- or three-year period. Many times the therapist will say to such a child, "You see, Alice, it's fun to loosen up with other kids, and nothing bad or scary happens when you do. You just feel better and get healthier and healthier."

Group psychotherapy with adolescents often is useful, especially since many of them cannot talk easily in one-to-one interviews with therapists. However, they may talk freely when they participate in a group of six to twelve teen-agers with similar problems. In such a group the therapist may be an active or passive participant, depending on the needs of the group. He frequently uses some of the current adolescent jargon and may even dress as they do. A therapist with a headband and beads is more likely to establish contact with adolescents than one in a suit coat, white shirt and necktie. A therapist who has the ability to work effectively with adolescents often restricts himself to this work and leaves treatment of parents and small children to other members of the clinical team.

The discussions of an adolescent group usually range widely, but the therapist tactfully keeps his goals in mind to substitute healthy interpersonal activities for the games the adolescents are playing. He never lectures and rarely censures, and much of his effectiveness lies in the warmth that the adolescents gradually develop for him, for he is perhaps the only adult they can truly communicate with. Imperceptibly and often unconsciously they adopt some of the goals the therapist represents.

Group psychotherapy with parents is commonly employed in child guidance clinics. It may be used in addition to individual sessions with the parents, or it may be the sole method of treatment. Such groups usually consist of three to eight couples who are having similar problems with their children and are playing the same kinds of games with them. In many instances the parents can see in others, and then recognize in themselves, unhealthy attitudes toward children that they would have difficulty seeing in individual treatment sessions. Together the parents talk out their interpersonal difficulties with their children and find new ways of relating to them. The therapist may let the parents explore their problems with little interference from him, or he may be fairly active, especially when he feels the group needs help in crystallizing points.

Family therapy is a special form of group therapy that has been developed in recent years. In it the parents and one or more of their children meet as a family group once or twice a week with the therapist in sessions that last from one to two hours. Many psychiatrists feel that family therapy is most useful in parent-adolescent problems of lesser severity. However, the full value of family therapy will become apparent only as it is applied over long periods of time to a wide variety of parent-child problems.

Individual Verbal Interview Treatment. Face-to-face verbal interviews have been tried with small children, but most therapists find play therapy much more useful. After the age of twelve or thirteen play therapy is no longer practical, and individual or group psychotherapy is used. The therapist who does one-to-one psychotherapy with adolescents must usually be a fairly active participant in the patient-therapist dialogue; he cannot sit back and expect the patient to carry the major burden of talking, as in psychotherapy with adults. Also, as noted above, the therapist must be able to adopt some of the attitudes of his adolescent patients in order to communicate with them. The therapist who puts his feet on the desk and inquires, "Well, man, what's been the action this week?" is more likely to have a useful session than a therapist with both feet on the floor who says, "Perhaps you might tell me about some of the problems you have encountered this week." Also, a background activity such as eating snacks and sipping soft drinks is useful while talking with adolescents.

Individual interviews with parents in child guidance clinics usually follow the conventional pattern of adult psychotherapy, with the patient doing most of the talking and the therapist occasionally intervening with interpretations and brief questions. Such psychotherapy may deal mainly
245

with the parent's relationship with the child. However, in some cases it is devoted to examination of the parents' own childhood or other areas of his life that directly or indirectly are affecting his relationship with the child.

Modified Forms of the Child Guidance Clinic Approach

The basic pattern of child guidance clinic work is carried into many kinds of child and adolescent services. It must often be modified to meet the practical necessities and limitations of various treatment situations, but the goals and fundamental methods remain the same. Thus, the basic model of child guidance clinic work may be employed in psychiatric services attached to juvenile courts, public and private schools, welfare agencies and many other institutions.

The Psychotherapy of Adults

In many cases the psychotherapy of an adult is basically an exploration of games he began in childhood and adolescence and is carrying into adulthood. The retrospective analysis of the games of childhood and adolescence is done in two main ways. First, by the patient's reminiscences and the therapists's interpretations, the patient gradually grasps what has happened in his past and how it is affecting his current relationships. What was hidden enters awareness—what was unconscious becomes conscious.

Second, the patient and the therapist have one interpersonal relationship, and usually only one, that is directly available for their scrutiny; the relationship between the two of them. The patient tends to bring into this relationship the same games he played with his parents and is now playing with his marital partner, his work colleagues, his social acquaintances and others. For example, the patient who in most situations plays a hard game of Ready or Not, Here I Come tries to bully the therapist and manipulate him, and the patient who plays Bang, Bang, You Shot Me Down tries to make the therapist feel guilty and inadequate and thus to dominate the treatment situation.

However, the patient-therapist relationship has a unique quality. In all other interpersonal relationships the game player arouses emotional responses from the people with whom he tries to play his game. They become angry at him, or they are frightened by him, or they lecture him, or they abandon him in disgust or bewilderment. In brief, either they become trapped in his game or they reject him. The therapist does neither. Instead, in an informed way he works to help the patient gain insight into his game and to solve it in the context of their relationship with each other. Through expression of his feelings, insight into his personality structure, insight into his past and current interpersonal relationships, and both analyzed and unanalyzed aspects of his relationship with the therapist, the patient has an opportunity to rid himself of his game and to substitute healthier ways of relating to others.

INDEX

251